MAKING MUSIC

Van Raalte Institute Visiting Research Fellows Lecture Series, no. 18

MAKING MUSIC
Hope College's Music Department, A History

Marc Baer
Visiting Research Fellow, 2018
Van Raalte Institute, Hope College
Holland, Michigan

Marc Baer and Allison Utting

Van Raalte Press
Holland, Michigan

© 2020 Van Raalte Press
All rights reserved

Van Raalte Press is a division of Hope College Publishing

Theil Research Center
9 East 10th Street
PO Box 9000
Holland, MI 49422-9000

vanraalte@hope.edu
www.hope.edu/vri

Printed in the United States of America

ISBN: 978-1-732-0854-3-5

LCCN: 2020939607

Jacob E. Nyenhuis, PhD, LittD
    Editor-in-Chief and Publisher

JoHannah Smith
    Project Editor
    Office Manager

Russel L. Gasero
    Layout and Design

Marena De Leau
    Cover Design

Dedicated to the memory of Charles C. Aschbrenner

(1936–2016)

Marc Baer taught for thirty-three years as a member of Hope College's Department of History. He subsequently served as the college's dean for Arts and Humanities and chaired the Department of Music; he is currently a senior research professor at Hope. This is his fourth book.

Allison Utting graduated from Hope College in 2018 with a major in secondary social studies education and a minor in history. She is currently an eighth grade history teacher in Byron Center, Michigan.

Contents

Acknowledgments — ix
Preface — xi
Introduction — xiii

1. The Making of a Department — 1
   - The First Generation, 1866-1894 — 3
   - Becoming a Department, 1895-1950 — 9
   - The Modern Era — 24

2. Pioneers to Professionals — 33
   - "Our Chief Musician," 1890-1940 — 36
   - 1940 and Beyond — 44

3. Experiencing Resonance: Students Making Music — 67
   - Sacred Beginnings — 71
   - Student-Inspired Initiatives — 74
   - Joining Ensembles — 79
   - Touring — 85
   - Performing — 89
   - Faculty as Mentors — 92

4. Where Music Dwells — 97
   - Early Years, 1866-1907 — 99
   - The Voorhees Era, 1907-1940 — 101
   - New Musical Spaces — 105
   - The Department is Homeless — 114
   - Home at Last, 1956-2015 — 116

5. The Year in Music — 123
   - True Impassioned Melody, 1866-1941 — 125
   - "The music you have made," 1941-2015 — 138

6. Finding Its Tune: A Musical Community — 155
   - Town for Gown — 159
   - Gown for Town — 162

Conclusion — 179
Appendix — 183
   Hope College Music Faculty, 1866-2016
Index — 201
Visiting Research Fellows Lecture Series — 213

Acknowledgments

Our book is dedicated to Charles C. Aschbrenner. His conception of a history of Hope College's Music Department has given birth to *Making Music*, our project being better for the legacy he left—the collection of a body of materials on which to base such a history. The other individual who deserves special thanks is Jack Hyde, who worked with Charles on his project. Jack both shaped the materials into a chronological narrative and carried out additional valuable research. As well, Jack answered our many questions about sources and interpretations.

Marc Baer, Visiting Research Fellow at the Van Raalte Institute (2018), and Allison Utting, recipient of a research assistantship from the Joint Archives of Holland, thank the directors of these two programs, Jacob E. Nyenhuis and Geoffrey D. Reynolds, for funding and supporting this project. Lori Trethewey, office manager of the archives, and Geoffrey Reynolds graciously gave of their time to help us locate and understand sources and to reproduce images.

Greg Olgers, Lynne Powe, and Tom Renner also helped us ferret out images in the Hope College collections. We thank Krisia Rosa and Lori Trethewey for transcribing our oral history interviews; Kiley Corcoran and Lian Robinson for their research assistance; Randy Kalmink, our Dimnent-spaces detective; and all the alumni and retired faculty who contributed memories of their time in the Music Department.

The following read through and commented on either individual chapters or the entire manuscript: Paul Trap, Robert Ritsema, Robert P. Swierenga, Holly Utting, Peter Walther, Jacob E. Nyenhuis, and Patricia Baer. We are deeply grateful for their help in making this book better. The same is true for our project editor JoHannah Smith.

Thank you all.

Marc Baer
Allie Utting
2019

Preface

In this book, we use (capital) *Music* to refer to the department, and (lowercase) *music* to refer to the performative. Nowhere is context more important—and vexing—than in Music's identity within the institutional context of Hope College. In various places, the following are used: School of Music, Department of Music, and Music Committee (once in the early twentieth century and then a second time in the 1940s). Using capital *Music* as a common reference seemed appropriate.

Equally worrisome was what name to use for the private high school associated with Hope College. What would ultimately be known as the College High School was first called Pioneer School (1851-54), then Academy (1855-99), and then Preparatory School (1900-1928), before being renamed the College High School in 1928. We often use *preparatory school* to cover a multitude of names. Until 1924 faculty taught in both the preparatory school and the college, and students from both schools lived in the same dormitories. And as far as music and even chapel attendance went, both faculty and students participated together. Other terms include:

- Originally called Memorial Chapel, we use the chapel's eventual name throughout, namely, Dimnent Chapel.

MAKING MUSIC

- Please note a distinction between Vespers as a music series and the annual Christmas Vespers (see ch. 2).
- First Church, in chapter 1 and elsewhere, is now Pillar Church.
- We use *department* throughout, the word most contemporaries used.

All images and sources in this volume are courtesy of the Joint Archives of Holland (JAH), except where otherwise noted.

Introduction

There's music in all things, if men had ears.
Lord Byron, *Don Juan*, 1824

There is more to music than meets the ear.
Jeremy Begbie, *Theology, Music and Time*, 2000

On October 22, 2015, the Jack H. Miller Center for Musical Arts opened on the east side of Hope's campus, and at that time, the college's Department of Music comprised thirteen full-time and twenty-eight part-time faculty. Such a remarkable building and staff could not have been imagined in 1862 when the college opened its doors to a handful of students.[1]

There has always been music at Hope College. Indeed, making music has been so pervasive, it is a wonder that Hope students have had time to do anything else. But if, as in the words of the student

---

[1] Hope was chartered in 1866, in which year part of the first class graduated.

newspaper, "We find music everywhere,"[2] then in the early years, it was also nowhere, at least in terms of either having a recognized physical space or being an established part of the college curriculum—or even having the appropriate faculty for such an academic department. *Making Music* addresses these topics, as well as a related set of concerns: which music, for whom, and to what end?

Like all historians, we began with questions. As the project evolved, many of our questions flowed toward the matter of *department*. John Nykerk is traditionally considered the founder of Hope College's Department of Music. Although it is true that Nykerk shaped what would become a department to fit a modern form, it is equally true that the department's foundation goes back to the first days of the college, because music has always been taught at Hope—even before the college graduated its first class. If music has existed from the beginning, then as historians, we want to point out how much context matters, because we often err by imposing our own experience onto the past. Thus, the music at Hope College has changed, just as the college has changed—music has served a changing Hope, and Hope has served a changing Music Department. Music made the department, not the other way around. To unpack all this, we approach various topics through six thematic chapters.

The first chapter tells the convoluted story of the era between the 1860s and the 1940s, when the college did not know quite what to do with music. Read any *Anchor* before the last few decades, and notice that the subject of music dominates its pages. But should the model of teaching music to students be that of the conservatory or the liberal arts college? To justify the major required a definition of Music's identity, that is, should the music taught to students have the academic rigor of philosophy or chemistry, or was it better to think first in terms of what today would be termed an extracurricular?[3]

If the story in the first chapter is complicated, then that of the second chapter is relatively simple: a recognizably modern faculty with a distinct character emerged fairly quickly from around 1945 to 1965, due to a strong working relationship and respect between the leadership of the department and that of the college. Yet from the late 1860s to the early 1890s, the outcome of that relationship could not be predicted.

---

[2] *Anchor*, 1 Mar. 1909.
[3] Cf. Robert W. Cavanaugh, "The History and Contemporary Problems of Music in American Institutions of Higher Learning," 4-5, 15-17, manuscripts-music folder, box 1, Cavanaugh Papers, H88-0020.

Introduction xv

Chapter 3 focuses on students as makers of music. To a large extent, this story is told through the eyes of the department. Students, however, have made music on their own in venues far beyond the department, for example, a class party after the Pull or fraternity men serenading the women of Voorhees—who then did their own spontaneous singing.[4] This pervasiveness was sometimes seen as a problem, as will be evident in several chapters.

One of the most intriguing questions from the late nineteenth through the late twentieth century, which at times flummoxed both the college and the department, involved physical location. Almost every department at Hope had a well-recognized building associated with it. For Music, however, it proved hard to determine where home was for the faculty who taught music and if there could be an appropriate building in which all musicians could both teach and perform. These issues are discussed in chapter 4.

It is safe to say that by 2015 musical performances ranked second in terms of audience, just after collegiate athletics. At the same time, what those audiences heard in the century and a half covered in this book was characterized by both change and continuity. Some significant events disappeared, for example, performances of Handel's *Messiah* and the All-College Sing. Other events, such as Christmas Vespers and the Musical Showcase, have become vital to the musical rhythm of the year. Although audiences from 1866 to the present have heard music at Hope College—graduation being a case—different years have brought different kinds of music. Chapter 5, "The Year in Music," explores the different types of music Hope College musicians have performed for audiences throughout the years.

The music of Hope College is held in high regard in West Michigan. Musical events at Hope are the bridge that links the college to the city of Holland—and beyond. The final chapter explores the relationship between campus and community and how it has developed from the 1860s.

Those who have ears, let them hear—and read.

---

[4] See Robert P. Swierenga, *Holland, Michigan: From Dutch Colony to Dynamic City* (Holland, MI: Van Raalte Press; Grand Rapids: Eerdmans, 2014), 3: chs. 28, 30; *Anchor*, 5 Oct. 1927; diary entries, 7-8 and 22 Oct., 1 Nov. 1927, HC diary 1927-, box 1, Mildred Schuppert Papers, W94-1183.

CHAPTER 1

The Making of a Department

> The Musical department of Hope College is as yet vacant.
> *Anchor*, 1890

> Although music is not one of Hope's major departments, the part which it plays enriching the life and activities of the campus is great.
> *Anchor*, 1943

> The Department of Music is an independent, autonomous department . . . of Hope College.
> *National Association of Schools of Music Visitor's Report*, 1968

In the early years at Hope College, the late June Commencement ceremonies took place over the course of several days. First came Baccalaureate, then Hope Preparatory School had their graduation ceremonies, followed the next day by the gathering of alumni, and then, on the final day, the college's graduating class was the focus of attention. In 1873, as part of the alumni assembly held in the college chapel, the

Fraternal Society sponsored an event which included three songs, *Soft Glides the Sea*, *There's Music in the Air*, and *Music from the Shore*. The next day saw the college graduation at First Reformed Church. Music was interspersed with orations and ceremonial elements.[1] Looking back five years later, one critic related the occasion to an earlier one: "The music (singing) was notably deficient in comparison with former years, and it seems as if the college would only once in a few years contain some leading musical genius ... who imbue all their comrades with a love and proficiency of that fine art." There followed a report of the Wednesday college graduation held at Third Reformed Church: a Grand Rapids organist played Mendelssohn's *Wedding March* and Meyerbeer's *Robert le Diable*, in this instance termed "a wonderful selection for such an occasion (!)." The article went on: "Then our organist gave us a potpouri [sic] of beautiful strains, commencing with the Overture of 'Wm. Tell,' shifting off to 'Norma,' and closed with some beautiful passages from 'Trobadoure.'"[2]

These remarks beg several questions, some easily answered, some not, and others which have led to the inquiry upon which this chapter is built. First, why did the *Holland City News* pay such close attention to the music at Hope's Commencement? The answer: simply because the college and preparatory school were important institutions in a city whose history was a mere three decades old. Second, why did a local newspaper editor think he was qualified to be a music critic? We will never know, but this editor habitually weighed in on musical matters.[3] There are also some questions worth pursuing for more in-depth answers: Why, given the sort of college Hope was in its early years, was there music, and so much of it, at ceremonial, as well as other, occasions? Who was responsible for changes in the college's music program? That is, were the significant forces top-down or bottom-up? Whom was a music program to serve—college students, preparatory school students, area high school students, local audiences, or some combination of the above? As a program, how should Music be organized? Should the music faculty resemble other Hope teachers—academically trained, with primary expertise in one subject?

Long before there was a department of music at the college, there was music at Hope. Today, a department means an established faculty,

---

[1]   *Holland City News*, 28 June 1873. As late as 1946, Commencement still took place over three days; minutes of the faculty meeting, 3 Dec. 1945, H88-0335.
[2]   *Holland City News*, 29 June 1878.
[3]   Ibid., 25 June 1875, 3 July 1876, 30 June 1877, 28 June 1879, 26 June 1880, 1 July 1882, 27 June 1885.

a dedicated building, at least one major with a defined curriculum, and a consistent name. None of these was the case for Music in the early years. But from the beginning, there was music, and it was everywhere. The theme of this chapter is that the making of music created the department, not the other way around.

The first generation, 1866-1894

Music was ubiquitous in the first decades of the college's existence. In addition to Commencement, there were special events, such as the 1887 Day of Prayer for the college, which included singing at the beginning, middle, and end of the day;[4] the YMCA meetings in the 1880s, which opened with singing;[5] and the Glee Club at the junior exhibition of the Class of 1892, which sang *La Marseillaise*, as well as songs in German and Dutch.[6] But in this chapter, the focus is more narrow: the opportunities that led to the making of the Music Department included daily chapel and other occasions and then eventually instruction. Each of these activities and their occurrence during the first three decades of the college's existence will be explored.

By the early 1880s, an organist played at Hope's daily morning chapel, and a chorister led singing. These two positions were filled by older college students appointed by the Hope faculty.[7] Music in chapel was regularly the subject of commentary. In 1892, for example, the student newspaper pronounced that the addition of a piano had improved the quality of the music, and in 1912, the paper complained about the lack of variety in vocal music, suggesting substituting a solo or a quartet for a hymn from time to time.[8]

In addition to daily chapel, there were other occasions for making music. Music played a vital role at college commencements, beginning with the first in 1866, when the entire graduating class of eight sang an ode written by Hope's first president, Philip Phelps Jr., and set to music by William Gilmore, a member of the class.[9] Earlier that week, as part of Commencement, there were orations "interspersed with singing by the college choir," and later, "The commencement music was

---

[4] Minutes of the general faculty, 3 Feb. 1887.
[5] *Anchor*, 1 Oct. 1887; *Intelligencer-Leader* 8 (20 June 1941), 11.
[6] Minutes of the collegiate faculty, 23 Feb. 1891. For more examples, see chs. 5 and 6.
[7] For example, minutes of the general faculty, 23 Sept. 1882, 21 Apr. 1883, 5 May and 21 Sept. 1885, 16 Sept. 1886.
[8] *Anchor*, 1 Nov. 1892, and 1 Jan. 1912.
[9] Wynand Wichers, *A Century of Hope, 1866-1966* (Grand Rapids, MI: Eerdmans, 1968), 71; see also 278-79; for the music, *Hope College Remembrancer* (1866), 20, Commencement and Baccalaureate collection, H88-0394.

instrumental and chiefly rendered by some of the graduating class."[10] A subsequent "college choir" turned out to consist of four men. Given Hope's size during its first generation, we should not imagine more was possible by way of vocal music, although it should be noted that this college choir—or better, quartet—went on the road, giving concerts in Holland, Zeeland, Vriesland, and Overisel.[11] The college faculty played a role in choosing music by determining who in the senior class would have specific duties at Commencement.[12] In later eras, this would be the responsibility not of the college faculty but of the Music Department.

The years after 1866 witnessed change, as well as continuity. At the graduation marking the twenty-fifth anniversary of the college, the Commencement ode of 1866 was sung by the alumni. There were piano solos; songs by a male quartet; a tenor solo; an organ voluntary, *Gloria*, by the composer Whitney Eugene Thayer; a duet; and pieces by Mozart and Luther Emerson. The audience sang the Dutch national anthem, which at that time was the college song, and a brass band paraded the streets of Holland.[13] Half a century later, although the chair of the department decried an attitude that saw music as a "filler inner" for programs, rather than a legitimate college major,[14] the situation at Hope was more complicated. Music, while not yet a major, was as much a part of the identity of the college as was the teaching of Latin or history.

Finally, there was instruction in both vocal and instrumental music—although not in the form of courses as such. William Gilmore was listed in the first college catalog as "Tutor in Music in each Department."[15] In that year, the departments were theological,[16] collegiate, and preparatory. A year later, Gilmore was joined by his brother John, a Hope senior.[17] Subsequent tutors were responsible for instruction in singing. Most of the college catalogs for this era stated that "Vocal Music is usually provided for. No charge is made for this;

[10] *Remembrancer* (1866), 5.
[11] *Excelsiora* 9 (31 May 1872).
[12] Faculty minutes, 29 Apr. 1878, and 5 May 1885.
[13] Commencement program, minutes of the collegiate faculty, 25 June 1890; *De Hope*, 2 July 1890.
[14] Robert Cavanaugh, "Contemporary Problems of Music Departments in Liberal Arts Colleges," *Association of American Colleges Bulletin* 38 (May 1952): 322.
[15] *Hope College Catalog* (1865-66), 28. Gilmore was a tutor in music 1862-69. In 1872 he returned to Hope from pastoring in Virginia to teach primary and female education and co-led the Female Department: Wichers, *Century of Hope*, 89; Elton J. Bruins and Karen G. Schakel, eds. *Envisioning Hope College: Letters Written by Albertus C. Van Raalte to Philip Phelps Jr., 1857 to 1875* (Holland, MI: Van Raalte Press, 2011), 150.
[16] In 1885 this became a separate institution, Western Theological Seminary.
[17] *Hope College Catalog* (1867-68), 32.

but lessons in Instrumental Music are at the expense of the student."[18] Like the work of these tutors, a "singing school" organized in 1871 by a student and later a "singing class" taught by a Grand Rapids musician were of a different purpose than academic subjects in which students were examined before moving on to more advanced work. A turn-of-the-century catalog spelled this out: "In both departments [college and preparatory school], written examinations are held at the close of each term or whenever a subject is completed."[19] Music, then, was not taught as an academic subject.

Catalogs between 1878 and 1882 list Tinis Kommers, an 1877 graduate, as teacher of vocal music in the academy. Since all Hope instructors taught both preparatory and college students, might Kommers be considered the first member of a Hope College music faculty? This seems to be a step up from the Gilmore brothers and subsequent tutors.

In the beginning, the primary purpose of the college was for the faculty—many of whom were ministers—to train future ministers.[20] There was no place in the classical curriculum for required courses in music. Although the cause-and-effect relationship is unclear, the changing vocations of Hope's earliest graduates likely opened the door for teaching music. Whereas the graduates of 1866—the first class—all went on to careers as either clergymen or teachers, starting with the second class, other occupations began appearing, including merchants, physicians, bankers, lawyers, and even an apothecary.[21] Thus the college continued to recruit tutors in music, usually upperclassmen, and from the college's earliest days, "vocal exercises" were required of all students, and vocal music was offered: "Gratuitous instruction in vocal music is regularly given to all interested. This has long been a source of benefit and *recreation* [emphasis added] to the students."[22] Music's academic marginality was evident not only in the connotation of *recreation* but also in the transient nature of staffing. In 1881-82 the responsibilities for vocal music were "temporarily filled" by Tunis Kommers (Class of 1877) and John George Van Hees (1881), two recent graduates, and John H. Kleinheksel Jr., a teacher of Greek, English, and algebra.[23]

[18] Ibid. (1878-79), 19.
[19] Ibid. (1900-1901), 51.
[20] Fifteen of the 28 men who taught at Hope ca. 1857-89 were ordained ministers: Preston J. Stegenga, *Anchor of Hope: The history of an American denominational institution, Hope College* (Grand Rapids, MI: Eerdmans, 1954), 213.
[21] *Hope College Catalog* (1873), 30.
[22] Ibid. (1865-66), 16, 26.
[23] Ibid. (1881-82), 7. For John Nykerk in this regard, see minutes of the collegiate faculty, 19 Apr. 1894.

Whatever music was at Hope in the first three decades of the college's existence, it was not of the order of academic subjects—moral philosophy, ancient languages, theology, the Bible—whose students were rigorously examined. Music instruction was farmed out to choristers such as Teunis Muilenburg (1889), a junior who was "giving music lessons to some of the students."[24] The same is true for leadership, which lay in the hands of the college president and faculty.[25] Music at Hope was more of an extracurricular activity than a taught subject.

As well, music *at* Hope was frequently less than music *from* Hope; that is, making music was often the work of outsiders. This is made evident by the history of commencements. In 1875 a Hope graduate of 1873 was given "a good mark for the success of the musical part of the entertainment," while Miss H. E. Colyer of Kalamazoo played the organ for that and the following year's Commencement. At subsequent graduations, performers from Allegan, Grand Haven, Grand Rapids, and Holland provided the music.[26] The *Holland City News* considered this pattern as positive. Commenting on Hope's 1879 Commencement, the paper pronounced: "The innovations in this city to take professional musicians to furnish the music for such occasions is a move in the right direction and has been a custom years ago at other colleges."[27]

If important benchmarks of a modern college are an academically trained faculty in a department offering majors to students, then Music at Hope, before the turn of the century, was far from that. Take the case of "Professor" G. C. Shepard. The 1884-85 catalog lists him as "instructor of vocal music and the voice." Two years later, the student newspaper reported that, "About fifteen of the students are attending Prof. Shepard's singing class." Shepard directed not only the music at the academy's Commencement but also a concert by his students and some Holland musicians that Monday evening in the college chapel. "Professor" in this case was an honorary not an academic title, and Shepard continued to reside and perform in Grand Rapids, even while teaching at Hope.[28]

Change, however, was on the horizon. In the college catalogs of the 1880s, John Nykerk is listed as tutor and instructor in vocal

---

[24] *Anchor*, 1 Feb. 1888.
[25] Minutes of the general faculty, 2 Oct. 1883, and see also the minutes of 21 Dec. 1883.
[26] *Holland City News*, 25 June 1875, 3 July 1876, 30 June 1877, 26 June 1880, 1 July 1882, 20 June 1883.
[27] Ibid., 28 June 1879.
[28] *Anchor*, 1 Nov. 1887; *Holland City News*, 11 Oct. 1884.

Young John Nykerk

music, having taken Shepard's place, and as offering classes in voice culture, the intersection of oratory and music—two of his passions.[29] He began leading music in the daily chapel service, while in the 1890s, he organized an orchestra as well as male and mixed singing groups, including the College Quartette, which gave concerts throughout West Michigan.[30] Although not academically trained as a musician, Nykerk was sufficiently serious about the subject to attend the 1888 Music Teachers' National Association conference held in Chicago.[31] John Nykerk, therefore, as the college's first true music professor, helped a discipline expand beyond an extracurricular activity. He was aided by a series of articles in the *Anchor* promoting music, and in 1888 alumni and students were urged to write college songs and create musical clubs.[32] But the student newspaper also pointed to the disconnect between music and Music at Hope, commenting in 1890: "The Musical department of Hope College is as yet vacant."[33]

[29] *Anchor*, 1 Nov. 1888; for his many roles, see also ch. 2.
[30] Gordan Mackay interviews with Laura Alice Boyd and Rev. James Wayer, biographical folder, Nykerk Papers, H88-0111.
[31] *Anchor*, 1 June 1888.
[32] Ibid., 1 Mar., 1 May, 1 June, 1 Sept., 1 Nov. 1888.
[33] Ibid., 1 Oct. 1890.

Did Nykerk found the Music Department? Since 1866 *department* has had many meanings. It originally referred to a division—the collegiate, the preparatory, the theological. It was a program, hence the "Normal (Education) Department," and it was gender specific, thus "Female Department." The term "Department" defined an academic program supporting courses—now majors—thus the Department of Biology provided offerings for the science course (major).

In terms of teaching, *department*, when referring to a program, usually meant at least one permanent, academically trained professor, responsible for examining either individual students or an entire class (for example, sophomores) in a given subject and reporting results at a faculty meeting. *Academic department* meant either a cluster of courses or perhaps an area of instruction in which there were no courses as such. When the college's Normal Department opened in March 1888, with the purpose of preparing teachers, the curriculum for the first two years included music, the first time Hope required that subject of any student. As well, the next year's catalog entry for the academy advertised "Religious Instruction And Music— In all the Classes."[34] Music, however, was not required of most Hope College students, much less available to them, given the heavy demands on their time.[35]

An important turning point came in 1891 with the hiring of Nykerk as a teacher at the academy, for he was the first long-term instructor who taught music. Catalogs in the early 1890s listed Nykerk as professor of music and principal of the academy and, eventually, as assistant professor of English. Under Nykerk, the college began to offer prospective students dramatically more options in the study of music.

> In harmony with the progressive spirit that has placed Music in the curriculum of our public schools, Hope College furnishes, without expense to the pupil, a course in theory of music, supplemented with an elementary course in harmony. Sight singing and voice culture receive special attention in class. The Glee Club and the Eupsalian Orchestra have, for the last three years, given added enthusiasm to this *department* [emphasis added]. All qualified students may become members of the above organizations. Private lessons in voice culture will be furnished at reasonable rates.[36]

---

[34] *Hope College Catalog* (1889-90), 21.
[35] Music offerings were not listed as possible electives for any of Hope's courses: *Hope College Catalog* (1908-9), 17-20.
[36] *Hope College Catalog* (1891-92), 28-29.

In the last decade of the nineteenth century, Hope College appeared on the verge of offering something like a major in music. The 1892-93 catalog held out this promise:

> To such as desire it, a four years' course in Vocal Music is furnished, comprising Voice Culture in class, Sight-Singing, Expressive Rendering, and the principles of Theory, Harmony and Counterpoint. This course is given to regular students and is provided without extra tuition.[37]

The 1894-95 catalog still listed Nykerk as professor of music, adding:

> A large class, under the direction of Prof. J. B. Nykerk, meets once a week, and receives drill in Voice Culture and Choral Singing. A primary class in Theory and Sight-Singing is conducted by Mr. J. J. Heeren [a Hope senior, who that year was chorister]. To these classes all students are admitted without charge. Further, fine opportunities are afforded for the study of Piano and Voice. Messrs. Post and Campbell of Grand Rapids, two of the most prominent and competent musicians in the State, each have large classes of private pupils in their respective *departments* [emphasis added].[38]

In terms of the college's vision for music, where did matters stand at the end of Hope's first generation? The 1894-95 catalog seems to suggest that, although there was not a music department as such, there were departments—a confusing nomenclature that will be explored in a moment. John Nykerk was a single identifiable music professor—about to move on to English. There were Hope students who taught other students and Grand Rapids musicians who taught Hope students. Music's curriculum hardly seemed stable.

Becoming a department, 1895-1950

In 1946 a new entity—the music committee—was created and given two tasks: to promote music on campus and to address the problems that had arisen from the role the department had played at the college.[39] This segment explores both developments and problems

---

[37] Ibid. (1892-93), 25.
[38] Ibid. (1894-95), 37.
[39] Faculty minutes, 4 Feb. 1946. For music as a problem, see *Intelligencer-Leader*, 20 June 1941; minutes, 14 June 1950, Board of Trustees (BOT) Papers.

from the late nineteenth century to the mid-twentieth century. Unlike the pre-1895 decades, what characterizes this era is a mix of bottom-up and top-down forces that shaped the department.

The first half of the twentieth century was a time of transition for Music, in which name, physical home, curriculum, and faculty were all fluid. The early years of this era include the founding of the School of Music and ensuing discussions about whether it might become a conservatory.[40] Hope undergraduates, as well as non-degree-seeking students, including those in the preparatory school and in the Holland area, were able to take courses in this school. In 1925 the college added a bachelor of music degree, and for the first time, Hope students could major in music. To understand these developments, the pages that follow address how Music was organized and the debate about the role music should play in the life of the college—whether to provide entertainment, to train future musicians or teachers of music, or some combination thereof. Answers to these questions would drive decisions about music faculty: Should they be professionally trained and teach only music, or—as in the past—could Music be staffed by faculty who taught a variety of subjects?

In 1895 John Nykerk moved from the academy to the college faculty as professor of English, but he continued to play a central role in shaping music at Hope. He directed the Glee Club, as well as daily chapel music for the better part of three decades. In the 1895-96 college catalog, Nykerk is listed as professor of English language and literature and "in charge of Vocal Music." For the academy, however, he is listed as teaching English and music.

According to college lore, in 1903 Nykerk founded the Music Department. He certainly played an important role in creating the School of Music, forerunner of the modern department, and he began the practice of inviting prominent musicians to perform at the college.[41] But Hope continued to employ a hybrid model, using outsiders and advanced college students to teach those in their first two years at the college, as well as students in the preparatory school. Putting lore aside, however, the foundation narrative is complicated, that is, that

---

[40] In this, Hope was part of a national discussion: cf. Earl Enyeart Harper, "Music in Liberal Arts," *North Central Association Quarterly* 15 (Jan. 1941): 265-66; Sondra Wieland Howe, *Women Music Educators in the United States* (Lanham: Scarecrow Press, 2014), 227.

[41] Gordan Mackay interview with Esther Snow, biographical folder, Nykerk Papers; see also *Hope Alumni Tattler* (May 1928), 8. The *Milestone* (1916), 83, claimed that Nykerk "organized the department twelve years ago."

seemingly obvious terms, such as *department* or even *founding*, cannot be understood in the context of Hope College without a deeper inquiry.

As in the late 1880s, so at the turn of the century, the *Anchor* continued to publish editorials arguing music should be more prominent at Hope.[42] Students pressured the college for more music courses, making Nykerk—a gifted singer who believed music was especially important—the effect as well as the cause of an expanding music program.[43] This was evident in an issue raised by students in 1899: vocal music offerings failed to be open to female students and to those less advanced in their work. "We have no doubt," the *Anchor* assumed, "that if such a class were organized, many would avail themselves of the opportunity and that, in the course of time, Hope would be able to boast not only of a well-trained chorus of male voices but also of a chorus of mixed voices."[44] By 1905—thanks to Nykerk—this vision had materialized.

How then did the college respond to student demand and to Nykerk's entreaties? New instructors were hired to teach piano, harmony, composition, strings, and voice. And after the early twentieth century, although the college no longer appointed advanced students to the positions of chorister and organist, it did continue to rely upon them. With the opening of Van Raalte Memorial Hall in 1903, Music had its first home. The 1905 college yearbook featured what it termed the "Department of Music."[45]

From the perspective of the *Anchor*, much had changed from the disparaging comment the paper had made fifteen years earlier:

> The Musical Department of Hope college is rapidly coming to the front. It is no longer an experiment. More than sixty pupils are enrolled in this department, and the work done by them is attracting wide attention.... The student recital given at the close of the former term by pupils of Mr. Pease, assisted by several of Mr. Post's pupils, gave evidence of the remarkable success with which the instruction in this department is attended. In the near future, the Choral Union will give its annual public entertainment. This organization consists of students of the department of music,

---

[42] *Anchor*, 1 Apr. 1901, 1 Apr. 1902, 1 Mar. 1909.
[43] See his essays on music in *Anchor*, Apr. and June 1890.
[44] *Anchor*, 1 Dec. 1899.
[45] *Milestone* (1905), 11. Missing from the page are Nykerk, who taught courses in voice culture and singing, and Judson Kolyn, the Hope junior who taught rudiments of music and sight singing.

Department of Music

Mr. Clarence Edward Pease,
Voice.

Mr. Henry C. Post,
Piano.

Mr. Josef Bistline,
Violin.

Miss Amy M. Yates,
Piano.

Miss Dorothy Raiguel,
Accompanist.

Department of Music (Milestone, *1905*)

together with other students of fair musical ability and is under the direction of Prof. J. B. Nykerk.[46]

Evoking a department, complete with recitals and concerts, in fact, obscures two critical factors: that Music was still reliant on students and outsiders as instructors and had still failed to provide a major. "A Department of Music has been in operation for two years. Eighty students attended this year, but as yet no credit is given for this work."[47]

While not inaccurate to claim Nykerk as Music's founder, it is perhaps just as correct to declare Hope president Gerrit Kollen as cofounder, based on a ca. 1895-96 brochure he had signed: "Those desiring a musical course can find no better opportunity anywhere. Messrs. Post and Campbell, two of the most competent instructors in this State, give lessons at the college in Piano and Voice."[48] Presumably, Kollen authorized Nykerk to associate the term "department" with the music program. The vital role of Hope College presidents in the growth of the department will be developed in the last part of the chapter.

The catalog of 1903-4 is the first to mention a School of Music at Hope College. For the first time, an official college publication detailed what was on offer and identified a vastly expanded curriculum in piano and violin. There was also a clear statement of purpose:

> From this description, it will be seen that Hope College is, first of all, offering a liberal classical course, which will serve as an adequate foundation upon which to build professional courses, which, in turn, prepare for the more active and practical duties of life.

Music also seemed to be an integral part of the college: "The School [of Music] will commence at the opening day of Hope College; will be subject to the Rules and Regulations of said institution, including the observance of all the holidays (legal as well as private) which are in connection with Hope College." The School of Music had some of the appearances of an academic department:

> Twice a year, there will be held an "Examination Day" and a "Public Lesson," which will be held on the evening of Examination Day....

---

[46] *Anchor*, 1 Apr. 1905.
[47] Apr. 1905 minutes, 1900-1910 folder, BOT Papers.
[48] "Hope College," correspondence, 1885-1912 folder, box 1, Gerrit Kollen Papers, H88-0088.

> The Public Lesson will be a concert given by the different pupils of the school. Examination Day will occupy the entire afternoon. ... The Musical Committee of Examiners will then consider the pupil's work and his or her advancement made during the past school term, and upon these considerations and the final decision of the teacher, it will be decided whether the pupil is able to enter the next class or not.[49]

Why had the School of Music been founded? There is a very good chance that what occurred was a meeting of minds between Nykerk and Kollen to "swing for the fences."[50] Nevertheless, the question remains: What was the School of Music to be?

In the new century, music at Hope continued to be omnipresent, and new traditions were added to older ones. The 1907 dedication of Voorhees Hall was "rendered still more agreeable by the beautiful songs sung by a chorus of Hope's maidens," whereas the Glee Club sang at the 1911 installation of Hope president Ame Vennema.[51] The literary societies were constantly making music.[52] In the fall of 1923, after the Pull, the freshman gathered in the Jenison Park pavilion, and after dinner, a ukulele trio performed, followed by two songs performed by their own Cornelia Nettinga.[53]

Although Music had not yet become an academic department, there is another element to this story, revealed in a single sentence in the 1903-4 catalog: "It is hoped that this department may before long develop into a Conservatory of Music."[54] In December 1904, President Kollen invited Henry Post to a meeting of the college faculty. Post, a highly regarded Grand Rapids musician, had begun teaching at Hope that fall. His appeal is worth noting in detail.

> Mr. Post thanks the college authorities for the kind treatment he and his colleagues had received. He spoke very hopefully about the opportunities Holland offers for the development of

---

[49] *Hope College Catalog* (1903-4), 49, 54-55.
[50] No evidence exists in the Nykerk or Kollen papers, and material in the Hope faculty and BOT minutes merely reports what was, rather than how it had come to be.
[51] *Anchor*, 1 July 1907, 1 Mar. 1913.
[52] For a sampling, see scrapbook, Ethel Leestma Swets Papers, H18-1988; Hope memory book, 1921-23 folder, Alice Hoffs Papers, H09-1686; minutes, 1909-20 folder, Meliphone Society Papers, H88-0416.
[53] Memory book, 1923-27, Susanne (Dragt) Vander Borgh Papers, H89-1059.1. First conducted in 1898, the Pull is an annual tug-of-war between the men of the freshman and sophomore classes.
[54] *Hope College Catalog* (1903-4), 49.

The Making of a Department

Frater Frolics (Milestone, *1941*)

a conservatory of music. He urged the desirability of establishing a definite course or courses of both vocal and instrumental work and of determining on definite credits for such work. He explained what immediate facilities were needed in the line of a couple studios or rooms and expressed the hope that soon there might be established a closer affiliation between Hope College and the work of his colleagues and himself in the direction of the establishment of a department of vocal and instrumental music.

The faculty then voted to create a committee, consisting of Kollen, Nykerk, and John Bergen, professor of Bible and elocution.[55] There is no record of this committee ever making a report. The next year, 1905, the Hope faculty's annual report to the college council (today's board of trustees) mentioned that a committee had been appointed to "consider the relation between the School of Music and the College, and the advisability of recommending to Council the adoption of a scheme of credits to be given to our students pursuing music courses, a practice now in vogue in Oberlin and other first-class colleges."[56]

Awarding credit for music courses would represent the first step toward a major.

---

[55] Minutes of the collegiate faculty, 6 Dec. 1904.
[56] Annual Report of Hope Faculty to the Council, minutes of the collegiate faculty, 18 Apr. 1905.

Launching the School of Music postponed a decision, or perhaps, less proactively, was simply mission creep. In that same 1905 faculty report to the college council, the value of the School of Music to Hope was evident:

> The College School of Music has, during the past year, almost doubled in attendance, about eighty students are now pursuing the courses offered.... The school proves to be a very popular and useful feature of the College curriculum ... as a local advertising scheme, a faculty recital, and a pupils' musicale were given during the past year, and one or two more will be given before the close of the session.[57]

Such schemes were successful, although for that year, there were only seventy-three students enrolled in the school—fifty-three were townspeople and the remainder Hope College or preparatory students.[58] A decade later, the *Milestone* made it clear how valuable the school was to the college: "Hope's music department ... attract[s] large numbers of students from neighboring towns, as well as from the city and college itself."[59] Since the majority of students in music schools in this era were women, expanding the music program was a shrewd move. In the three decades between 1904-5 and 1934-35, the proportion of females in the school ranged from just over half to three quarters.[60]

The numbers speak to the value of the school arrangement for the college, and the reverse may well have been true. But the reality remained— as in the past, the school employed no full-time, resident faculty. In 1905-6 three faculty resided in either Grand Rapids or Chicago, while the history of music course was offered by Edward Dimnent, professor of Greek language and literature.[61] Without credit being awarded for courses applied to a major in music, the school had an odd identity. Although in 1915, it boasted about the rising number of students, the college's *Bulletin* suggested music was not like other programs: "At this date it is impossible to classify the students in the School of Music, but the number thus far enrolled is fully one hundred."[62] To bear out this

---

[57] Ibid.
[58] Kiley Corcoran, "Who Were the School of Music students?" Making Music folder, Music Department (MD) Papers, H88-0378.
[59] *Milestone* (1916), 83.
[60] Howe, *Women Music Educators*, 223; Corcoran, "Who Were the School of Music students?"
[61] *Hope College Catalog* (1905-6), 67-68.
[62] *Hope College Bulletin* (Nov. 1915), 6.

complication, catalogs of this era listed the School of Music separately after the college and preparatory departments.[63] Was the school *in* but not *of* Hope College?

The signs should not be missed of Music beginning to function like an academic department: it had an identified space (first Van Raalte Hall and then in 1907 Voorhees); the faculty was a bit more permanent, rather than constantly coming and going (Henry Post, for example, taught 1903-10); and the curriculum became more clearly defined, although not yet leading to a major. The college could make a valid argument that Music provided value for the money.

> Thorough training under capable teachers may be had in Piano, Pipe Organ, Voice Culture, Violin and the ordinary branches of Musical Theory. Besides the private work of the studio, ensemble practice and public appearance, together with numerous opportunities to hear distinguished artists, constitute for the Hope College student musical advantages of the highest order. Rates of tuition will be found very low considering the character of the instruction offered.[64]

The 1922 *Milestone* praised the ever-fervent John Nykerk about his project, remarking on "the larger number of students enrolled and by increased appreciation of music by the student body," while including pictures of a twenty-member orchestra and a fifteen-member band.[65] The financial foundation of Music, however, may still have been a problem. A 1920s presentation by the Hope Dramatic Club in Carnegie Gymnasium was advertised to "Benefit the Music Department of Hope College."[66]

There were hints of institutional growth—indeed, expansion—for example, the *Anchor* reported the department planned to offer a four-year conservatory course leading to a certificate, but there was also this ominous remark in an official publication: "In the near future, the School of Music will be more definitely united, organized, and systematized, so that our students may engage in the branch of aesthetic study with larger results and under more favorable conditions."[67] Reading between the lines, in spite of student pressure and Nykerk's prodding, there

---

[63] *Hope College Catalog* (1914-15), 65-71.
[64] *Hope College Bulletin* (Aug. 1916), 8.
[65] *Milestone* (1922), 124, 126-27.
[66] Scrapbook, Alice Hoffs Papers.
[67] *Anchor*, 2 Oct. 1918; *Hope College Bulletin* (Nov. 1919), n.p.

remained a disconnect between the School of Music and the college. A 1921 *Anchor* editorial was particularly biting:

> The School of Music is sometimes thought to be a mere appendage, with little connection with the college. The freshmen, it is true, never know of its existence until the second semester, but nevertheless, the school fills a great need. . . . Would that a course in music were a required course for graduation. . . . The average student is sadly deficient in the art that charms the soul and drives away all cares.[68]

It was, the student newspaper suggested, time for something new.

In the 1920s, many American higher-education institutions began offering bachelor's degrees in music, which gave rise to the National Association of Schools of Music and in turn to its role as accreditor.[69] But a new major, and with it the new bachelor of music degree, was a bold move for the still small and relatively poor Hope College. Offering a major in music without a departmental structure and an adequate corps of instructors seems risky from our vantage point. Why, then, did the college announce in 1925 that it would take that step? It may have to do with the optimism of the 1920s, as embodied in Hope president Edward Dimnent building a chapel seating fourteen hundred at a time when Hope's student body numbered four hundred. It may have been the result of Nykerk's lobbying.[70] In 1925 the *Anchor* asked students to respond to the following question: "What do you think of the Degree in Music that is being offered by Hope College?" The paper printed the response of four students, including the first to earn the new degree, Cornelia Nettinga, who would graduate from Hope in 1927, with a bachelor of music in voice:

> A degree will give the student recognized standing in the musical world, just as any other degree does. Besides, if a degree is given, there will be a greater incentive toward the study of music. Many may seek musical training who would not think of it otherwise because it offers opportunities for positions which would not be available without it. Then, too, it will help bring students to Hope

---

[68] *Anchor*, 4 May 1921.
[69] Burnet Tuthill, *NASM—The First Forty Years* (Washington, DC: National Association of Schools of Music, 1973). Oberlin, for example, first offered the BM in 1903: Howe, *Women Music Educators*, 223.
[70] *Anchor*, 15 Oct. 1919; *Milestone* (1921), 70.

Cornelia Nettinga, first recipient of a bachelor of music degree (Milestone, *1927*)

who would not come otherwise and thus enlarge the influence of the institution.[71]

In 1925 an *Anchor* headline read, "Plans for Degree in Music Matured." The article noted the instructors in piano, voice, violin, organ, cello, and music education, as well as the opportunities to participate in glee clubs, an orchestra, and other ensembles.[72] The problem was supporting the BM program, given the now historic pattern of relying on part-time outsiders. Of the eight faculty listed for 1925, Nykerk taught English (chairing that department) and served as dean of men; his role as secretary of the School of Music was administrative. The remaining seven were part-time instructors, few of them were living in Holland and therefore were drawn to outside interests. By 1927 four of these seven were gone. Sustainability would have been a problem even in the best of times.

In the nine years the BM program existed at Hope, the School of Music produced nine recipients of the degree.[73] In 1934 the board of trustees accepted a recommendation of its committee on degrees: "Discontinuance of the degree Bachelor of Music as we are not in a position to give the proper credits for the degree."[74] Quite simply, the college was using income from nonmatriculated students in the School

[71] *Anchor*, 14 Oct. 1925.
[72] Ibid., 23 Sept. 1925; *Hope College Catalog* (1927-28), 18. For the rather stringent entrance requirements for the BM, see *Hope College Catalog* (1927-28), 93-94.
[73] For a student's perspective on that program, see Charles C. Aschbrenner interview with Carlyle Neckers, 2002, Oral History Project folder, box 4, MD Papers.
[74] Board minutes, 25 Apr. 1934, 1931-45 folder, BOT Papers.

of Music to fund faculty for the BM program. In 1928-29 there were 119 students enrolled in the School of Music, but in 1932-33, in the midst of the Great Depression, the number was down to forty-one, a drop of two thirds.[75] In 1934 the faculty committee on courses decided that "after this school year, no further Bachelor of Music degrees be granted, but that such students as have completed the present Bachelor of Music requirements be given the AB [bachelor of arts] degree with Music as Major."[76] The last graduates were in 1935.

The interwar era was characterized by ambiguity as far as a music program at Hope was concerned. On one hand, the BM had disappeared, and the 1935 report of the Special Committee on Curriculum and General Education had conceptualized what today is the four-division structure of academic departments, which had failed to mention music. On the other hand, a 1936 Hope faculty meeting approved a motion that "the matter of credit to be allowed for courses in Applied Music be referred to the staff of the Music Department."[77] The following year, the Music Department's proposal on credits was approved by the Hope faculty, while a request to create the basis for a music education major was handed off to an ad hoc committee "with power to act."[78] In a 1937 Hope faculty meeting, Hope president Wynand Wichers recommended and the faculty approved that students in Chapel Choir and the department's band be able to earn up to four credits for time spent on what was heretofore understood to be an extracurricular activity.[79] In retrospect, these developments pointed to the creation of an autonomous academic department.

The years 1940-41 witnessed another transition. In college publications, "School of Music" was replaced with *department*. The proximal cause was the closing of Hope High School, which had been an important feeder for the School of Music. Inconsistency regarding Music, however, continued. For the first time, a Hope catalog listed Music alphabetically in terms of faculty, but when it came to the section on each department's courses, Music was still at the end, rather than listed alphabetically between mathematics and philosophy. Linguistic confusion remained, as evident in comparing two programs for musical events: two days apart, in June 1940, one listed the School of Music,

---

[75] Corcoran, "Who Were the School of Music students?"
[76] Faculty minutes, 1 June 1934.
[77] Faculty minutes, 28 Mar. and 15 June 1935, 5 Nov. 1936.
[78] Ibid., 8 Jan. 1937.
[79] Ibid., 10 Sept. 1937.

Musical Arts Club (Milestone, *1942*)

the other the Department of Music.[80] There was also muddle regarding space: the description in the catalog section on college buildings no longer included a reference to Music's studios being in Voorhees; in fact, no building was indicated as Music's home until 1942, when Columbia Hall was listed as "the Music Building."[81]

At the same time, prior to World War II, there was evidence of expansion in Hope's music program. In 1940 the college began offering a major in music education.[82] Encouraged by new music faculty member Robert Cavanaugh, in October 1941, the Musical Arts Club organized itself to, in the words of its president, "perpetuate music and the interest of music on Hope's campus."[83] The club began sponsoring musical events, explored in chapter 3.

The college made a significant decision in 1946 to create the Music Committee, with Robert Cavanaugh designated as chair. The committee also included the other music faculty, who, along with Cavanaugh, were to choose two additional members and "draw up a statement of functions," or as the *Anchor*, reporting on a decision of the college faculty, put it: "to further the development of music on the campus and to handle the problems that pertain to the Music Department of the college."[84] This Music Committee was an odd construct, recognizing

[80] Programs, scrapbook 1938-41, box 5, Paul Hinkamp Papers, H88-0073.
[81] *Hope College Bulletin* (1942-43), 19. For Columbia Hall, see ch. 4.
[82] Ibid. (1940-41), 62.
[83] *Anchor*, 29 Oct. 1941.
[84] Ibid., 27 Feb. 1946.

both how deeply embedded music was in the life of the college and that Music was still not a department with responsibility for managing its own affairs. The committee is best understood as a transition between the college's first eight decades and its last seven.

From the beginning, the Music Committee took on characteristics of a regular academic department, and in their first meeting, members decided that "all public performances of students representing Hope College musically, must be passed upon by a member of the Music Committee."[85] Making music at Hope was hereafter to be dependent on a somewhat unusual "department." The committee included nonmusic faculty to either determine or at least propose curriculum, staffing, building use, and other matters traditionally decided upon by academic departments, for example, that "a college band should be organized immediately."[86] Music, however, was moving toward becoming a recognized academic department: February 4, 1948, is the last time the heading "Music Committee" appears in departmental minutes; thereafter, the heading is "Music Faculty Meeting."[87]

In addition to these developments, there was, of course, an ongoing discussion as to what role music should play at the college. A 1943 *Anchor* editorial, "Music Department is Worthy of Far Greater Support," argued that "Although music is not one of Hope's major departments, the part which it plays enriching the life and activities of the campus is great." The thrust of the article, however, is not curricular, but it prodded more faculty and students to attend events sponsored by the department.[88] By now the college offered a BA in applied music, with a new curriculum that went into effect fall 1948, while continuing to stress music as extracurricular: "Students interested in music find abundant opportunity to gratify their desires through membership in one or more of the musical organizations," including Chapel Choir; Women's and Men's Glee Clubs; the Hope College Messiah Chorus, which included students, faculty, and community members; the Madrigal Singers; the orchestra; and the band.[89]

The growth of enrollment in Music after World War II kept pace with the growth of the student body and, combined with the student musical groups, contributed to making Music a department, as that term has been used since the mid-twentieth century. Academic

[85] Music Committee minutes, 17 Sept. 1946, box 1, MD Papers.
[86] Ibid., 19 Feb. 1946.
[87] See music faculty minutes, 1947-48.
[88] *Anchor*, 19 May 1943.
[89] *Hope College Bulletin* (Mar. 1948), 32, 93.

institutions in general, and Hope in particular, regularly discuss how to reinvent themselves. Should Hope College become a university? Should it have a graduate school or an evening college? These questions were all raised during the early to mid-twentieth century.[90] Music was no different in this regard. Some proposals failed to find support, for example, to become a conservatory; others succeeded for a season and then passed away, such as the Glee Clubs; and still others struggled but continued to bear fruit, for example, the orchestra.

Decades of confusion about whether Music was a school or a department paralleled ambiguity about its leadership.[91] Curtis Snow is not listed in the catalogs from 1929 to 1935 as head of the Music Department. Yet the faculty resolution after his death termed him "head of the Department of Music." This was followed in the eulogies delivered by President Wichers and former president Edward Dimnent, as a "very fitting recognition of Professor Snow's success in building up a strong Musical School."[92] Snow was replaced on the music faculty by Kenneth Osborne, named director of the department (or school) until he left the college in 1940, with Robert Cavanaugh his successor. Until Cavanaugh was appointed department head in 1950 (when he was on leave to complete a doctorate), there was no designated head, and Cavanaugh chaired the Music Committee after its 1946 formation. It may be too simple an interpretation, but apparently Music became a department like others when Cavanaugh became its head—in 1950.

In 2002 Jantina Holleman recalled that after Cavanaugh had returned from service in World War II, he "was sort of made the unofficial head of the department."[93] Not until the 1950-51 catalog is Cavanaugh—or anyone else—listed as department head. A 1949 *Anchor* article stated that "Professor Robert Cavanaugh has left for the year to continue his studies at the University of Michigan toward his Doctorate of education in music. Mr. Morrette Rider has been appointed active [*sic*, acting] chairman of the department in his absence."[94] In a letter

---

[90] Faculty minutes, 8 Apr. 1921, 2 Nov. 1928, and 30 Oct. 1930; *Hope College Bulletin* (Feb. 1931), 16; John W. Hollenbach to Morrette L. Rider, 14 Aug. 1951, correspondence 1947-53 folder, Morrette L. Rider Papers, H88-0130; cf. Jacob E. Nyenhuis *et alii*, *Hope College at 150: Anchored in Faith, Educating for Leadership and Service in a Global Society* (Holland, MI: Van Raalte Press, 2019), ch. 2.
[91] The following discussion may be of little interest to any reader who has never been a department chair.
[92] Faculty minutes, 13 June 1936.
[93] Charles C. Aschbrenner interview with Jantina Holleman, 2002, Oral History Project folder, box 4, MD Papers; cf. *Anchor*, 16 May 1969.
[94] *Anchor*, 22 Sept. 1949.

Robert Cavanaugh

[handwritten annotation: Chapel choir & several of my courses]

from Rider to college librarian Mildred Singleton, the acting chair stated: "The Music Department of Hope College in its present form is one of the newest departments of the college."[95] The first official college document demonstrating that there was a department of music came from the board of trustees: "In view of his current leave of absence to continue his studies at the University of Michigan, it was VOTED to inform Mr. Cavanaugh that he will be appointed head of the department of Music upon his return to active duty next fall at the salary commensurate with that position."[96] Students (who were always making music, as well as demanding academic opportunities to make more) and key faculty (especially John Nykerk, Curtis Snow, and Robert Cavanaugh) in many ways had willed the department into existence.

The modern era

Becoming a department was more of a process than an event. The process began in the late nineteenth century and became complete in

[95] Rider to Singleton, 7 Nov. 1949, correspondence 1947-53 folder, box 3, Rider Papers.
[96] Executive Committee (EC) minutes, 12 Jan. 1950, minutes 1945-55 folder, BOT Papers.

the mid-twentieth century. Without evidence of an official decision to clarify that what had been called a department for six decades was indeed a department, at some point between 1947 and 1950, the Department of Music simply *was*.

In her 2002 interview, Jantina Holleman attributed to President Lubbers the realization that Music needed "a stronger presence and structure." She went on to mention that Lubbers promoted accreditation by the National Association of Schools of Music.[97] Much like the Kollen-Nykerk partnership, Lubbers and Cavanaugh worked well together to promote Music. Holleman also helpfully connected the vague department designation and leadership to the indistinct curriculum when she arrived in 1946. "You took music courses, but you couldn't properly get a degree in music . . . nothing that really added up to what you would call a degree in music. . . . It was not very well organized, and kind of catch-as-catch can, I think." Holleman thought private lessons rather than rigorous coursework characterized the music program at Hope."[98] This older model of lessons and activities, such as glee clubs and Chapel Choir, without a set major of required taught courses, was related to the absence of a critical mass of professional faculty (see ch. 2). In the interview, Holleman also spoke to this problem of expertise, recalling that, although she was hired to teach piano and music education, "I was asked to take over the music history [course] on a moment's notice." "You improvise," she stated (a telling comment).[99] Improvisation was typical of the 1866-1950 era of Music, versus the professional rigor evident from the 1950s to the present.

Did becoming a department then make a difference in terms of Music's identity? One answer came early on. In 1950 the department decided how to conduct comprehensive examinations: "The test should be written by our own faculty, not by some outsider, who is unfamiliar with our course requirements."[100] For almost nine decades, music at Hope had included outsiders; indeed, music could not have flourished without them. Becoming a department likely was the result, not the cause, of a changed identity, for the examination issue was followed the next year by the decision that a proposed Education Department course for music majors be taught by the Music Department.[101]

[97] Aschbrenner interview with Holleman.
[98] Ibid.
[99] Ibid.
[100] Music faculty minutes, 27 Apr. 1950, box 1, MD Papers.
[101] Ibid., 18 Feb. 1952.

26 MAKING MUSIC

This new identity as a department was reflected elsewhere. Regarding the band, in 1955 Morrette Rider argued it was first and foremost a departmental ensemble and thus "outside activities of the band should not interfere with these functions, and there should be limitation on such outside activities."[102] If ensembles were to be understood as the department's monopoly, the same notion underscored Music's sense of their new home. What was later named the Nykerk Hall of Music opened in 1956. Following discussion of a request in 1957 from the Drama Department to use the building's auditorium, the music faculty determined "to be very cautious in this subject."[103] The following year, Holleman was asked to communicate to the leadership of the college's YMCA that "the Music Department is responsible for giving approval to music representing the College on deputation teams."[104] To encourage music majors to identify more closely with their department, the faculty began requiring all majors and minors to participate in Musical Arts Club meetings and in the early 1960s moved to establish music fraternities and sororities.[105] The management of their curriculum, building, and students pointed to the forging of a new identity within the modern department's first decade of existence.

There are other pointers to Music's new identity. The department's faculty secretary, Esther Snow, charged with taking notes at faculty meetings, used the header "Music Committee" through February 1948. Jantina Holleman assumed the responsibilities of faculty secretary in September 1949 and initially used the header "Music Faculty Meeting," but two months later and thereafter, "Music Department Minutes." Esther Snow was faculty secretary again in 1950-51 and reverted to "Music Committee" for two meetings but thereafter used "Music Department." This evidence speaks to the difficulty of adapting to the new identity, which was a process rather than an event—more vacillating than linear.

Larger forces also helped define Music's new identity, beginning with the department's curriculum. The student newspaper reported in spring 1950 that "The Music Department . . . has recently adopted a complete program of studies leading to graduate studies in music in the

---

[102] Music Department minutes, 2 Nov. 1955, box 1, MD Papers.
[103] Music faculty minutes, 21 Jan. 1957, box 1, MD Papers; see also ibid., 20 Oct. 1977.
[104] Music Department minutes, 16 Oct. 1958, box 1, MD Papers.
[105] Ibid., 3 and 31 May 1951; 26 May 1958; 11, 18, and 25 Oct., and 1, 8, 15, 22 Nov. 1960; 17 Jan. 1961.

fields of Applied Music, Secondary Music, and Elementary Music."[106] Music education courses—then labelled as public-school music—had first been first offered in 1925. By 1950-51 the BA in music education had three tracks—secondary vocal music education, secondary instrumental music education, and elementary school music.[107] In terms of the applied music major, aimed at those whose vocational goal was performance, students were required to take courses totaling sixteen semester hours in applied music within a forty-credit major and to have a successful jury every semester prior to performing junior and senior recitals. Students had to apply to become majors, to be voted up or down by the music faculty.[108] In 1949 Holleman wrote, "Our music curriculum has attained serious standards only this present year."[109]

As a department, Music purposefully engaged both campus and community. In 1950 Holleman was tasked by her colleagues with exploring the possibilities of a music day at Hope to attract prospective students. The following year, Harvey Davis organized a Haydn performance in partnership with Tulip Time. The department took part in the planning for a fine arts festival at Hope.[110] All the while, the department continued to provide music for graduation and other ceremonial occasions. By 1964 music ensembles included over three hundred students drawn from departments across campus, and the department staged seventy-five concerts and recitals per annum.[111]

In some instances, however, the outward focus led to constriction. Beginning in the late 1950s, the department began to express concerns about the decades-old *Messiah* production, ending it two decades later.[112] As a strong identity developed, Music grew bolder, in one case challenging one of Hope's most important traditions. In 1951 chair Robert Cavanaugh was directed to "write a letter to the Student Council concerning more effective regulations for the All College Sing," an event which, albeit made music, also devoured students' time.[113] In the early 1960s, concerns were raised about how much time the Homecoming recital and Christmas Vespers were demanding, and at one point, the

[106] *Anchor*, 20 Apr. 1950.
[107] *Hope College Bulletin* (1950-51), 74.
[108] Ibid. (Feb. 1947), 93, 96, and (Feb. 1949), 88; Music faculty meeting, 11 Oct. 1949, box 1, MD Papers.
[109] "Piano Teaching Activities," (1949), Music Department curriculum folder, Holleman Papers, H88-0075.
[110] Music Department minutes, 20 Feb. and 17 Mar. 1950, 20 Feb. 1951.
[111] *Holland Sentinel*, 28 Mar. 1964.
[112] Music Department minutes, 18 Dec. 1958, 10 Mar. 1960.
[113] Ibid., 19 Mar. 1951; see also ch. 5.

department moved to eliminate both.[114] This evidence reveals a major shift in Hope College culture, from music made everywhere to musical production as the responsibility of professional faculty.

The beginning of a critical mass of full-time, academically trained faculty came after World War II, a topic explored in the next chapter. By 1959 the department had seven full-time members. Growth in personnel was accompanied by two related developments. Typical of modern departments, Music continued to press for additional staff as the number of students it served grew and as the faculty recognized national trends.[115] At the same time, however, Cavanaugh expressed a concern that reflected the debate undergirding the founding of the department just after the turn of the twentieth century: "The Department is becoming oriented to the professional student, rather than filling the service needs of the liberal arts college."[116] That debate continued, even while the requests for new staff were successful, so that by 1970-71, the department comprised twelve full-time faculty (an increase of over 70 percent since 1959), who, besides performing themselves, were preparing students for their recitals, leading ensembles on tours, staging Vespers, engaging sabbatical projects, and providing summer camps for high school students.[117]

In the late 1950s, the department began discussing reviving the bachelor of music degree.[118] In the early 1950s, Cavanaugh and the department appeared to be opposed to the degree as inappropriate for a liberal arts college,[119] but recreating the BM was an inevitable outgrowth of the growing professionalization of departmental faculty. In 1967, after five years of discussion, the board of trustees approved the BM after the department had asked college faculty to support it, which they did by a vote of 58-25. According to Morrette Rider, "We considered this matter a subject for the entire faculty," harkening back in time to the academic culture at Hope a century earlier. Music's argument, that the department needed "stronger and deeper training of a professional

---

[114] Ibid., 16 Mar., 18 Oct., and 22 Nov. 1960; 18 Sept. and 30 Oct. 1963.
[115] Ibid., 15 Nov. 1967.
[116] Ibid., 6 Dec. 1967.
[117] Robert Ritsema to music alumni, 22 Feb. 1971, Ritsema Papers, H99-1357.5.
[118] NASM—Self Survey Report, 1959, box 4, MD Papers; Music Department curriculum folder, Holleman Papers.
[119] Cavanaugh, "Contemporary Problems of Music Departments," 325-27; "Questions and Answers Pertaining to the Proposed Music Department Curriculum" (n.d.), correspondence 1954-64 folder, box 1, Cavanaugh Papers.

nature" won the day.[120] The return of the BM led a decade later to a reworking of the degree's curriculum, with new courses in piano skills and music education.[121]

The reinstatement of the BM was related to maintaining the National Association of Schools of Music (NASM) accreditation. The quest for such recognition began in the late 1940s, when music professor Milton Johnston attended the NASM annual meeting to determine the requirements for accreditation. President Lubbers responded to the report Johnston gave him: "I think we are making headway, and we will be pleased to apply for accreditation as soon as we feel we are ready for it." But then he added: "I would not be interested in slavishly modifying our music offerings for the sake of membership in the National Association."[122] The first evidence that the department was willing to seek accreditation came in 1957, resulting in a 1959 application for associate membership in NASM.[123] In May 1959, Dr. Roy Underwood, director of the Division of Fine Arts at Michigan State University and a member of NASM's Commission on Curricula, visited Hope's campus. Cavanaugh was notified in August that the commission supported Hope's application and was passing its recommendation on to NASM's executive committee, which approved the college's BA in music education and applied music for a two-year probationary period, prior to an application for full membership.[124]

The report of the NASM visitor revealed the state of the department at midcentury: "The instructional staff is highly competent, both from the standpoint of training and teaching ability. One quickly notes a loyalty to the institution, pride in the department, sincere interest in the students, and a desire to constantly improve their teaching." Underwood went on: "It was evident that the music students had great respect for their instructors."[125] His one dissonant note was a recommendation to drop the applied major because it had produced just a single graduate every two years. As a sign of its strong identity, the department pushed back, responding that the applied major was

---

[120] *Anchor*, 7 and 14 Oct. 1966; *Alumni Magazine* 20 (Jan 1967): 21; "Music Curriculum" (ca. 1978), music curriculum 1966-90 folder, box 1, MD Papers.

[121] "Music Curriculum."

[122] Johnston to Lubbers, ca. Dec. 1947, and Lubbers to Johnson, 21 May 1948, Johnston biographical file. See also Aschbrenner interview with Holleman.

[123] Music Department minutes, 21 Jan. 1957; NASM Self Survey Report folder, box 4, MD Papers.

[124] Thomas Williams, secretary, NASM, to Cavanaugh, 12 Aug. and 18 Dec. 1959, NASM application folder, box 4, MD Papers.

[125] NASM—Visitors Report and Response folder.

the only option for a student interested in becoming a performer or proceeding to graduate school as preparation for college teaching.[126]

NASM accepted Music's argument, and two years hence granted full membership to Hope's Music Department. In 1969 that membership was renewed. One sentence in the NASM visitor's findings is revealing: "The Department of Music is an independent, autonomous department . . . of Hope College."[127] After just over a century, the process of music becoming a department was now complete.

In 1951 criticism was raised in a department meeting about the Music Box column in the student newspaper, focusing on its less-than-professional tone.[128] The gossipy column, written by students, had been a regular feature of the *Anchor* for decades. During that time, the *Anchor*'s coverage of music on campus was remarkable, nearly filling the first page of many issues. In their complaint, the department articulated a desire to move from a college culture, which saw music everywhere—representative of the century after 1866—to a modern professional milieu, wherein making music was mostly the responsibility of the department. The success of the Music Department, ironically, is seen in contemporary issues of the *Anchor*, which reveal meager coverage of music at Hope.

By the 1960s, thanks to upward and downward forces, Music had a modern curriculum and once again two degrees, now with five majors. Music had been accredited by the nationally recognized professional body in the discipline and resided in Nykerk Hall—the first building created at the college with music in mind. All this happened during the 1950s and 1960s as Music took on an identity as a modern department, evidenced by a professional faculty, and defended its interests against those of other departments, for example, Music itself, rather than a college-wide body, would examine its own majors.[129]

Although music shaped Music up to the 1950s, this bottom-up top-down arrangement declined shortly thereafter. Hence the paradox of the modern era: the waning of independent music making corresponded to the rise of Music making music. The chapters which

---

[126] Ibid., and Cavanaugh to Thomas Williams, 7 Jan. 1960, NASM application folder.
[127] NASM visitor's report, 1968.
[128] For both, see, e.g., *Anchor*, 1 Mar. 1951; cf. Music Department minutes, 3 Mar. 1951.
[129] Morrette Rider to Ernest Ellert, 27 Apr. 1950, correspondence 1947-53 folder, Rider Papers. Ellert, a professor of German, chaired the committee on comprehensive examinations.

follow will explore this concept from distinct angles. For now, two points need to be made.

First, the department eliminated some historic ensembles, for instance, glee clubs and the marching band and replaced them with others like jazz studies and the wind ensemble. In this, Hope's Music Department followed national trends in higher education.[130] Other fixtures also disappeared because of broader cultural shifts, for example, the All-College Sing.

Second, in 1936 the musical abilities of the 152 incoming freshmen were surveyed: 70 percent could sing, and over 60 percent could play at least one musical instrument. These students would bring musical skills learned in school and at home to Hope's campus and use them in a variety of settings.[131] In contrast, a recent national survey reported participation in college ensembles of just under 15 percent of undergraduates, because, according to the respondents, they did not have the time.[132] The students may well have been signifying music was not as important to them as it was in the century before the 1960s. The Hope music program's coming of age paralleled a decline in making music outside the department's control. Among former music majors interviewed for this book, the closer we came to the present, the less evidence there was of students making music on their own.

Most people want to know two things: where is home, and does someone care about me? For Music, the answer to the first, explored in chapter 4, is Nykerk Hall of Music in 1956 and then Jack Miller Center for Musical Arts in 2015. For faculty, the sense of the second is understood as *valued*. Here the answer lies in the long list of Hope presidents, beginning with Gerrit Kollen, who supported music programs and personnel.

After the 1946 acquisition of Walsh Hall for Music—thanks to the initiative of President Lubbers—according to Jantina Holleman, "There was a tremendous espirit de corps in those days. We had a sense of being a part of something new." She went on to praise Lubbers—"He knows

---

[130] J. Perry White and George N. Heller, "Entertainment, Enlightenment, and Service: A History and Description of Choral Music in Higher Education," *College Music Symposium* 23 (Fall 1983): 10-20; Paul Tanner, "Jazz Goes to College," *Music Educators Journal* 57 (Mar. 1971): 57, 105, 111-13.

[131] Faculty minutes, 5 Nov. 1936; cf. Howe, *Women Music Educators*, chs. 3, 7-8.

[132] Roger Mantie and Jay Dorfman, "Music Participation and Nonparticipation of Nonmajors on College Campuses," *Bulletin of the Council for Research in Music Education*, no. 200 (Spring 2014): 41-62; see also Dimitra Kokotsaki and Susan Hallam, "Higher education music students' perceptions of the benefits of participative music making," *Music Education Research* 9 (2007): 162.

music is important . . . and was a great support and encouragement to us"—and repeated this for presidents Calvin VanderWerf and Gordon Van Wylen.[133] The NASM report of 1968 confirmed that "The administration supports the Department to the fullest extent," evidenced by their backing an addition to Nykerk Hall and adding a music librarian to the department.[134]

In his 1894 inaugural address, President Kollen, referring to Christian colleges, stated: "I do not mean to say that all branches should be taught in our colleges as they are in institutions with almost unmeasured resources but that whatever is taught should be taught equally well."[135] Regarding the teaching of music, every succeeding president would echo Kollen's remarks.

---

[133] *Hope College Magazine* 31 (Spring 1978): 9. For President Dimnent in this regard, see Aschbrenner interview with Neckers.

[134] NASM—1968 visitors report, esp. 2, 12.

[135] 27 June 1894, addresses, 1894-1913 folder, box 1, Kollen Papers; see also *Holland City News*, 30 June 1894.

CHAPTER 2

Pioneers to Professionals

Even when [Curtis Snow's] physical resources were diminishing . . .
he was a musician without peer . . . a superb teacher . . .
because he continued to be a student.
President Wynand Wichers, 1936

The development of one's potential is what you're trying to achieve
in a student, to have them see what they can achieve with what
they've been given. And you have to know yourself what
it means to develop what you've got.
Jantina Holleman, 1978

It is the teaching of piano, as well as my own performance,
that gives me my professional identity.
Charles C. Aschbrenner, ca. 1995

What was John Gilmore? In the second catalog published by Hope College, readers who recognized William Gilmore's role on campus discovered that, "Music is now aided by his brother Mr. John Gilmore."

The younger Gilmore was an 1868 Hope graduate who subsequently became a farmer in the Grand Rapids area. Fifteen years later, the 1882-83 catalog listed him as "in charge of vocal music."[1] Should we understand John Gilmore to have been one of the pioneering faculty in Hope's music program?

The answer to an apparently simple question can be drawn from several early 1880s Hope College faculty meetings, for apparently not all was well in Music. In preparation for the 1882-83 academic year, Hope president Charles Scott responded to a concern raised, indicating that "arrangements had been made with Mr. John Gilmore to give 25 lessons in vocal music to the students during the year."[2] Scott's statement made it clear that in the 1880s, Music was not treated like a typical department, where faculty had considerable autonomy. Three months later, just after the start of the 1882-83 academic year, professors Henry Boers and John Kleinheksel were "appointed a Committee to ascertain from Mr. John Gilmore of Grand Rapids his terms etc. for giving instruction to the students in vocal music once a week for the year and that Prof. Scott be requested to lay the matter before the Executive Committee of the Council."[3] Negotiations were apparently successful, for a local newspaper reported that Gilmore had arrived on campus on October 13 to "take up his duties."[4]

From today's vantage point, this story seems odd: for the most part, faculty do not negotiate with colleagues outside their teaching areas, and the necessity of reporting back to the council (now the board of trustees) may seem ominous. Another clue regarding the crisis in music instruction is in the report of a faculty meeting less than four months later. Gilmore had changed how vocal music was taught, provoking a student rebellion. Consequently, the faculty created a committee to "examine the merits of the old and new systems & if deemed advisable, return to the old." This and a subsequent committee in effect told Gilmore how to teach vocal music and what textbook to use.[5]

John Gilmore's fraught tenure as a teacher of music was short lived. The following year, the catalog listed Harman Van Slyke Peeke, a senior in the preparatory school, as "in charge of vocal music." What

---

[1] *Hope College Catalog* (1867-68), 32, (1882-83), 5. For William Gilmore, see ch. 1.
[2] Minutes of the general faculty, 27 June 1882.
[3] Ibid., 23 Sept. 1882.
[4] *Holland City News*, 14 Oct. 1882.
[5] *Excelsiora* 13 (3 Nov. 1882): 31; minutes of the general faculty, 9 and 19 Jan. and 29 Mar. 1883.

then was John Gilmore in 1882-83? Certainly not a faculty member as understood by professors today.

Throughout the Gilmore affair, the college faculty—not an autonomous department—sought to address the problem. Music had neither a single professor nor any full-time instructors; individuals were hired in what might be understood as a hit-or-miss approach. What then, regarding Music, does *faculty* mean? For our purposes, it is contextual. This chapter will address how the music teaching staff evolved in both earlier and modern eras.

In the 1880s, *instructor* and *tutor* were used interchangeably,[6] but the use of *professor* is particularly confusing. Hope recognized certain individuals as professors but referred to others as instructors. Professors were heads of departments, which meant they examined Hope students in specialized fields, such as history or mathematics. But, *professor* could also refer to a title that individuals—musicians in particular—used for themselves to designate a teacher of music for paying students who were never examined in music—thus "Professor" G. C. Shepard, who was a Grand Rapids performer in the 1880s, taught vocal music at Hope.[7] The Gilmore episode reveals *faculty* in the modern sense was not the right term for him.

To staff Hope College's music offerings in the early years, West Michigan musicians were hired to teach an instrument or lead a vocal group. They did not attend the college's faculty meetings and were not pictured in early *Milestones* as Hope instructors.[8] Except for John Nykerk, these "faculty" were all outsiders: they were not graduates of Hope, few lived in Holland, and their professional training had been private rather than in an academic institution.

In the first half century of the college's existence, to be a member of the faculty meant one was a man or woman for all seasons. In the 1890s, along with his role with music, John Nykerk also taught English and even geology, and in the 1920s, Martha Barkema and Nella Meyer taught both music and French. Until the 1930s, Hope faculty taught both preparatory and college students.[9] Looking back from the twenty-

[6] Compare John Nykerk's title in the 1885-86 *Hope College Catalog* and the general faculty minutes for 21 Sept. 1885.
[7] *Anchor*, 1 Nov. 1887. Until the 1930s, most such "faculty," rather than hold college degrees, had studied music with another performer/teacher. Howe, *Women Music Educators*, 231-32.
[8] Compare *Milestone* (1905), 11, with *Hope College Catalog* (1904-5), 15-16, 29.
[9] Clarence Kleis, Class of 1919, had presidents Dimnent and Wichers as teachers at both the preparatory school and Hope College; Nancy Swinyard interview with Clarence Kleis, 1977, Hope College Living Heritage Oral History Project. See also,

John Nykerk, 1920

first century, the faculty landscape at Hope is unrecognizable. It was not until Music became a department with a critical mass of academically trained professors that its form and function would resemble that of a modern department. This chapter reconstructs the history of who brought this about.

"Our Chief Musician," 1890-1940

In his eulogy at the service for Curtis Snow, former president Edward Dimnent characterized the organ professor as "Our Chief Musician."[10] The term offers an important insight into an era that began with John Nykerk and continued until the hiring in 1940 of Robert Cavanaugh, when the Music Department was so small and staffed mostly with part-time faculty, that one person held it together. Subsequently, a critical mass of professional faculty ensured that survival was no longer at stake. At issue in the pioneers' era was who contributed to the flourishing of Music—and music.

"Some Recollections About the Hope College Preparatory School," Jay Folkert Papers, H88-0053.2.

[10] Robert Snow, *Musikalisch Frau Schnee: A Brief Biography of the Life of Esther MacFarlane Snow* (2002), 19, biographical folder, Esther Snow Papers, H88-0140; see also faculty minutes, 13 June 1936.

John Nykerk was the son of a pastor in Overisel, graduating as valedictorian of the academy Class of 1885 before attending Hope College. In some ways, Nykerk was closer to the post-1940 generation than he was to his own, studying at Chautauqua Institution in New York and Oxford University, pursuing vocal studies in New York City and Boston, and attending professional conferences.[11] As a student and subsequently a member of the faculty, he was a maker of music, both in terms of performance and composition.[12] Although he never published, he did write two essays for the *Anchor*, in which he discussed the educational value of music.[13]

In other ways, Nykerk was a classic case of the early music faculty: a graduate of Hope who—between stints of teaching high school—was a tutor or instructor in vocal music. He accepted his appointment as tutor with mixed emotions: "I feel that I have to take hold of a severe but not unpleasant task, but I am confident that with God's help, I can make it a success."[14] In 1895 he was asked to join the college faculty as professor of English and be in charge of vocal music.[15] Nykerk remained at Hope until he retired in 1936. He also chaired the English department (1910-36) and served as dean of men (1918-36).

Despite these responsibilities, music remained a personal passion: Nykerk was a vocalist—a baritone who did concert and choral recitals in Michigan and well beyond—and he conducted the college's orchestra. Soon after taking up his professorship, he organized the college's first glee clubs.[16] According to the student newspaper, "Professor Nykerk is ever encouraging everyone to consider the advantages that are being offered in music."[17]

Nykerk played a vital role as secretary of the music committee, which launched what became a major, and two decades after his death, the committee became the Department of Music. In this role, he hired

---

[11] *Anchor*, 1 June 1888, 15 Sept. 1926.
[12] Booklets, *Hope College Alumni Songs* and the *Hope College Songbook*. Several of his songs were still well known in the 1930s: biographical folder, Nykerk Papers.
[13] *Anchor*, Apr. and June 1890.
[14] Nykerk to Rev. Peter Moerdyke, 30 June 1885, correspondence 1885-1934 folder, Nykerk Papers.
[15] The 1900-1901 *Hope College Catalog*, 9, 19, lists him as in charge of vocal music for the college and music for the preparatory school—as well as professor of English for both.
[16] *Milestone* (1928), 96; Gordan Mackay interview with Rev. James Wayer, biographical folder, Nykerk Papers; *Hope College Catalog* (1889-1900), 54-55; *Holland City News*, 29 Nov. 1934.
[17] *Anchor*, 15 Oct. 1919.

dozens of faculty, who supervised lessons and taught courses. As a measure of his success, by the mid-1920s, the School of Music enrolled over 120 students.[18]

As the chief musician of his era, Nykerk led the music in Winants Chapel every morning until 1929, when these duties were assumed by Curtis Snow. In so doing, Nykerk maintained the nineteenth-century connection at Hope between faculty and faith.[19] Mrs. W. H. Loomis, who taught several music courses, said in chapel in 1928, that "Music is a gift from God. It is just as much a part of this universe as the sun, moon, and stars," and Nykerk certainly would have echoed that statement.[20]

Although he had an exacting reputation as a professor, Nykerk combined organizational genius with rare ability as a teacher. Alice Hoffs thought Nykerk was "one of the most influential professors I've ever had at Hope ... [and] a great influence on my life." She recalled how he combined musical with literary knowledge.

> One time, he asked me to play a song for chapel, and at that time, they had a grand piano up there on the stage, and I was all seated at the piano ready to start, and he asked me what I was going to play. So I told him, and he immediately thought of a poem.... And here I was, sitting on that bench all that time while he had to recite that poem to the audience. Of course, I was embarrassed. But he did know a lot about all those things.[21]

Today almost no one remembers John Nykerk, except for the competition bearing his name, which he launched in 1936, his final year on the Hope faculty. At the end of that year, his colleagues passed a resolution honoring him for his unique contribution to Hope over four decades, pointing out that it was "rare that a man be privileged to engage in so wide a variety of activities, literary, musical, civic, and religious, and that he attain outstanding distinction in all of these."[22]

---

[18] Ibid., 15 Sept. 1926; Corcoran, "Who Were the School of Music students?"
[19] All faculty were expected to present talks in chapel from time to time: faculty minutes, 10 Nov. 1933; see also HC diary 1927-, box 1, Schuppert Papers.
[20] *Anchor*, 14 Mar. 1928; *Musical Monitor* 4 (Nov. 1914): 81; for Nykerk, *Anchor*, June 1890, and booklets, *Hope College Alumni Songs* and *Songs of Hope College*, biographical folder, Nykerk Papers.
[21] Gordan Mackay interviews with Emma Pieters and Rev. James Wayer, Hope College, biographical folder, Nykerk Papers; Larry Wagenaar interview with Alice Hoffs, 1999, Alice (Brower) Hoffs Papers.
[22] Faculty minutes, 13 June 1936.

Curtis Snow at the Skinner organ

Earlier, the Class of 1921 had honored Nykerk by dedicating the 1920 *Milestone* to him, who, in their words, had "affiliated himself with the students of Hope both as friend and instructor."[23] In 1963 the music building was named after him, and now there is a plaque in his honor in the Dimnent Chapel narthex, and a departmental scholarship bears his name.

Nykerk's most important hire was Curtis Snow in 1929. He was Hope's first full-time appointment in music as college organist and instructor in organ and piano. From the 1880s through the early twentieth century, students had been the designated organists for chapel services, and since 1911, although organ had been taught occasionally, organ teachers had come and gone, and for some years, in spite of the college's claim to offer instruction in organ, no professor had actually taught it.[24] The new Dimnent Chapel with its remarkable organ demanded the college improve its overall quality. Snow was the beneficiary, and in his brief time on the faculty, he established the high place of organ studies at Hope College.

In contrast to Nykerk, Curtis Snow and his wife, Esther, were neither Hope graduates nor members of the Reformed church. Prior

---

[23] *Milestone* (1920), 5.
[24] See, e.g., *Hope College Bulletin* (May 1916), 150-55, and (Nov. 1928), 21-28.

to their arrival, neither had completed a college degree. At age fifteen, Curtis Snow was appointed assistant organist at a church in his Massachusetts hometown. Subsequently he studied organ in Boston before moving to Iowa to accept a position at an Episcopal church in Sioux City as organist and director of a men's choir. In 1917 he enlisted in the Army, was discharged in 1919, and then returned to his church position; in 1922 he joined the faculty of the Conservatory of Music at Morningside College in Sioux City. At the same time, he served a Presbyterian church in the city as organist and choir director, performed at concerts in the Midwest and beyond, and wooed and married Esther Mac Farlane, a fellow church organist.[25]

Snow learned about the opening at Hope from a friend in Orange City, Iowa. He was hired and arrived in Holland just in time to participate in the June 1929 dedication of the magnificent Skinner organ and then played in that year's Commencement.[26] Thereafter, according to Wynand Wichers, Snow virtually lived in Dimnent Chapel, just a block away from his Twelfth Street home. At his memorial, Wichers praised Snow:

> [for] constantly bringing into this place great organists from various parts of the country, partly for his own education and enlightenment and enjoyment and also to build up on this Campus an acquaintance with those who were foremost in their profession and a devotion to that which was outstanding.[27]

Snow had accomplished for organ what Nykerk had for vocal and instrumental music.

Raising the stature of organ music at Hope, however, is not Snow's only legacy. In fall 1929, he formed the Chapel Choir, which performed regularly at the daily religious services. Snow chose and then drilled the sixty students at two one-hour practices per week, with one of his choir members deeming him a "fine conductor."[28] A month into his first semester of teaching at Hope, Snow launched Vespers, a series of bimonthly Sunday afternoon musical performances. An individual with apparently boundless energy, Snow, in fall 1934, assumed leadership of

[25] *Hope College Bulletin* (Feb. 1931), 62, and (Feb. 1938), 58.
[26] *Anchor*, 18 Sept. 1929; Commencement program, 19 June 1929, dedication 1929 folder, Dimnent Memorial Chapel Papers, H88-0393.
[27] *Holland City News*, 9 Jan. 1936.
[28] *Milestone* (1930), 144; clipping, Hope College Career (1929-31) folder and diary entry, 16 Dec. 1929, HC diaries 1929-34, box 1, Schuppert Papers.

Hope's band and even procured uniforms for them. Despite an overly full schedule on campus and in the community, Snow continued to perform once or twice a month at Vespers and in concert work across the Midwest.[29]

As a teacher, Snow's focus was on preparing church organists to be exceptional artists and practical theologians. He expected excellence from his students, and to that end, they regularly performed for area churches, in preludes at Hope's daily chapel services, and at public recitals, which culminated in senior recitals.[30] Snow's first organ major, Richard Niessink, completed the BM in 1932. Toward the end of her life, Ethel Leestma Swets, another organ major who had worked under Snow, remembered him as "the whole department of music."[31] She may have meant he was the only full-time faculty member, but most likely, she intended something more profound than that. His photograph is in her college scrapbook, next to which she wrote, "My wonderful organ Prof."[32] Following the Chapel Choir's performance at the 1933 Baccalaureate service, Snow had the students to his home, where they presented him a copy of Robert Schauffler's *Beethoven* (1929).[33]

After two years on the faculty, Snow was promoted to professor of organ and piano. While at Hope, he earned his undergraduate degree and began work on a master of music degree at the University of Michigan. Despite the sudden onset of tuberculosis, he ran the race until the very end. He was "determined not to give up the work he loved so well,"[34] and though he was too ill to stand, he directed the Civic Chorus in late November 1935. At just forty-one years of age, Curtis Snow died on New Year's Eve 1935. Repeating the phrase of the college president, a faculty resolution termed Curtis Snow "our 'Chief Musician,' head of the Department of Music, brilliant organist, masterful conductor of the Chapel Choir and Civic Chorus, and instructor in the Science of

---

[29] Events—recitals (organ) folder, box 3, MD Papers; programs, box 2, Curtis Snow Papers, H88-0142; diary entries, 25 Apr. 1930, 16 Mar. 1932, HC diaries 1929-34, box 1, Schuppert Papers.

[30] *Hope College Bulletin* (1929-30), 56. Mildred Schuppert recorded all these occasions in her diaries: HC diary 1927- and HC diaries 1929-34, box 1, Schuppert Papers.

[31] *Holland Sentinel*, 15 Apr. 2007.

[32] Scrapbook 1929-36, Ethel Leestma Swets Collection; see also Baer and Utting interview with Swets' daughters, Marcia Buck and Faith Curtis, 21 June 2018, Making Music folder.

[33] Scrapbook 1929-36, Ethel Leestma Swets Collection.

[34] Entry for 25 Nov. 1935, Holland Civic Chorus Record Book, 1930-38, Curtis Snow Papers.

Music."[35] President Wichers summed up his contributions and pointed out how Snow was a model pioneer and that one person, even in a short time, could make a difference.

> He never would be satisfied until everyone had learned to love music. It is no wonder, therefore, that as the months and years went along, that this appreciation of music amongst our Student Body was constantly increasing, so that all facilities were taxed to capacity.... And so, we pay tribute to him today as our music master.[36]

In 1940 Snow was remembered in an organ scholarship that bore his name, and in the next decade, an auditorium was named after him in the Nykerk Hall of Music. There is currently a lounge in the Jack Miller Center which honors his memory.

While Curtis Snow taught at Hope, his wife, Esther, served the music program as an accompanist and an occasional soloist. After her husband's death, this widow with four small children filled a void and played an important role in the development of Hope's music department.

Esther Snow was not the first female to teach music at Hope. Indeed, the path was well worn: Snow's predecessors included eighteen women from 1904 on, each of whom had taught for at least a year—making Music one of the most female-welcoming departments at the college in the first half of the twentieth century. Whereas the female music faculty had averaged just under six-and-a-half years teaching at Hope,[37] Esther Snow stayed for seventeen years as a full-time faculty member, on top of her part-time work when her husband was alive. Esther Snow's leadership of the department during the dark days of the Great Depression and the Second World War was especially significant.

Before coming to Hope in 1929 with her husband, Esther Snow had had private classes in organ and piano; studied at the Morningside College Conservatory, Sioux City, Iowa; and completed further work at the Oberlin Conservatory of Music, Oberlin, Ohio. Between 1919 and 1923, she was the organist for two different churches in Sioux City. Snow survived her husband's death, certainly financially and perhaps psychologically as well, because the college took her on to help teach

---

[35] Faculty minutes, 13 June 1936.
[36] *Holland City News*, 9 Jan. 1936; *Anchor*, 15 Jan. 1936.
[37] For two cases, Grace Fenton and Helene Karsten, see *Anchor*, 2 Oct. 1918; *Holland Evening Sentinel*, 6 Mar. 1961; Aschbrenner interview with Holleman.

Esther Snow and the Women's Glee Club

organ and piano students. She was appointed instructor in piano and theory in 1937, taking Sarah Lacey's place teaching piano and other music courses. In 1940 Snow began teaching music theory and pipe organ and served as the college organist—replacing the faculty member who had succeeded her husband. She also taught a methods course for music education students.

Her role in the department expanded during World War II. As men departed to serve their country and the college became strapped for money, the remaining faculty had to do more with less. Snow led a women's sextet, advised the Musical Arts Club, directed the Chapel Choir and the Women's Glee Club, and served as an accompanist and organist for, as she put it, "all college services . . . all musical events and activities."[38] The Women's Glee Club was a major responsibility for a single mother: there were two or three rehearsals every week in the fall semester and then five per week in the spring, endless performances, and for Snow, spring tours on twelve occasions between 1941 and 1954; in 1953 she joined Robert Cavanaugh on the inaugural Chapel Choir tour to the East Coast.[39]

As was true for her husband, Esther Snow was also deeply involved in the city of Holland musical communities. She served as organist and choir director for Hope Reformed Church and for the *Messiah*

---

[38] Snow, *Musikalisch Frau Schnee*, 26; Esther Snow personal file.
[39] *Anchor*, 22 Jan. 1953; Esther Snow personal file.

44   MAKING MUSIC

productions for a quarter century and performed regularly in the Vespers programs. Snow earned her undergraduate degree at Hope in 1941, majoring in music. Arthritis made her organ playing difficult, and in 1954, she took a leave to finish her MA at Michigan State University and then returned to Hope to teach German. During these years, she and history professor Paul Fried provided academic leadership for the Vienna Summer School. Snow was widely praised by both the students she mentored and her colleagues, and after she passed away in 1974, her family endowed a scholarship in her name for students attending the Vienna program.[40]

1940 and beyond

During World War II, three female faculty members—Grace Fenton, Helene Karsten, and Esther Snow—kept music alive at Hope by ensuring that the glee clubs remained vital, teaching courses, and contributing to community events, such as the *Messiah*. But without someone to chart new courses, Music drifted until the end of the 1940s, when Robert Cavanaugh emerged as departmental leader.

Replacing Grace Fenton in 1940, Robert Cavanaugh began a long and distinguished career in Hope's Music Department, punctuated by service in the Navy from 1943 to 1946. In time, he assumed guidance of both glee clubs, the Chapel Choir, and the Choral Union; he taught theory and other subjects, and he took the lead in staging *Messiah* concerts.

Cavanaugh did not grow up in the Reformed Church, nor did he attend Hope; he graduated in 1937 from the University of Wisconsin—in English—and then earned a BM in 1939 and a master's in music in 1940 from the American Conservatory of Music in Chicago. Cavanaugh straddled the categories of pioneer and professional but resembled more the latter than the former: he remained at Hope for thirty-six years, engaged in some scholarly work, and was the first music professor with an earned doctorate, received in 1953.

[40] Libby Hillegonds, "Reminiscences of the 1940s," in *Hope at the Crossroads: The War Years*, ed. Eileen Nordstrom and George D. Zuidema (Holland, MI: Hope College, 2008), 59; Marc Baer interview with Roger Rietberg, 9 Aug. 2018, and Beverly Mulder to Marc Baer, email, 14 Aug. 2018, Making Music folder; Aschbrenner interview with Holleman; interview with Barbara Timmer, Communication 357 Video Projects, H03-1302.5; Snow, *Musikalisch Frau Schnee*, 29; Stephen I. Hemenway, *Hope Beyond Borders: The Life and Letters of Paul Fried* (Holland, MI: Van Raalte Press, 2014), 271-72.

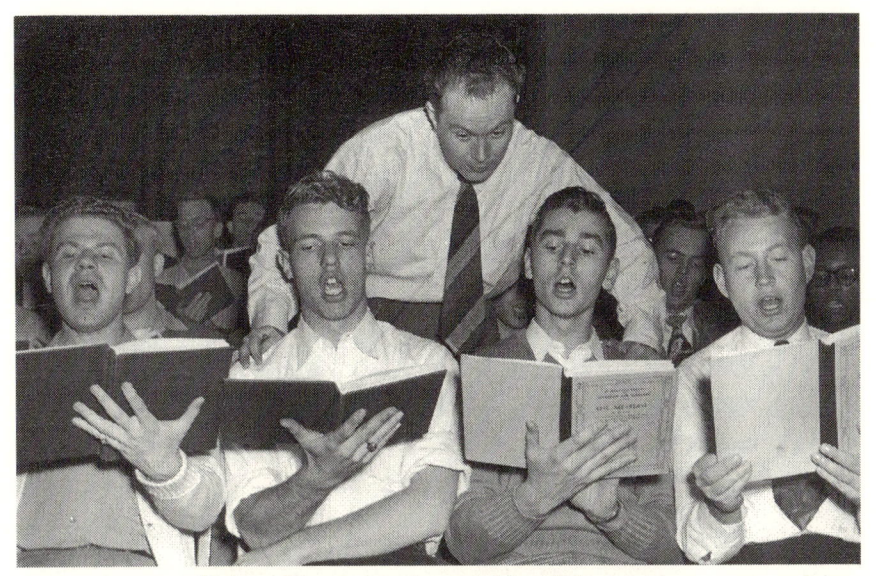

Robert Cavanaugh and *Messiah* chorus

When Cavanaugh joined the department, only Esther Snow and James Mearns, another new hire, taught full time. Lubbers recalled: "Most of the staff were part time, brought in for a few hours to teach their specialty."[41] Cavanaugh and Lubbers developed a solid working relationship, which helped the music professor succeed in everything he turned his hand to: vocal ensembles, music curriculum and faculty, developing the case for building Nykerk Hall, securing associate and then full membership in the National Association of Schools of Music, making music for the West Michigan community, and composing the song that would be sung by the Hope nation for the next several decades.

Cavanaugh began as director of the Men's Glee Club, taking them on tours and performing with them (except for a brief hiatus in the late 1940s), and he led the Chapel Choir for thirty-four years. He set the bar high, once telling the members, he did not care "if the choir gets every note wrong, just so it is to the glory of God," and an early student recalled him giving "us all lessons in repertoire, discipline, and growth into more mature young men."[42] According to George Zuidema '49, Cavanaugh "had outstanding choral groups including Chapel Choir and the Men's Glee Club," and professor of piano Joan Conway put it

---

[41] Irwin Lubbers, "Robert A. Cavanaugh: A Tribute," biographical material folder, Cavanaugh Papers.
[42] *Anchor*, 19 Mar. 1976.

simply: "The choirs worshipped him; they really loved him."[43] In 1953, following an invitation by the Protestant Council of Greater New York for the choir to be featured at the Easter sunrise service at Radio City Music Hall, Cavanaugh began taking the Chapel Choir on tours.[44]

Cavanaugh served as head of his department 1950-59, 1961-62, and chair 1963-69. Lubbers praised his leadership, as did this student: "He was always a very organized person and got things done."[45] Among Cavanaugh's several legacies is one perhaps no longer associated with his name, the *Alma Mater Hymn*, which he composed in 1947. It was printed in an *Anchor* issue that year, along with this comment: "It really is a thrill to have the *Alma Mater* sung at the end of each concert."[46] Robert Cavanaugh passed away in 1976, and was memorialized with the Cavanaugh Senior Music Award, the naming of the choral rehearsal room in the Jack Miller Center, and the Cavanaugh Apartments on East Fourteenth Street.

Referring to the faculty who had arrived after World War II, Jantina Holleman recalled, "We came into the music department when it wasn't really a department at all." Robert Cavanaugh made it so, but he could not have done this by himself.[47]

During the Great Depression, Holleman's mother won a piano in a jingle-writing contest. Her parents, South Dakota farmers, had their telephone and electricity turned off to save money for piano lessons for Holleman and her brother. While in high school, Holleman won a statewide music contest and began teaching piano to her peers. She went on to attend Morningside College and the State Teachers College in Springfield, South Dakota. Having earned her teaching certificate at age nineteen, Holleman taught music to first and second grade children for two years in Reliance, South Dakota, subsequently graduating in 1943 with a bachelor's degree from Iowa's Central College. She then became a music teacher at the high school in Sioux Center, Iowa, where she taught for another two years before moving to New York City and entering a graduate program in music education at Columbia University. Following her graduation in 1946, Lubbers recruited her to

---

[43] Zuidema, *Hope at the Crossroads*, 232; Baer and Utting interview with Joan C. Conway, 25 June 2018, Making Music folder. See also Bob Hoeksema to Cavanaugh, 8 Apr. 1966, correspondence, 1965-69 folder, box 1, Cavanaugh Papers.

[44] *Anchor*, 22 Jan. 1953; Zuidema, *Hope at the Crossroads*, 232.

[45] Lubbers, "Cavanaugh: A Tribute"; Baer and Utting interview with Robert Ritsema, 28 June 2018, Making Music folder; cf. Harper, "Music in Liberal Arts," 269.

[46] *Anchor*, 22 May 1947.

[47] Press release, 1 Apr. 1987, news releases and clippings folder, and Piano Teaching Activities (1949), Music Department curriculum folder, Holleman Papers.

Jantina Holleman

join the Hope faculty, where she would remain for the next four decades. Holleman's teaching coincided with an influx of World War II veterans. She almost certainly drew upon her time teaching children on the plains of South Dakota to interest these young men in the study of music. As she put it in 1978, "Music is a never-failing source of joy, I think, and you want the students to have some of that, to develop inner resources and capabilities." She knew that joy well through her own solo recitals and other performances—at chapel, in her church, and with the Symphonette.[48] As well, her joy came from two other sources: "a very direct, personal contact with students" and in helping to shape curriculum development in music education, church music, choral conducting, and perhaps the most important, because it touched so many students, the introduction to music course.[49] Holleman even held court at a weekly gathering to listen to records, attracting an average of ten students.[50]

This enthusiasm carried over into two important initiatives during her time at Hope College. In 1947 Holleman formed the Madrigal

[48] *Hope College Magazine* 31 (Spring 1978): 9; Piano Teaching Activities (1949), Music Department curriculum folder, Holleman Papers.
[49] *Hope College Magazine* 31 (Spring 1978): 9; press release, 1 Apr. 1987, news releases and clippings folder. Holleman Papers.
[50] Piano Teaching Activities (1949).

Singers. Their first concert took place in May 1947 when among other pieces they performed Thomas Arne's *Which Is the Properest Day to Sing?*[51] One of the original members, Duane Booi '49, recalled that Holleman had recruited a dozen students for the ensemble, who then sang for the Vespers series and other college events. "Jantina was a no-nonsense person, but she made singing fun and was very well liked."[52] Then in 1952, Holleman founded the College Chorus (at first called the Chancel Choir), attracting one hundred twenty-two students.[53]

Holleman raised funds to furnish the music building, which opened its doors in the fall of 1956; managed its music library; and chaired the committee planning the 1970 Nykerk Hall addition.[54] Beginning in 1972, she served as coordinator of piano activities, embracing a list of duties akin to chairing a small department. All the while, Holleman maintained a busy schedule of solo performances on campus and in the community. Holleman was also active on the scholarly front, in 1954 studying at the Music Conservatory in Amsterdam on a Fulbright Fellowship and then returning to Europe in the 1960s, with a grant to study harpsichord and piano.[55] Jantina Holleman became an elder at Third Reformed Church in 1974, the first woman to serve in that capacity in her congregation. She retired in 1987 and passed away in 2012.

Like Robert Cavanaugh, Morrette Rider also did not graduate from Hope College or grow up in the Reformed Church. Having been raised in the state, Rider attended the University of Pennsylvania before transferring to the University of Michigan, earning a BM in 1942 before his World War II Army service with the Signal Intelligence Service in China and India. He returned to the University of Michigan and completed his MM in 1947. While Rider was in graduate school, Cavanaugh contacted the dean of Michigan's School of Music, inquiring about potential candidates for a position at Hope in instrumental music and teaching a variety of other subjects. The dean suggested, "[Rider] is one of the few men we have had who has had a major in strings and a good deal of

---

[51] *Anchor*, 22 May 1947.
[52] Duane Booi to Marc Baer, 14 July 2018, Making Music folder.
[53] *Anchor*, 6 Nov. 1952; press release, 1 Apr. 1987, news releases and clippings folder, Holleman Papers.
[54] Press release, 1 Apr. 1987; letters to music graduates, 7 May and 9 July 1956, to Cavanaugh, 30 June 1967, minutes Music Dedication Committee, 18 Sept. 1970, Music Building 1956-70 folder, Holleman Papers; *Hope College Magazine* 31 (Spring 1978): 9.
[55] *Anchor*, 23 Oct. 1954; *Hope College Magazine* 31 (Spring 1978): 10.

Morrette Rider

[handwritten: directed the musicals that I was in]

work in the wind instruments and some experience conducting band." After an interview, Rider was offered the position.[56]

Rider's most important legacy is in establishing the excellence of instrumental music at Hope, which had suffered for decades for lack of a strong leader.[57] In 1947 he hit the ground running, offering a concert in Dimnent Chapel in November with thirty-one instrumentalists and a vocal quartet; thereafter, the orchestra gave three major concerts per year.[58] In 1949 Rider founded the Hope College Symphony, and the Hope Symphonette followed in 1953.[59] By 1957 the Symphonette was so respected that Michigan State University's public television station broadcast one of their concerts.[60] Meanwhile, Rider led the band to spend less time on marching so that its members could focus on their music, designating some members as the Concert Band, thereby distinguishing "pep" from "stage" bands.[61]

[56] Earl Moore to Cavanaugh, 25 Apr. and 1 May 1947, Rider to Cavanaugh, 3 May, Lubbers to Rider, 20 June and Rider to Lubbers, 24 June 1947, correspondence 1947-53 folder, Rider Papers.
[57] Instrumental ensembles—orchestra, 1921-72 folder, MD Papers; Aschbrenner interview with Holleman.
[58] Programs, instrumental ensembles—orchestra, 1921-72 folder, MD Papers.
[59] Programs, instrumental ensembles—Symphonette, 1953-74 folder, MD Papers.
[60] *Michigan State News*, 22 Nov. 1957.
[61] *Anchor*, 13 Nov. 1947; programs, ensembles, instrumental, band, 1926-82 folder, MD Papers.

According to student Evie Van Dam, "Whenever I think back . . . and remember what the orchestra and band formerly were and what they are now, the comparison is a marvelous revelation. . . . In fact, when I was a freshman, the orchestra wasn't even in existence."[62] Robert Ritsema, music major at the time of Rider's arrival and subsequent faculty member, recalled that after Rider came to Hope, the orchestra program took off.[63]

In a letter to Lubbers urging an overdue promotion, Rider listed his achievements:

> The instrumental music program of the college was started by me in 1947 and has grown to three large organizations, two faculty ensembles, numerous small groups, an instrumental music enrollment of more than 150 students and a faculty of two full-time and four part-time teachers. I feel that I had an important part to play in the accrediting of our department by the NASM and also in the building of our teacher education program. Our new building is in large part an outgrowth of this development.[64]

With that record and with his doctorate earned in 1955 from Columbia University, it is inexplicable that it took five more years for Rider to be promoted to professor. This is even more odd given that Rider was the most widely published faculty member in the history of the department.[65]

Experience on several professional music and arts organizations may have whetted his appetite for administration. Rider was appointed by President Vander Werf as Hope's dean of academic affairs, remaining in that position until 1975, when he moved west to be the dean of the School of Music at the University of Oregon. He retired from the university in 1986 and passed away in 2008.

President Lubbers knew Anthony Kooiker from his time at Central College in Iowa and personally recruited him to Hope. Kooiker joined Hope's music faculty in 1950, teaching piano, music literature, and music theory. A year later, Lubbers wrote, "The prestige of the music department has been greatly enhanced by his appointment," and

---

[62] *Anchor*, 24 Mar. 1949.
[63] Baer and Utting interview with Ritsema; see also Wilbur Brandli '46 to Rider, 22 Apr. 1974, correspondence 1956-86 folder, box 1, Rider Papers.
[64] Rider to Lubbers, 7 Oct. 1960, correspondence 1953-68 folder, Rider Papers.
[65] See articles 1962-75 folder, Rider Papers.

Anthony Kooiker,
Town Hall concert, 1954

ANTHONY KOOIKER
PIANIST

TOWN HALL — FRIDAY EVENING AT 8:30 NOVEMBER 26, 1954

he alerted Norman Vincent Peale and others in New York City about an upcoming concert Kooiker was to perform there.[66]

A small-town Iowan, Kooiker served as organist in a local Reformed Church and taught piano lessons on the side in his early teens. He began his undergraduate studies at Morningside College and then as a junior in 1942 transferred to Northwestern University and earned a BM; he earned an MM from the University of Rochester's Eastman School of Music in 1944 and taught at Central College 1943-47. From 1947 to 1950, he toured as accompanist with the noted violinist Albert Spaulding before coming to Hope, where he would remain for thirty-seven years, teaching piano, directing the Women's Choir, and with Jantina Holleman, orchestrating the Christmas Vespers program.

First and foremost, however, Kooiker was a performer. Having been on the New York stage both in the Town Hall and Carnegie Hall, in 1954

---

[66] *Anchor*, 25 Mar. 1948; Kooiker to Lubbers, 12 July and 18 Aug. 1948; Lubbers to Kooiker, 11 and 25 Aug. 1948; Lubbers to Peale and others 23 Mar. 1951, correspondence folder, and biographical materials folder, Anthony Kooiker Papers, H88-0089; memo, Lubbers to Hollenbach, 2 Dec. 1948, Milton Johnston, Hope biographical file; *Grand Rapids Press*, 29 Jan. 1986.

he achieved the enviable feat of a Town Hall solo concert, performing works by, among others, Bach, Brahms, Debussy, and Ravel.[67] Then in 1967, he performed in Carnegie Hall, playing works by Liszt, Bloch, and Beethoven. In the Holland area, Kooiker frequently performed, drawing significant artists and encouraging student and faculty recitals.[68] Later, during his time at Hope, he went on concert tours to Yugoslavia and the Netherlands. While performing on national and international stages, he took time to organize the Hope College Trio, which included Robert Ritsema on cello and Harrison Ryker, then subsequently Charles Gray, on violin, playing a chamber music repertoire.

Kooiker was highly regarded as a scholar and recording artist, as well as a performer. While teaching at Hope in 1962, Kooiker was awarded a doctorate from the University of Rochester. Having received a Danforth grant in 1959, he researched early keyboard music, which resulted in *Melothesis*, a 1967 book on Restoration-era music. In 1986 Kooiker recorded a solo album featuring works by Rachmaninoff and Debussy.

Joan Conway termed him "a brilliant man,"[69] and like his colleagues, his former students remembered him fondly. Nick Pool '56, pronounced, "He's been more than a teacher; he's been a mentor, a counselor, and a really fine influence in the lives of a great many people." Edna Ter Molen '60, recalled "his commitment to excellence."[70] Kooiker retired from the college in 1987 and died two decades later. His colleagues honored him with a memorial concert and a scholarship in his name, as well as a classroom in the Jack Miller Center. His former home on Twelfth Street was acquired by the College and moved to Fourteenth Street: it was then designated as Kooiker Cottage.

Freshman Roger Rietberg, recruited in 1940 by Cavanaugh in his first year of teaching, joined the Men's Glee Club and the Chapel Choir. In 1976, as a music professor at the college, Rietberg assumed the directorship of the Chapel Choir, taking over from Cavanaugh.

Rietberg grew up in Grand Rapids, where in kindergarten he had had his first experience directing, in this case, a band. After studying piano with a talented cousin, he gravitated to the organ. Rietberg entered Hope in 1940, leaving in 1942 for World War II service as a radio operator with the Army Air Corps in Italy. Following the war,

---

[67] Events—recitals (faculty) folder, box 2, MD Papers; *Holland Evening Sentinel*, 11 May 1964; *Anchor*, 15 May 1964.
[68] Press release, 1 Apr. 1987, news releases and clippings folder, Holleman Papers.
[69] Baer and Utting interview with Conway.
[70] *Holland Sentinel*, 9 Sept. 2001.

Roger Rietberg

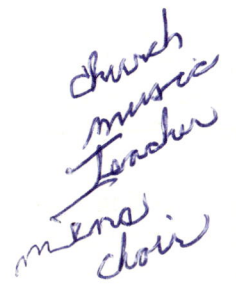

he returned to Hope, graduating in 1947 with a degree in music. He went on to earn a master of sacred music degree in 1949 from Union Theological Seminary. Meanwhile, he directed music at First Methodist Church in Red Bank, New Jersey, 1948-50, before returning to Holland's Third Reformed Church, where he served as minister of music from 1950 to 1954. After he accepted an offer from Hope in 1954 to succeed Esther Snow, the choirs became Rietberg's passion,

When Jantina Holleman founded it, the Chancel Choir (now the College Chorus) had over a hundred members and maintained that level of support well into the future because so many students wanted to sing but were unable to make the cut for the seventy-member Chapel Choir.[71] Rietberg assumed the leadership of the Chancel Choir in 1953, a year before joining the Hope faculty, getting the *Anchor* to announce that he "cordially welcomes anyone who enjoys singing to join the chancel choir."[72] The choir performed a variety of concerts, mixing the sacred music of Bach, Brahms, and Beethoven with contemporary secular artists. As a student, Robert Ritsema was a member of Rietberg's choir, which he recalled as a joyful experience, as did other former students.[73]

Rietberg eventually gave up the College Chorus to lead the Chapel Choir, directing it between 1975 and 1990, as well as the Men's Chorus.

---

[71] *Anchor*, 6 May and 1 Oct. 1953; Roger Rietberg personal file, H90-1087; Baer interview with Rietberg.
[72] *Anchor*, 1 Oct. 1953.
[73] Baer and Utting interview with Ritsema; emails to Marc Baer, Melissa Johnson, 4 June, Christopher Turbessi, 6 June, and Thomas Folkert and Ken Neevel, 21 Aug. 2018, Making Music folder.

His choir members called him "coach." As he recalled, this happened spontaneously sometime in 1976, shortly after his first tour as director, remarking that "Prof." had already been taken by Cavanaugh.[74] Kari Schaafsma '90, had a different interpretation: "Something that's really significant about Coach is the unity that he builds.... The unity that we feel and the closeness that builds make the choir just like a team."[75] Under Rietberg, in addition to performing at morning chapel, the choir staged concerts. For example, in fall 1977, they did Vaughn Williams' *Mass in G Minor*, whereas in spring 1980, with the College Chorus and Hope Symphonette, they performed Gabriel Fauré's *Requiem*.[76] Beginning in 1976, Rietberg led tours, first to various parts of the United States and Canada, then to Europe and the USSR. According to Rietberg, the choir singing Russian music combined with his awareness that other college choirs were going to the Soviet Union informed his decision to travel there.[77]

Rietberg taught courses in music theory, choral conducting, organ, and church music. He taught and directed simultaneously on multiple fronts, continuing as organist and choir director at Third Reformed Church.

In 1960 Rietberg received a Danforth Grant, allowing him to research organ repertoire and choral technique at Union Theological Seminary. Between 1964 and 1968, he left Music to serve as associate director and then director of admissions, having earlier travelled the country recruiting for Hope. Rietberg then returned to the Music Department full time, until he retired in 1990. He went out in style, in his final semester leading the audience at the DeVos Musical Showcase in singing the *Alma Mater Hymn* and conducting a last Chapel Choir concert in April. He is honored by a classroom in the Jack Miller Center named after him, as well as the departmental Chapel Choir Award.

Roger Davis never met an organ he did not like. He served as the college's organist for twenty-seven years and performed in church recitals across the Midwest and in the Netherlands; he taught organ to a generation of Hope students; he built some organs, and from the time he was a teen, he rebuilt others; and he wrote what has become the standard beginning organ book.

---

[74] Baer interview with Rietberg.
[75] *News from Hope College* (Apr. 1990), 6.
[76] Press release, 1 Nov. 1977; program, 27 Apr. 1980, vocal ensembles—Chapel Choir, 1970- ongoing folder, box 2, MD Papers.
[77] Vocal ensembles—Chapel Choir, 1970- ongoing folder; Baer interview with Rietberg.

Roger Davis at the Skinner organ

[handwritten: not the one in the chapel]

Davis grew up in Ohio, graduating in 1957 with a BS in instrumental music education from the University of Akron, his hometown college, specializing in horn, organ, and string bass. He earned his BM in organ in 1961 from the Oberlin Conservatory of Music, and in 1963 an MM from Northwestern University. He had played string bass in the Akron Symphony Orchestra and had served as the organist and choir director for a Cleveland suburban Congregational church and then at a community church in Chicago. Davis joined the Hope faculty in 1963, eventually replacing Roger Rietberg.

As well as teaching organ, church music, music history, and music theory and serving as the college organist, Davis conducted the College Chorus for twenty years. The highlight of that time was bringing the French composer and organist Maurice Duruflé to conduct the chorus and orchestra in his *Requiem*, and for a decade, Davis also headed up Christmas Vespers. Recalling his colleague's Vespers efforts, Robert Ritsema thought that Roger Davis was the one who really brought that to the standard it is today.[78]

Davis built on the legacy of Curtis Snow to the point that Ritsema pronounced the organ experience for Hope students "the envy of other schools of our kind throughout the country," while Beverly Mulder

---

[78] Baer and Utting interview with Ritsema.

recalled Davis as "a great man, quirky, but so kind to me."[79] In part, this came out of Davis's own experience as a musician: "Since I perform myself, I am aware of the problems involved in methods of practice and self-discipline."[80] Davis was instrumental in the college's planning and acquisition of the Dutch Pels and Van Leeuwen tracker organ, which in 1971 was installed in the Dimnent balcony, having made the case that the chapel had the best acoustics in Holland.[81] Davis gave the first public recital on it that May, a variety of Baroque, Romantic, and modern works.

His other legacy is the *Organist's Manual*, published in 1985. The purpose of this book is to provide both beginners and experienced organists a single source of technique and a collection of compositions.[82] Roger Davis died in 1990 at his home in Holland; he was fifty-five. Friends and family created an organ scholarship for Hope freshmen in his name.

When he was five, Charles Aschbrenner began studying piano with his mother. Oboe lessons with another teacher soon followed, and this began a competition between the two instruments for his heart and mind. Aschbrenner performed his first piano recital when he was twelve. As a student at Illinois Wesleyan, he was first-chair oboe with the Bloomington-Normal Symphony and, after transferring to the University of Illinois, he played the oboe with the school's symphony. Majoring in piano at Illinois, Aschbrenner became drawn to the work of George Gershwin, and the piano became his primary instrument.

Aschbrenner grew up in suburban Chicago, graduating in 1959 with a BM from the University of Illinois. He taught at Stephens College, 1959-61, modeling the modern Renaissance man by teaching piano, dancing in a production of *Carousel*, singing in a production of *The Mikado*, and, of course, playing the oboe. After the stint at Stephens, in 1963 he earned an MM at Yale, joining Hope's Music Department that same year, succeeding Helene Karsten.

During his years at Hope, Aschbrenner made a significant impact in two areas. The first concerned piano—his primary instrument. Within the department, he served as chair of the piano area, while also performing both as a soloist and in partnership with Joan Conway. The

[79] *Anchor*, 31 Jan. 1990; Beverly Mulder to Marc Baer, email, 14 Aug. 2018, Making Music folder.
[80] *Hope College Catalog* (1976-77), 12.
[81] Press release, 2 Mar. 1971, Roger E. Davis biographical file.
[82] Roger E. Davis, *The Organist's Manual: Technical Studies and Selected Compositions for the Organ* (New York and London: W. W. Norton, 1985), ix.

Charles C. Aschbrenner teaching

duo was sought after across the Midwest. As a solo artist, Aschbrenner performed not only on the televised church service the *Hour of Power* but also abroad. On sabbatical in 1986, he spent a month in Mexico, lecturing on Chopin and Schumann, whereas the following year, he went on an eighteen-day concert tour of Portugal, playing a program that included Schumann's *Carnival*, Chopin's *Ballade No. I*, and other music by American composers.[83]

Aschbrenner's second area of impact was pioneering instruction in eurhythmics at the college. The focus of Dalcroze eurhythmics lies in training musical faculties—tone and rhythm—to interact with bodily movements, to balance knowing music intellectually and feeling it physically.[84] For the pianist, it answers the question, "What do I do with my body when my hands are on the keyboard?" Aschbrenner spent his 1974 sabbatical in New York City becoming a certified Dalcroze instructor, subsequently teaching eurhythmics at Hope for the next three decades.[85] Elizabeth Johnson '05 recalled how Aschbrenner taught:

[83] *Anchor*, 25 Sept. 1986, 9 Dec. 1987.
[84] Michael L. Mark and Charles L. Gary, *A History of American Music Education*, 3rd ed. (Lanham, MD: Rowman and Littlefield Education, 2007), 436-37; James A. Keane, *A History of Music Education in the United States*, 2nd ed. (Centennial, CO: Glenbridge Publications, 2010), 367-70.
[85] *Grand Rapids Press*, 13 Oct. 1994; *Holland Sentinel*, 30 Aug. 1998; *Hope College Catalog* (1992-93), 248.

In the class, we were guided through various rhythmic training exercises, such as putting meter of three on one side of our bodies and meter of two on the other. We experienced movement, always barefoot and free-flowing, as he improvised on the piano, and were guided in ear-training and fixed-do solfège practice. Mr. Aschbrenner created a space of peace and a love of music, and it greatly affected my musicianship.[86]

Teaching students how to feel their art goes back to John Nykerk, who in 1890 argued that music helped train the emotions: "The true educator strives to develop the whole man, body, mind, and spirit."[87]

Aschbrenner presented the method at the 1982 Michigan Music Education Association conference, subsequently developing a lecture, "Pulse Patterning for Pianists," first given at the 1993 meeting of the Music Teachers National Association. According to a colleague, Aschbrenner "discovered how the whole body involves itself in a specific way to generate the regular pulses underlying a healthy and musical pianistic performance."[88]

Like those who had gone before him, Charles Aschbrenner was beloved by those he taught. In an April 2008 gathering, former students from the 1960s through the 2000s celebrated their teacher, joining his current Hope students and faculty colleagues in a unique Showcase of Performing Arts. According to Thomas Folkert '87, Aschbrenner "exemplifies what the Hope College Music Department has been about for years, bringing out the innate musical abilities of young men and women and nurturing them into fine musicians." Beth Quimby-Hopkins '99, added that Aschbrenner was "never pushing, never nagging, gently yet firmly guiding me, offering support in all areas of life when I needed it."[89] Charles Aschbrenner was emblematic of Music's new model faculty: he had not attended Hope as an undergraduate; the quality of his professional work was remarkable; he had remained at the college for several decades; and he was an innovator.

Aschbrenner retired in 2008 and passed away in 2016. He is honored by a scholarship in his name, as well as a piano practice room in the Jack Miller Center.

---

[86] Elizabeth Johnson to Marc Baer, email, 7 Aug. 2018, Making Music folder.
[87] "Music: Its Educational Value," *Anchor*, June 1890.
[88] "Charles Aschbrenner and Pulse Patterning," Piano Technique Reviews, PianoTechnique.org.
[89] *Holland Sentinel*, 29 Apr. 2008; see also Joseph Turbessi to Marc Baer, email, 26 May 2018, Making Music folder.

Robert Ritsema, 1986

How does one become a cellist? It helps to grow up on a musical farm. Robert Ritsema was introduced to the instrument by his farmer father, a self-trained vocalist, choir director, and organ repairman, who one day brought home a cello, telling his young son, "That is what you're going to play." Thereafter, an Olivet College, Illinois, professor drove fifteen miles to the farm to teach him. That the lessons had a positive impact was demonstrated when, at age fourteen, Ritsema debuted as a soloist with the Olivet College orchestra.[90]

Ritsema arrived at Hope as a student in 1953, and by the time of his graduation, he had played trombone in the marching band, joined the new Symphonette, practiced piano in Walsh Hall, and played other instruments in the basement of the chapel. In those days, he recalled, "We had to practice wherever we could find a room."[91] The Symphonette's first spring break tour in 1955 was "the highlight of the year," and Morrette Rider was an important mentor: "I owe him an awful lot. . . . he just sort of took us all in as his children."[92] Following Hope, Ritsema earned an MM (1959) and eventually a doctorate (1971) from the University of Michigan; his work included high school orchestra director and teacher at a college in Wisconsin. In 1967 Ritsema received

[90] *Grand Rapids Press*, 1 Feb. 1996; *Holland Sentinel*, 6 May 1999; Baer and Utting interview with Ritsema.
[91] Program, instrumental ensembles—Symphonette, 1953-74 folder, MD Papers; Baer and Utting interview with Ritsema.
[92] Baer and Utting interview with Ritsema; program, instrumental ensembles—Symphonette, 1953-74.

a phone call from Robert Cavanaugh who was about to lose Rider to the dean's office and wondered if he would be interested in the position of orchestra conductor.[93] Returning to his alma mater, Ritsema would serve as conductor of Hope College instrumental ensembles for the next thirty-two years.

Ritsema expressed the same thinking about the relationship between teaching and performance as enunciated by all faculty of his cohort: "You could not be a good teacher unless you were actually involved in doing the thing too."[94] His departmental responsibilities were demanding; over the years, they included teaching music history courses, introduction to music classes, courses in conducting and music theory, orchestration, string methods, and applied lessons on the cello. In addition to teaching, he conducted the orchestra and Symphonette and some semesters filled in for the band director.[95] In November of his first semester teaching at Hope, he directed an ambitious orchestra program, including works by Beethoven, Georges Enesco, and Leonard Bernstein.[96] Jantina Holleman thought Ritsema "a superb musician and a leader. He's brought the orchestra to near professional status. It's taken 50 years to get to this point."[97] His leadership was affirmed by the president of Elon College, who, having listened to Hope's orchestra perform at the Music Educators National Conference in 1970 termed it "the finest small college orchestra I can ever recall hearing."[98]

Despite all the ensembles he had taken on tours (in 1999 he estimated he had "spent about two years of my life on a bus with the Symphonette when you put all those weeks together"), Ritsema continued to perform, recalling nearly a hundred occasions from 1967 to 1999 when he gave faculty recitals at Hope.[99]

Ritsema spent a total of twelve years leading his department: he first served as chair from 1969 to 1973, under a new system of rotating

---

[93] Baer and Utting interview with Ritsema.
[94] Ibid.
[95] Melissa LaBarge interview with Ritsema, 22 June 2000, Hope College Living Heritage Oral History Project.
[96] Program and 13 Nov. 1967 press release, instrumental ensembles—orchestra, 1921-72 folder, MD Papers.
[97] *Holland Sentinel*, 6 May 1999.
[98] Malvin Artley to Robert Ritsema, 18 Mar. 1970, biographical folder, Ritsema Papers; 9 Jan. 1970 press release, instrumental ensembles—orchestra, 1921-72 folder, MD Papers.
[99] LaBarge interview with Ritsema; *Anchor*, 27 Jan. 1999; press release, 1 Apr. 1999, instrumental ensembles—Symphonette, 1975-2001 folder; biographical folder, Ritsema Papers.

leadership inaugurated by Cavanaugh. "A lot of the people in the department at that time were still people whom I had as professors. So that was a little awkward."[100] In this first term, Ritsema experimented, working with John Tammi of the Theatre Department to stage Hope's first complete opera in 1972, John Gay's *Beggar's Opera*, performed at the DeWitt Theater. David Bast, who had played Macheath, recalled, "I wasn't a very good singer. I was especially weak on the higher notes. To paraphrase Groucho, I wouldn't want to go to a musical that had me as the lead"; others, however, praised the music, one local newspaper calling it Hope's "most ambitious production to date." There was notable praise for Ritsema's eighteen-piece orchestra.[101]

In the years between 1988 and 1996, Ritsema served again as department chair. Good hires resulted in what he considered to be the two key factors in departmental excellence: studio teaching and high-quality ensembles.[102] Colleague Joan Conway said: "Ritsema was a great chair, and . . . the pillar of the department through all those years. I think he always tried to be fair and see all the sides, which wasn't easy."[103] For the college and community, his most important legacy is the Musical Showcase. This began with a joint Symphonette and Chapel Choir European tour in 1987, the two ensembles then meeting up at the end for a joint concert in the Netherlands. In the spring of 1989, after two years of planning, Ritsema brought both these large ensembles, as well as smaller groups, together at DeVos Hall for the first Musical Showcase.

Robert Ritsema's career in Hope's Music Department is a model of one word: service. He served his students; the West Michigan community; his church, Fellowship Reformed, as choir director from 1970 to 1988; and his profession. He retired in 1999 and is honored with the Ritsema Instrumental Rehearsal Room in the Jack Miller Center.

Like Ritsema, Joan Conway was a high school basketball player in an era when women's collegiate sports were not fully embraced; this may have displayed the personal drive that led to her success as a world-class musician.

Conway grew up in Pennsylvania, where from age twelve she was an accompanist at minstrel shows and churches. She graduated in 1957 from Lebanon Valley College and went on to earn an MM in 1959 from the Manhattan School of Music. Conway then spent the next decade

---

[100] Baer and Utting interview with Ritsema.
[101] David Bast to Marc Baer, email, 7 Aug. 2018, Making Music folder; *Holland City News*, 2 Nov. 1972.
[102] Baer and Utting interview with Conway.
[103] Ibid.

Joan Conway, 1985

in New York City, teaching and performing as a soloist, an ensemble member, and an accompanist in Carnegie Hall, Town Hall, and other prominent venues.

In 1969, when she was exploring college teaching opportunities, Conway performed at the Bay View Summer College and Conservatory, a Chautauqua-type setting in Northern Michigan. Robert Cavanaugh contacted the head of the Bay View program, seeking recommendations to fill a piano position at Hope. After Conway returned to New York City, professor Anthony Kooiker called to ask her to come to Hope for an interview. She recalls playing a Mendelssohn piece in Nykerk Hall's Snow auditorium—and the rest is history.[104] She and her colleagues hired in the 1960s reinvented the music program. Three themes stand out from Conway's tenure.

First, Conway was a performer, continuing at Hope what she had begun in Manhattan.

> I played with a string quartet from Philadelphia . . . [and] at Lincoln Center Library. I'd keep going back and doing that, and one sabbatical, of all things, I moved to Kalamazoo. . . . I could not believe what I played that sabbatical . . . I played with a clarinetist in the Chicago Symphony, and the principal cellist in Grand Rapids, and the concert master there and principal cellist in Flint.

[104] Ibid.

So, I kept all those things going while teaching, and it's not easy, because I like to spend time with my students.[105]

She also began performing with other musicians, most notably her colleague Charles Aschbrenner. According to Conway, "Dual piano playing was perhaps the hardest ensemble there is, because both pianists had to be exactly synchronized."[106] Beginning in 1982, Conway and Aschbrenner sponsored a two-piano camp for five summers at Hope. Never one to turn down a challenge, Conway was also a member of two other groups: soprano Laura Floyd and clarinetist Russell Floyd joined her in the Floyd-Conway Trio, and the Joan Conway-Phyllis Rappeport Duo played piano pieces written for four hands.[107]

Second, Conway was the first music faculty member since Curtis Snow, three decades earlier, to put substantial time into coordinating faculty recitals. "When I came, it was kind of rough and tumble. It kind of fell together," she recalled. "Somewhere along the line, like three or four years in, I started doing it." Conway recruited Hope art professor Delbert Michel to create a cover for the program, which she called "Musical Landscapes," and then used it for brochures for three decades, during which time, she pestered her colleagues to sign up for Sunday musicales. "We ended up having some really wonderful achievements for a school our size," she remembered. They included a whole year of major Schubert chamber works during the bicentennial year 1976-77, performances of American composers, a year featuring the works of Robert Schumann, and another year celebrating the ninetieth birthday of Aaron Copland.[108] The goal was not only to introduce students to more music but also to present teachers as performers.[109]

Third, Conway provided a model of musicians committed to interdisciplinary work, an archetype that went back to John Nykerk. On the one hand, there was art, not only drawing upon the talent of Del Michael but also on several occasions turning Snow Auditorium into a combined art gallery and recital space. "I got Maintenance to go up on ladders and hang wires all around. We had some Hope artists one year. Another year we had five local women artists . . . and we hung their

---

[105] Ibid.
[106] *Holland Sentinel*, 3 Nov. 1980.
[107] Edna Carmean, "Joan Conway," 1996, biographical folder, Conway Papers, H01-1415.
[108] *Anchor*, 27 Oct. 1985; *Grand Rapids Press*, 22 Sept. 1996; *Holland Sentinel*, 26 Sept. 1996; Baer and Utting interview with Conway; Aaron Copland to Department of Music, 1 May 1989, Aaron Copland folder, Conway Papers.
[109] Carmean, "Joan Conway."

stuff, so it gave a little class to that place."[110] And what was clearly more than a lark because of the time commitment, Conway began studying Japanese, eventually coleading a Japan May term.

When the bas-reliefs adorning the exterior of Nykerk Hall were moved to the Jack Miller Center, they were placed at the north end of the lobby, with *Performance* and *Teaching* together. Considering Joan Conway's career at Hope, it is appropriate they are next to each other. When asked about the balance between teaching and performing, Conway replied, "I love teaching, and I love performing, and I love chamber music, and I love playing for singers." When pressed, she confided that teaching was her first love. According to Robert Ritsema, "If you look back at all the teachers in a studio, she would be the one I would point to as being the really outstanding one."[111]

In 1992 Joan Conway was named Teacher of Year by the Michigan Music Teachers Association. Four years later, she was given an award by her alma mater's alumni association, the presenter reminding the audience that Conway had performed on many stages, adding "But she is never appreciated more than at her recitals at Hope College."[112] Conway retired in 2001; a piano scholarship honors her years at Hope, as does the practice wing of the Jack Miller Center.

It is appropriate to conclude this chapter with the 1960s cohort, which may be characterized as a new faculty model: Roger Davis, Robert Ritsema, Joan Conway, and—especially—Charles Aschbrenner, for his vision of a written history of Music at Hope College was the inception of this book.

The early Hope music teachers with the greatest impact had remained at the college for a considerable length of time: they set the bar high for their students, found a balance between teaching and performance, and juggled performances on local, national, and global stages.

A key element of their vision as music faculty was to combine performance and teaching, thereby offering an invitation to younger colleagues, themselves a new faculty model, thus fostering a liberal arts college model rather than a music conservatory.[113] The concept of the

[110] Baer and Utting interview with Conway.
[111] Baer and Utting interviews with Conway and Ritsema.
[112] Carmean, "Joan Conway."
[113] See George Hauptfuehrer, "The Music Department in the Liberal Arts College," *Association of American Colleges Bulletin* 34 (Dec. 1948): 480; Aschbrenner interview with Holleman; press release, 1 Apr. 1987, news releases and clippings folder, Holleman Papers; Hollenbach to Rider, 20 Nov. 1950, correspondence 1947-53 folder, Rider

"performing professor" began with Nykerk and continues to this day. In the late 1970s, Music chair Stuart Sharp spoke about such faculty:

> Performance keeps the teacher in touch with the demands of making music. It enables one to maintain a good perspective, and one's sensibilities remain keen. The performing professor can empathize with what's involved in presenting a senior recital, for example.[114]

It was not always easy, as evidenced in a report from 1950, reflecting on how rapidly the department had grown in the previous decade, during which time, they had been housed in three different buildings.

> The Music Department is one of the most rapidly expanding departments on the campus: it now offers more than twice as many courses as it did in 1940.... The music faculty has doubled in number, while the total number of students who are taking music lessons has tripled during this same ten-year period.... Sixteen seniors will be graduated this spring with a major in music. This is the largest number of music students to receive their diplomas in the history of Hope College.[115]

There were also increased demands placed on faculty. Jantina Holleman, hired in 1946, recalled, "I had far more piano students than I was supposed to have," thirty-five instead of the promised twenty-five. "But everybody was teaching extra things."[116]

When the department reached critical mass—between 1945 and 1965—faculty could enrich each other in conversation, through excellence in performance, and in teaching; this cross fertilization is true of the other arts departments at Hope College as well. Music could now flourish, without over dependence on the pioneer type, such as Nykerk, to hold things together. The later music faculty discussed in this chapter, from Cavanaugh to Conway, fostered a new character for Music, evident by comparing them as a group with their predecessors.

Papers; Kooiker to Lubbers, 4 May 1954, correspondence folder, Kooiker Papers; "Music Department Report for the Year 1968-1969," correspondence 1965-69 folder, Cavanaugh Papers; Summary of Music Department Opinions, 1971 folder, box 1, MD Papers; Robbi Hartt to Marc Baer, email, 9 Aug. 2018, Making Music folder.

[114] *News from Hope College*, Apr. 1978.
[115] *Hope College Bulletin* 88 (May 1950).
[116] Aschbrenner interview with Holleman.

In the first era—that of the pioneers—the focus of most faculty was outside of Hope, for example, in a Grand Rapids studio. In the second era—that of the professionals—the focus was simultaneously inward—on students—and outward—as professionals on stages beyond Hope. The inward focus might be understood—without too large a dose of hyperbole—as the performing professor loving his or her students and modeling how faith and thinking can be complementary. This motivation began early: "The large place music has on Hope's campus was staked out in imagination and faith by Dr. Nykerk when Hope was primarily a preparatory school."[117] It has continued through our own time, evident in Jantina Holleman's prayer at a faculty meeting:

> Enlighten us to understand what it may be to serve Thee with our minds. May we count wisdom of greater value than knowledge; may we acknowledge that the fear of thee is the beginning of wisdom [Psalm 111:10]. . . .We pray especially that we may learn to love our students . . . [and] may we be a witness to them of the good news of thy gospel.[118]

---

[117] *Alumni Bulletin Hope College* 1 (1937), 3.
[118] Prayer for faculty meeting, 31 Jan. 1983, writings and speeches, 1949-94 folder, Holleman Papers.

CHAPTER 3

Experiencing Resonance: Students Making Music

> Now, classmates, raise a rousing song, with voices full and clear and strong, the song of jubilee! Oh, Mother Hope, to thee we sing, and thus a grateful tribute bring.
> *Anchor*, 1888

> Thank you for asking for the best we had in us, not only as singers but as people.
> Ann Van Dorp to Robert Cavanaugh, 1967

> [Hope's Music Department] was a place that all of us could grow as musicians together and grow in our faith together as well.
> Victoria Longfield, Class of 2015

It all began with a Sunday evening walk and an organ. For years, Ethel Leestma had excelled at the piano until a bout of warts threatened her future musical career. Hoping to widen her horizons, her father brought her to the family's home church, Grace Reformed in Grand Rapids. Sitting her down at the organ, he told her to play. Although,

Ethel Leestma on practice organ (Milestone, *1932*)

initially, she was unsure of how to do that, after hearing the power and volume of the crescendo pedal, she was hooked. By her senior year of high school, Leestma's talent for the organ had earned her a scholarship to Olivet College, an honor she politely declined for the opportunity to play on the Skinner organ in the newly opened Dimnent Chapel and to work under Hope's new organ professor, Curtis Snow.[1] When Ethel Leestma entered Hope in 1929, her musical prowess quickly earned her a reputation among the freshman class, and under the close mentorship of Snow, her talent and love for the organ continued to flourish.[2]

In addition to playing the organ in chapel a month after she arrived on campus in 1929, joining the college's first Chapel Choir as a freshman (singing at Wynand Wichers' inauguration in October 1931), and serving as the secretary-treasurer of the orchestra during her four years at Hope, Leestma also accompanied on both piano and organ for various concerts and the recitals of other students, as well as performing her own recitals.[3] In Dimnent Chapel, in June 1930, she played works by, among others, Charles-Marie Widor, César Franck,

[1] News clipping, 21 May 1929, scrapbook, Ethel Leestma Swets Papers; *Anchor*, 22 Jan. 1930.
[2] News clipping (n.d.), scrapbook, Ethel Leestma Swets Papers; *Anchor*, 22 Jan. 1930; *Holland Sentinel*, 15 Apr. 2007.
[3] Scrapbook, Ethel Leestma Swets Papers; newspaper clipping, memory book, box 3, Schuppert Papers.

Félix-Alexandre Guilmant, and Maurice Ravel.[4] Her junior recital, before a large audience, was particularly noteworthy. Commenting on her playing a Bach piece, the campus newspaper stated:

> Miss Leestma displayed excellent technical mastery of the instrument and fine musicianship. Particularly in the Adagio of this group there was nice balance and a great deal of finesse.... The most salient improvement in Miss Leestma's playing since last year was the increase in poise and confidence which lent to her performances a general tone of greater maturity.[5]

On June 13, 1933, Ethel performed her senior organ recital in front of approximately 150 people in Dimnent Chapel. It was enthusiastically reviewed.

> Introducing her program with Rameau's intricate *Minuet and Gigue*, Miss Leestma continued to the heaviest part of her program in *Fantaisie and Fugue in G minor*, by Bach, and *Sixth Symphony*, by Widor. Playing these numbers, as well as the rest of the program, entirely from memory, Miss Leestma displayed an advanced technique in the Bach number, interpretive ability in the meditative adagio movement, and the particularly beautiful intermezzo of the Widor composition.[6]

Eight days later, Leestma was awarded her bachelor of music degree in both piano and organ, the first BM student at Hope to graduate with a concentration in two instruments. She went on to play the organs in several churches, but as her daughters attested, it was playing on Dimnent's Skinner organ that remained one of her greatest joys in life.[7]

Although noteworthy, Ethel's Leestma's story is far from unique. Over the last century and a half, thousands of students like her have come to Hope College with a passion for making music and have seen that passion nurtured, challenged, and strengthened by faculty and fellow students. This chapter tells of their experience at Hope College, organized by subject: chapel connections, student initiatives, ensembles, touring, performing, and faculty-student collaboration. The ensembles,

---

[4] Programs, scrapbook, Ethel Leestma Swets Papers.
[5] *Anchor*, 4 May 1932.
[6] Newspaper clipping (n.d.), scrapbook, Ethel Leestma Swets Papers.
[7] Baer and Utting interview with Marcia Buck and Faith Curtis, 21 June 2018, Making Music folder.

organizations, and opportunities discussed here include both those either sponsored or directed by Music faculty and those created by students. Musical ensembles introduced by other departments, such as the praise band and gospel choir sponsored by Campus Ministries, although important to music at Hope, are outside the scope of this book.

Not one of the developments considered in this book—not the faculty, the buildings, or even Music itself—would have been possible without the ever-present commitment of the student body to music. From the beginning, as seen in chapter 1, it was student interest in music that necessitated the formation of the School of Music and, eventually, a department; buildings and faculty followed. The current Department of Music is very much the result of decades of student involvement in music making rather than the product of administrative transactions hoping to produce an interest in the subject. In other words, student passion preceded the department's institutionalization by several decades. Music is different than any other department in this respect.[8]

The department is also exceptional for the broad range of students it has served. A departmental brochure of the mid-1960s speaks to the wide variety of students who made music at Hope:

> Hope College maintains several large musical ensembles, all active in training and performance. The Chapel Choir, the Chancel Choir, the Orchestra, the Band, and the Symphonette have a total student membership of over three hundred students. These organizations are open to all students, with the majority of members majoring in fields other than music, so that it is not uncommon to find a math major and an elementary education student sharing the same desk in the violin section of the orchestra, or a future coach and future physicist singing side-by-side in the choir.[9]

Three hundred students represented just under 20 percent of the student body at that time.

---

[8] The exception may be athletics, for which, see Gordon Brewer, *But How You Played the Game!: A History of Intercollegiate Athletics at Hope College* and *Journey of Hope: Names and Games Remembered* (Holland: Hope College, 1992, 2002); Thomas Renner, *In Pursuit of Excellence: A History of Intercollegiate Athletics at Hope College—1970-2020*, forthcoming; Nyenhuis, *Hope College at 150*, 2: ch. 8.

[9] Brochure, "The Music of Hope College" (1966), brochures-music at Hope College folder, box 1, MD Papers.

Men's Glee Club

The 1947 Men's Glee Club provides another window into the level of diversity often found in musical groups at Hope, both in terms of background and vocational interests. That year, most of the ensemble was made up of nonmajors who found joy in singing. They came from all over the country, as well as from India and Saudi Arabia. Members included future engineers, ministers, architects, doctors, historians, journalists, hospital administrators, biologists, and lawyers. Their background in music ranged from high school glee clubs to the New Jersey All-State Chorus and the Navy's Great Lakes Blue Jacket Choir. Junior baritone Arthur Van Eck '48 had spent three years as a Marine pilot in World War II. Although he had been planning to go into ministry, he was very interested in music and served as the business manager for the Glee Club. Senior second tenor A. Dale Stoppels, prior to attending Hope, had sung in Holland High School's a cappella choir, served three years as a naval officer during World War II, and after graduation pursued a career as a lawyer.[10]

Sacred beginnings

Early in the history of Hope College, student experiences in making music were frequently connected to the crafting of chapel services. Chapel and music were so intertwined, especially in the early years of the college and through the late twentieth century, that it is difficult to separate them. Before the mid-twentieth century, most

---

[10] "Information Regarding the Hope College Men's Glee Club," scrapbook, box 4, Cavanaugh Papers. See also "The Hope College Women's Glee Club, 1950," informational flyer, vocal ensembles—glee clubs folder, box 2, MD Papers.

music students, and Hope College students in general, planned to pursue careers in ministry or teaching upon graduation.[11] As a result, for these students, sacred musical experiences were meaningful not only personally but also professionally. The "famous College Quartette," organized by music professor John Nykerk, supports this assertion. The quartet—consisting of Albertus Broek, Gerhard John Dinkeloo, Anno Dykema, and James Wayer—performed in Holland, Hamilton, and Fennville. Three of the men went into the ministry, and Dinkeloo became a public school music teacher.[12]

Students were frequently involved in producing music for chapel. Every academic year, two students were selected by the faculty to fill the positions of chorister and organist. In 1881 Sarah Gertrude Alcott of Holland, a senior and one of Hope's first two female graduates, played the organ in morning chapel, whereas senior Pieter Ihrman served as chorister.[13] Hope preparatory school students were also occasionally selected. Beginning in her sophomore year of high school, Sarah L. Jones acted as college organist from 1885 until Peter Swart, also a high school sophomore, succeeded her in the fall of 1887.[14] In January 1930, Mildred Schuppert played the organ in chapel, and that fall Hazel Paalman sang Mendelssohn's *O Rest in the Lord* in the chapel service. In 1930 professor Curtis Snow's students, including Ethel Leestma, filled in for him for a week as chapel organist. Snow had previously asked students to submit titles of their favorite hymns to him. "This will make the chapel service more interesting for the student body," the *Anchor* commented, "besides aiding Mr. Snow in picking the type of hymns desired by the students."[15]

With chapel attendance either expected or required during the first century of the college's history,[16] the desire for music of high quality to complement the sermon encouraged both the more formal organization of Music at Hope and the formation of the first student musical groups. The *Anchor* frequently addressed the students' desire for better and more varied music in chapel services.

[11] For Hope's first sixty years, 46 percent of graduates went into ministry and 32 percent into teaching: *Hope College Catalog, May Bulletin* (1926), 86.
[12] Gordan Mackay interview with Rev. James Wayer, biographical folder, Nykerk Papers.
[13] *Hope College Catalog* (1881-82), 7.
[14] Ibid., 1885-88.
[15] Diary entry, 9 Jan. 1930, HC diaries 1929-34, box 1, Schuppert Papers; *Anchor*, 30 Oct. 1929, 11 Feb. 1930.
[16] Chapel attendance was expected and encouraged until Edward Dimnent became president in 1918; he made it compulsory: Nyenhuis, *Hope College at 150*, 277.

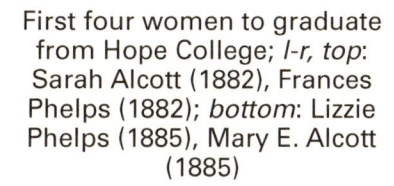

First four women to graduate from Hope College; *l-r, top*: Sarah Alcott (1882), Frances Phelps (1882); *bottom*: Lizzie Phelps (1885), Mary E. Alcott (1885)

> Why can we not have an anthem by a select choir or a quartette or a solo by the professor of music now and then in our morning chapel services? It would vary the monotony and lend more interest and prominence to those exercises as to not make them seem like a necessary evil or a disagreeable routine. . . . Besides, it might in some degree make up for the lack of a Glee Club or a Conservatory of Music.[17]

Two years later, the student paper expressed the same sentiment: "If we need anything, fellow students, it is to become better acquainted with music. How pleasant it would be if our chapel exercises were enlivened with better singing."[18] Indeed, many of the early musical groups were founded and led as a result of student initiative, including the choristers, organists, and accompanists. A note from an 1887 college faculty meeting reveals the several roles students played in the early organization and production of music:

> Request Mr. P[eeke] to continue for the present as Chorister, and that he and Mr. Nykerk be requested to organize a Chapel choir. Regarding chapel choir, Mr. Nykerk reports that he and

[17] *Anchor*, 1 Jan. 1893.
[18] Ibid., 1 Mar. 1895.

Mr. Peeke have had this matter under consideration but that they recommend the appointment of a precentor. Faculty urged president to request Mr. J[ohn] Lamar [a preparatory school junior].[19]

Select students were given nearly equal authority when it came to producing music for chapel in the early years of the college. By the early twentieth century, this influence would disappear with the formalization of the department and the professionalization of its faculty, but its legacy inspired future student-driven initiatives.

Although students were heavily involved in the production of sacred music for spiritual purposes, they also performed secular—even popular—music at other events, particularly Commencement. In fact, a sampling of music programs at Hope shows the extent to which early music offerings promoted a blend of secular and sacred. To take one example, in a 1937 concert of the Girl's Glee Club, the program was divided into a "Sacred Program," for example, *The Lord is My Shepherd*, by Schubert, and a "Secular Program," for instance, *The Light of Dawning*, by Tchaikovsky and Gottlieb Federlein.[20] This legacy would continue well into the twentieth century, carrying over into other occasions of students making music.

Student-inspired initiatives

Fueled by their desire to make music, students often took the creation of musical experiences into their own hands. Before the professionalization of Music's faculty in the 1950s, and especially before the rudimentary establishment of a department at the dawn of the twentieth century, students had helped ensure that musical instruction was offered at Hope. In 1871 junior Helenus Nies established a "singing-school." It was free of charge and met in the chapel at four o'clock on Tuesday afternoons.[21] Recognizing the desire of students for music instruction, the college began recruiting music tutors, including Nies and Cornelis Van Oostenbrugge, Class of 1876.[22] Teunis Muilenburg, Class of 1889, gave students music lessons as a senior, in addition to

---

[19] Minutes of the general faculty, 14 Jan. 1887. A precentor is an individual, not necessarily ordained, who leads worship.
[20] Hope College Girl's Glee Club (ca. 1937), vocal ensembles—glee clubs folder.
[21] *The Excelsiora* 1 (9 Mar. 1871), 19.
[22] *Hope College Catalog* (1871-72), 38, for Nies. For Van Oostenbrugge as tutor of music, see *Catalog* (1876-77), 22, 44.

serving two years as chorister.[23] During her four years at Hope, Ethel Leestma taught organ to at least two fellow classmates. She saved two of their performance programs; on one she wrote, affectionately, "My organ pupil at Hope."[24] Student instructors tended to be upperclassmen, although Harman Van Slyke Peeke, Class of 1887, oversaw vocal music in 1883 as a freshman and later served as the college's chorister.[25]

Hiring academically trained music faculty removed the need for student instructors, but it did not dampen the pioneering spirit of the students. Students passionate about music were often behind some of Hope's first musical organizations. In 1888 "Twelve of the college Republicans [there were then 39 students at Hope] organized a glee club and sang campaign songs at the Republican speeches."[26] A staple in the first century of the college, glee clubs were repeatedly demanded by students. The first Hope College Glee Club was discontinued after being active on campus from 1890 through 1893. Students wasted little time calling for its return. In comparing an advertisement for songs from Rutgers, the *Anchor* pondered:

> Are there not voices in our midst to compose another glee club, which shall sing good old songs with the clear ringing voices of college men? College songs the world over have a hearty reception when well sung, and men from other colleges have told us that they dwell with fondest memories upon the hours they spent together at the close of well-spent days singing the good old songs. Unless we change quickly, fellow students, we will go into life without any of these things to recall in later years. May we have another glee club before many moons have waned.[27]

Three closely linked notions emerged from this challenge: (1) certain music stimulated an emotional response, (2) well-known songs were particularly resonant, and (3) music made memories. Thus, when in 1916 two students arranged for publication of the *Hope College Song Book*, at least nine of the titles included works that to some extent had been composed by students years before. The *Alumni Song of '85* contains this chorus:

---

[23] *Anchor*, 1 Feb. 1888.
[24] Program, scrapbook 1929-36, Ethel Leestma Swets Papers.
[25] *Hope College Catalog* (1883-84), 12; minutes of the general faculty, 5 May 1885, 16 Sept. 1886.
[26] *Anchor*, 1 Nov. 1888.
[27] Ibid., 1 Feb. 1894, and see also, 1 Mar. 1888, 1 Oct. and 1 Nov. 1895.

> May affection but deepen as time rolls along,
> As yearly we join in a reunion song;
> Here's to the days! Here's to the days!
> Here's to the days we love![28]

In 1895, the year following the *Anchor*'s challenge, the paper inspired students with the need for a glee club: "How the right college spirit would be aroused if another Glee Club would cause the old college songs to resound through Winants' Halls."[29] That fall the appeal was acknowledged, and John Nykerk agreed to serve as director of the newly organized Glee Club. The group met once a week, with Nykerk drilling them in voice culture and choral singing.[30]

Not just the Glee Club benefited from student creativity. Marinus A. Hoffs '24, the future husband of Alice M. Brower '23, came to Hope with three other young men from Iowa and formed a quartet.[31] Another student-initiated ensemble, the Prins-Baker Quartet (known also as the Hope College Quartet and the Collegian Quartet), likely began in a fraternity house. The quartet comprised two brothers from Holland, Peter N. '20 and Teunis W. Prins '20, and two cousins from Passaic, New Jersey, Peter G. '20 and Tunis Baker '23, all members of the Fraternal Society. Might the idea of a quartet have been born on the occasion the four young men sang the first self-referential verse of the *Frater's Song*?

> Let's sing once more, my merry Fraters;
> Tune your hearts to music loud and long:
> Ev-'ry heart it needs must thrill,
> Ev-'ry soul with rapture fill,
> As we join in the Frater's song,
> As we join in the Frater's song.[32]

Be that as it may, the quartet met with considerable success in the late 1910s, their reputation surviving in newspaper clippings in Peter Baker's memory book. According to one clipping, the Collegian

---

[28] *Alumni Song of '85*, in *Hope College Song Book*, 9, Songs of Hope College. Nyenhuis, *Hope College at 150*, 2, app. 11, 1225-56, reproduces all the songs from *Hope College Alumni Songs*, as well as two alma mater hymns, and both the Centennial Hymn, "Hope Thou in God," and the Sesquicentennial Anthem, "I Will Lift up Mine Eyes (Psalm 121)."
[29] *Anchor*, 1 Mar. 1895.
[30] Ibid., 1 Dec. 1895; *Hope College Catalog* (1895-96), 35.
[31] Larry Wagenaar interview with Alice Hoffs, 1999, Alice Hoffs Papers.
[32] *Hope College Song Book*, 11.

Collegian Quartet
(Milestone, *1917*)

Quartet was "rapidly rising to prominence and distinction through their excellent work. Many engagements have been filled during the past few months, and from all quarters they receive a constant flow of invitations to present their excellent program."[33] An important component of the pre-World War I revival of the Glee Club, the quartet disbanded in 1920, when three of the four members completed their years at Hope, but not before the group had performed throughout West Michigan.[34]

The high point of student singing initiatives was the 1916 Pageant of Hope.[35] Harris Meyer and Arthur Cloetingh (both Class of 1916 and on the student leadership team that cooperated with a faculty committee to stage the event) compiled the *Hope College Song Book*,[36] which includes seven songs, either recently written or put to music by

---

[33] "Collegian Quartette at Forest Grove," newspaper clipping, scrapbook 1915-20, Peter Garret Baker Papers, H88-0003.5. See also *Milestone* (1917), 87, 92.
[34] First Annual Program, Hope College Glee Club and newspaper clippings, scrapbook 1915-20, Peter Garret Baker Papers. Their graduation was delayed by military service during World War I: *Milestone* (1918), 89, 94, and (1919), 93. Tunis Baker did not receive his degree until 1923: *Alumni Directory*, 1951.
[35] See ch. 5.
[36] Cloetingh was "Master of the Pageant," and Meyer, "Composer and Director of the music": *Milestone* (1916), 111; cf. faculty minutes, 4 Feb. 1916.

Hope students or alumni, as well as eight apparently new fraternity and sorority songs.[37] This autonomous spirit has continued into the twenty-first century, taking form in two student-led a cappella groups, Twelfth Street Harmony (2001) and Luminescence (2003); both are still sponsored by the Music Department.[38]

Much of the success of these student-initiated ensembles, and of Hope musical ensembles in general, may be attributed to the efforts of a few impassioned individuals, rather than to broad student participation. As with all collegiate organizations, it was unreliable student interest that most frequently plagued Hope musical ensembles. Senior Carolyn McCall's decision to revive a twenty-five-voice student choir in 1978, a move she credited to a shift in "student interest," speaks to the variable nature of undergraduate priorities.[39] Despite the inconsistency, dedicated students have done much to promote excellent music and its appreciation on campus.[40]

The Musical Arts Club was established in 1941 as an organization for any musically inclined student; it sought to develop "a fuller appreciation [for] and interest in music" on campus.[41] Contemporary music, operas, and individual composers were among the topics of discussion at the group's monthly meetings. In addition, the club sponsored musical films and live music—including the 1945 Homecoming—a school song contest in 1949, and the All-College Sing in 1950.[42] Arlene Peterson and Chung Sun Yung, winners of piano and instrumental scholarships respectively, performed at a November 1949 Musical Arts Club meeting. Peterson played the first movement of Beethoven's *Sonata No. 9*, and Yung performed the *Minuet*, by Boccherini, and Simonetti's *Madrigale*. One member of the group would typically serve as a critic at these meetings.[43]

Before disbanding in 1952, the Musical Arts Club had been responsible for sponsoring a series of vespers services, including the annual Christmas Vespers; decorating Dimnent Chapel for the Christmas season; and providing ushers for concerts and recitals. The club's goal in sponsoring the vespers series was to "give music students of Hope an opportunity to perform in public and to bring to

---

[37] *Hope College Song Book*, Songs of Hope College.
[38] Rebecca Fox Blok to Marc Baer, personal communication.
[39] *Anchor*, 15 Sept. 1978; see also Aschbrenner interview with Holleman.
[40] *Anchor*, 16 Oct. 1947.
[41] *Milestone* 1954 (n.p.); Aschbrenner interview with Holleman.
[42] *Milestone* (1945), 53, and (1949), 144; *Anchor*, 13 Jan. 1949, and 14 Dec. 1950.
[43] Minutes, 19 Nov. 1949, Musical Arts Club, H88-0419; *Milestone* (1942), 86.

public attention the work of the music school."[44] The group typically had a member of the Music faculty serve as an advisor, but when the possibility of getting a professor to take Robert Cavanaugh's place was discussed at a 1949 meeting, the group decided to leave the position open, suggesting students were capable of leading.[45]

Joining ensembles

Early in the college's history, student musical groups were formed to fill the need for good music at chapel, but they quickly expanded their repertoire of songs and instrumental offerings. Throughout Hope's history, dozens of ensembles were formed. From the Jazz Band and Knickerbocker Quartette to the Girl's Ukulele Club and Madrigal Singers, each ensemble provided students with the opportunity to pursue experiences in making music that catered to their individual interests and talents. As a result, being part of a musical ensemble defined the musical experience of many students.

Like any other competitive venture, musical group participation can be both stressful and fulfilling, combining the demand for difficult performances with friendships and lasting memories. The nerve-wracking experience of auditioning was comically captured in 1948 by the *Anchor*'s Music Box columnist:

> Those who happened to be passing through the basement of the chapel on Thursday or Friday of the opening week of school probably wondered why there were so many frightened looking people seated in front of Prof. Cavanaugh's room. No, it wasn't a chow line or married vets looking for an apartment. These poor people were waiting to try out for the different choral organizations on the campus. They were admitted one at a time and once inside, the nervous applicant found himself surrounded by critics, namely, seated from left to right: Miss Holleman at the piano, Mr. Cavanaugh, Mrs. Snow, and Miss Paalman. . . . The first step in the procedure was singing scales. I think the object of that phase was to see [at] which high note it was still possible to emit a reasonable amount of volume without turning blue in the face. The final step was to sing one part of the hitherto undisclosed hymn.[46]

---

[44] *Anchor*, 10 Dec. 1941, 19 May 1943.
[45] Minutes, 24 Oct. 1949, Musical Arts Club.
[46] Newspaper clipping (1948), scrapbook, box 4, Cavanaugh Papers.

Anyone who has ever auditioned will both smile and sweat in reading this passage.

Although anxiety inducing at the time, many alumni look back fondly on their experiences in these ensembles and attest to their value, both in music and in life. One of them was Robert Kranendonk '50.

> Of course, I happily joined the Men's Glee Club. Early on, I began to appreciate the joy of singing in harmony with men my age. It was an education with fun. . . . Membership in other musical organizations soon followed, including Ms. Paalman's Chapel Chorus and Jantina Holleman's Madrigal Singers. They all contributed to a greater appreciation of "good" music.[47]

Another student, Susan Eenigenburg '67, spoke of her experience as a member of the Chapel Choir in a letter to the group's director:

> I wanted to tell you that this was the most meaningful experience of college life for me, that what I saw and felt in our group was far more significant than the books I have studied or the classes I have attended. I wanted to tell you that my eyes, ears, and heart were constantly open to appreciate and feel the constant love and concern shared by the group.[48]

Some students were attracted to Hope College because of the possibility of performing with such ensembles. Like Ethel Leestma, Lauren Noetzel '67 declined a scholarship to another college to attend Hope. In a letter to Cavanaugh, she reflected:

> When I was a very young girl—maybe twelve or so years old—I heard the Choir in Chicago. I decided right then that I would go to Hope College so I could sing with you. When I graduated from high school, I decided to . . . give up a four-year scholarship to a state school and to go to a junior college so I could spend at least two years in the choir.[49]

---

[47] Robert Kranendonk, "Music Maker," in *Hope at the Crossroads: The War Years*, ed. Eileen Nordstrum and George Zuidema (Holland, MI: Hope College, 2008), 240.

[48] Susan Eenigenburg to Cavanaugh, 12 Aug. 1967, correspondence 1965-69 folder, box 1, Cavanaugh Papers; see also, Leander Ling-chi Wang to Cavanaugh, 28 Sept. 1961, Chapel Choir scrapbooks 1961-62 folder, box 6, MD Papers; Robbi Hartt to Marc Baer, email, 9 Aug. 2018, Making Music folder.

[49] Lauren Noetzel to Cavanaugh, 25 July 1967, correspondence 1965-69 folder, Cavanaugh Papers.

Choral Union and John Nykerk

Such reflections are a testament to the quality of the ensembles as well as the experiences that resulted from membership in them. Throughout the years, Hope music ensembles have met with success, making music on Hope's campus and beyond, and collectively enriching the lives of students. Five groups stand out in this regard.

Originally a singing class for mixed voices, the Choral Union was organized by music professor John Nykerk in 1900, becoming Hope's first permanent musical organization. Described in 1905 as the "leading attraction of Hope College" and as "one of the most prominent features of college life," the Choral Union met once a week in Winants Chapel to study oratorios and cantatas.[50] It consisted primarily of students skilled at vocal music as well as other students who could read music and showed a "fair amount of musical talent." Every year, the Choral Union gave several public concerts, often singing at Commencement and performing Mendelssohn's *Elijah* in June 1905, Holland's first-ever oratorio. By 1908 the group's reputation for stellar performances led the *Holland City News* to publicize their upcoming concert as the "musical event of the year."[51] Nearly every spring, the Choral Union

---

[50] *Milestone* (1905), 151.
[51] *Holland City News*, 28 May 1908.

performed oratorios, including *Elijah* and *Song of Hiawatha*, by Samuel Coleridge-Taylor, until in 1915, the group disbanded.

The Hope College Glee Club was an early feature of music on campus and one that garnered considerable student support. Although the first one had dissolved, two new glee clubs were formed in 1915, realizing a "long-cherished dream."[52] The Men's Glee Club, under the direction of Stanley Deacon, consisted of sixty members, and the Ladies Glee Club, also directed by Deacon, had thirty members. In the spring of 1917, the Men's Glee Club held its first annual program—admission fifteen cents.[53] World War I threatened the stability of the Men's Glee Club, with key members leaving the college for military service.[54] Following the war, the clubs solidified into ensembles, typically comprising about thirty students. By 1928 Hope's Glee Clubs had come to dominate the state glee competition so thoroughly that its director decided to replace it with a critiqued recital, because, complained the *Anchor*, "Hope always wins."[55] A once fledgling society had become one of the college's most renowned musical groups, further helped by going on tours.

The Glee Clubs weathered the financial storms of the Great Depression and the enrollment plunges of the Second World War. Jantina Holleman, who joined the Hope faculty in 1946, recalled the Glee Clubs as "THE organizations."[56] Their end came in 1954, when both the men's and women's clubs were absorbed into the Chapel Choir, at times reappearing as a men's or women's chorus.

Founded in 1929 by Curtis Snow, the Chapel Choir is the longest continuously running musical group on campus. Harkening back to an earlier time, the choir was formed with the primary purpose of singing at morning chapel services and on special occasions.[57] The original choir was made up of fifty-four voices, but it has grown continuously since its conception. In 1940 Robert Cavanaugh assumed responsibility for the choir, and later, the *Anchor* enthusiastically claimed that "under his leadership, the Chapel Choir has taken its proud place among the finest college choirs of the nation."[58] The Chapel Choir went on its first

---

[52] *Anchor*, 13 Oct. 1915.
[53] Program, newspaper clippings, advertisement, scrapbook 1915-20, Peter Garret Baker Papers.
[54] Ibid.
[55] *Anchor*, 28 Nov. 1928; see also, *Hope Alumni Tattler* 1 (May 1928): 3.
[56] Aschbrenner interview with Holleman.
[57] *Anchor*, 30 Oct. 1929.
[58] Press release, 11 May 1965, Tulip Time and municipal programs 1936-95 folder, box 3, MD Papers.

tour in the spring of 1953, subsequently performing at such venues as the Hollywood Bowl, Radio City Music Hall, Disneyland, McCormick Place in Chicago, and the White House.[59] In 1967 the choir went on its first European tour, performing in Belgium, the Netherlands, West Germany, Switzerland, Italy, Yugoslavia, and Austria.[60] For a time, freshmen were not eligible to audition, and singing with the College Chorus came to be a prerequisite for subsequent membership in the Chapel Choir.[61]

Formed in 1890, the Eupsalian Orchestra, Hope's first instrumental ensemble, performed concerts in Holland, Allegan, and Fennville before disbanding in the spring of 1893.[62] In its place, a large orchestra developed from some of the best players in town joining the remaining members of the old orchestra.[63] Once again exhibiting initiative, in 1900 students organized a nine-instrument orchestra and recruited a local bandmaster, William Breyman, to lead them.[64] In another display of the college's perpetual struggle to sustain instrumental ensembles, a new orchestra was formed in 1908. By 1915 it had grown to fifteen members, playing the processional at that year's Commencement.

World War I had the same effect on instrumental and vocal ensembles: by 1919 the orchestra was down to eight members, but by 1922, its numbers had recovered. The *Anchor* enthused: "The string section is especially strong, consisting of eleven violins, three cellos, and in all probability, a double bass. . . . For the past three years, Hope College has had an orchestra which has not been surpassed by any organization of its nature in the state."[65] The following year, the orchestra went on its first tour, performing in Grand Haven, Muskegon, and Grand Rapids. It dissolved in 1924, after its core members graduated. The "Le Petit Symphonie" of nine members performed until 1925, when the Hope College Orchestra was once again reestablished. The orchestra continued to perform for the next two decades, but without strong faculty leadership, the instrumental program at Hope floundered until 1947, when Morrette Rider joined the Hope faculty.[66]

---

[59] Ibid., 16 May 1967, vocal ensembles—Chapel Choir, 1931-69 folder, box 2, MD Papers.
[60] *Anchor*, 11 Nov. 1966.
[61] Music correspondence, 1966-90 folder, MD Papers.
[62] *Anchor*, 1 Mar. 1893.
[63] Ibid., 1 May 1893.
[64] *Hope College Catalog* (1900-1901), 54. For William Breyman, who led two different orchestras in Holland, see Swierenga, *Holland, Michigan*, 3:2067.
[65] *Anchor*, 3 May 1922.
[66] For Rider's impact, see ch. 2.

Men's Orchestra (Milestone, *1919*)

In a history of the Music Department published in the *Anchor* in 1923, John Nykerk reported that two decades earlier, senior Peter Swart had organized a band at Hope, another example of student-initiated music at the college.[67] The band's principal purpose was "furnishing pep" on campus, and thus they performed at many Hope College sporting events.[68] In the 1910s and 1920s, band membership followed the trajectory of the orchestra; the band pictured in the 1916 *Milestone* had twenty members, but it was soon followed by instability. Likely from the effects of World War I on college enrollment, in 1920 several members of the Holland community were needed to fill out the band. "Whoever heard of a college without a band?" grumbled the *Anchor* in 1929; in the late 1920s, lack of interest—institutional and student—necessitated recruiting conductors from both Hope College and Western Theological Seminary, and some band members were seminarians.[69]

In 1934 Curtis Snow founded the Hope Marching Band, with the goal of eventually turning it into a symphonic band.[70] His untimely death inaugurated a decade-plus drift, with non-Hope staff and even students attempting to maintain a viable band. There were, however, good years, especially from 1939 to 1941. The 1939 band comprised over fifty students—including drum majorettes and a drum major—and

[67] *Anchor*, 5 Dec. 1923; see also *Hope College Catalog*, 1893-94.
[68] For examples, see *Anchor*, 7 and 16 Oct. 1925, 13 Oct. 1932, 5 Oct. 1938.
[69] Ibid., 23 Oct. and 6 Nov. 1929; *Milestone* (1916), 87, (1928), 97, (1929), 95, and (1930), 143.
[70] *Hope College Bulletin* (Feb. 1935), 18; Snow, *Musikalisch Frau Schnee*, 18.

Hope College Band (Milestone, *1926*)

in these years, it performed as a marching band for football games, at concerts, and in Tulip Time.[71] On the eve of World War II, however, there were repeated turnovers in directors, and as with the orchestra, it was only after Morrette Rider joined the Music faculty that the band became a premier ensemble.[72]

Touring

Possibly even more than membership in musical ensembles such as the orchestra and band, participation in spring break tours came to define the experience of many Hope students who made music. Robert Ritsema recalled that the 1954 tour with the Symphonette, termed by the *Milestone* as "an elite arm of the Orchestra," was his favorite memory of his undergraduate years at Hope, and he believed that he was not the only alumnus who felt this way. "Hundreds of kids have said that, over the years, when they look back on their college experiences, [touring] was their top remembrance."[73] Nearly every spring since 1925, at least one ensemble—either a glee club, or the Hope College Chapel Choir, Orchestra, Symphonette, or Wind Ensemble—travelled for up to three

---

[71] *Milestone* (1939), 105; program, scrapbook 1941-43, box 6, Hinkamp Papers.
[72] *Milestone* (1940), 85, and see ch. 2.
[73] Baer and Utting, interview with Ritsema; *Milestone* (2003), 220.

weeks, often performing more than a dozen concerts along the way. The tours provided thousands of students an opportunity to showcase their musical talents before a wider audience than those on campus or in the local community.

The Glee Clubs were the first of Hope's musical groups to tour. Typically, the Women's and Men's Glee Clubs would travel, alternating yearly between the East and the West. On their first tour in 1925, the Girls' Glee Club travelled to New Jersey and New York for three weeks, performing twenty-four concerts along the way. Following the stock market crash in October 1929, spring break tours were halted. From 1929 to 1936, the Glee Clubs were able to tour only once—in the spring of 1932. Touring opportunities were limited during World War II, but thanks to Esther Snow, who assumed directorship of the Girls' Glee Club in 1942, the ensemble held together, and she managed to produce several performances beyond Holland.[74] Glee Club tours continued until 1954, when the Chapel Choir absorbed the ensembles.

Chapel Choir first toured a year prior to that, in 1953, and found success. Seventy-two students, as well as professors Robert Cavanaugh and Esther Snow, had travelled to the East Coast, where performances included a concert of sacred music at the University of Rochester and the Easter Sunrise Service in Radio City Music Hall.[75] In a letter to President Lubbers shortly after the tour, John Soeter '27 wrote:

> I join a large number of folks in sending this word of deep appreciation. Once again, we know that Hope is on the march. After the concert, a group of us were discussing the affair. The suggestion was made that it might be a good idea to record some of the numbers rendered. Alumni and Church folk alike would probably buy records. . . . Fritz Yonkman and I also agreed that a record of the best Hope songs would also be treasured.[76]

By 1965 the Chapel Choir had already performed in half of the fifty states and the Canadian province of Ontario and had traveled over fifty thousand miles.[77] A report in the *Anchor*'s Music Box column provided comic insight into life on the road:

[74] Program for tribute concert, 12 May 1967, ensembles, vocals, Women's Chorus folder, box 2, MD Papers.
[75] Ensembles, vocal—Chapel Choir correspondence, 1952-72 folder.
[76] Ibid., John J. Soeter to President Lubbers, 8 Apr. 1953, Ensembles, Vocal—Chapel Choir Correspondence, 1952-72 folder, MD Papers, box 2.
[77] Press release, 11 May 1965, Tulip Time and municipal programs 1936-95 folder, box 3, MD Papers.

If you want to give any of the boys a going-away present, we offer a few suggestions. What with only one suitcase a person, and 13 singing engagements, and everyone sweating a gallon each concert, we might suggest some Deodorant.... Or if any of you wish, you might pack a lunch, because someone is bound to get hungry.[78]

While on tour, students were housed with alumni and members of the churches where performances were held. The hosts frequently spoke to the character and quality of the students they accommodated, responding like Rev. Harvey Hoffman '32, pastor of Second Reformed Church in Hackensack, New Jersey, in a letter to Lubbers:

The people without exception enjoyed entertaining the choir members in their homes. They have unanimously expressed their favorable comments on the caliber of young people who represent Hope College. I can assure you that the reputation of the College is enhanced by the appearance of the Chapel Choir, under such expert direction as that of Dr. Cavanaugh and Mrs. Snow.[79]

Although such interactions served as splendid publicity for the college, the tours represented much more than that to the students who participated. To many, they were the learning experience of a lifetime. On tour, some students were afforded the opportunity to explore places they may not have otherwise seen. Robert Ritsema recalled the thrill of being in Radio City Music Hall for the first time, a place this Illinois farm boy had never expected to see.[80] Others learned how to interact with community members, church leaders, and faculty outside their academic sphere. Philip Huizenga '54 confidently stated, "I've said it before, but will say it again, that I sincerely believe I learned as much about meeting and getting along with people on the trips as I did in all the rest of my experiences at Hope (this isn't meant to belittle the rest of Hope!)"[81] In 1972 students even got the chance to sing for President Richard Nixon and First Lady Pat Nixon when the Chapel Choir

---

[78] *Anchor*, 27 Mar. 1947.
[79] Harvey B. Hoffman to President Lubbers, 10 Apr. 1953, vocal ensembles—Chapel Choir correspondence, 1952-72 folder. For a similar insight from the West Coast a decade later, see Leonard Wezeman to Lubbers, 8 Apr. 1955, in ibid.
[80] Baer and Utting interview with Ritsema.
[81] Philip Huizenga to Cavanaugh, 16 Jan. 1956, correspondence 1954-64 folder, box 1, Cavanaugh Papers.

Chapel Choir at the White House

performed at the White House, wearing their striking Eames robes.[82] Lynne Walchenbach '73, described the experience as "thrilling," while also admitting, "It's scary to sing before the President."[83]

Most importantly, the tours gave students a chance to have fun and learn from one another. After his return from the 1924 Girls' Glee Club East Coast tour, Nykerk amused a morning chapel audience with stories of the "girls' wanderlust, their pranks, and their ice cream sodas, the latter he generously furnished."[84] Antics abounded on tours, especially within the Men's Glee Club. During the 1947 tour, Milton Hinga wrote a theme song entitled "Cavinyaugh, dear old Cavinyaugh," while Arthur Van Eck '48, recalled, "Many of the veterans in the Glee Club were always eager to arrive at the next venue so that they could get to the Library, a code word for a place to 'bend the elbow' for a while."[85] A clipping in Robert Cavanaugh's scrapbook divulges another amusing story:

[82] *Holland Evening Sentinel*, 23 Nov. 1970; on the robes see Paul Trap, "The Eames Robes used by the Hope College Chapel Choir," Chapel Choir papers folder, box 3, MD Papers.
[83] "Singing for Nixon 'More Like Social Event Than Religious One,'" newspaper clipping, *Flint Journal* (n.d.), Hope College White House scrapbook, box 3, Cavanaugh Papers.
[84] *Anchor*, 4 Mar. 1925.
[85] Ibid., 8 May 1947; Arthur O. Van Eck, "One Veteran's Entry into Hope," Nordstrom and Zuidema, *Hope at the Crossroads*, 214.

When the Glee Club stopped in Mohawk, New York, being a little off schedule, they had to don their tuxedos in the kitchen of the minister's parsonage. Chuck Stoppels, a little more speedy than the rest in dressing, peeked into the living room and saw there a rather good-looking young lady, with whom, he announced to the fellows, he intended to get a date for the evening. He engaged her in conversation, soon reaching the point where he was just about to ask her for a date, when she, sensing of course what was coming, tactfully explained, before he could ask that she was Mrs. Dekker, wife of the minister of that church.[86]

Such memories anchored tour veterans to other alumni, their faculty leaders, and the college as a living institution.

Performing

In fostering a department welcoming to all students with an interest in music, Music has been strategic in extending opportunities based on merit, not major. In the process, students with a wide variety of relationships with music have been able to experience the thrill of performing, sometimes in front of a single professor and on other occasions before thousands at DeVos Performance Hall. No matter the size of the audience, however, performing was a significant rite of passage for students who made music at Hope.

These presentations took multiple forms, including student recitals, ensemble concerts, and performances initiated by both students and faculty. Since the early twentieth century, senior music students have been required to give a complete recital and, later, juniors a half recital.[87]

According to Jantina Holleman, "This requirement is one of the most challenging for any young performer; like writing a thesis, or competing in the Olympics, it requires much study, and practice, practice, practice."[88] Over the years, these recitals have been held in a variety of locations, including Winants Chapel, Dimnent Chapel, Walsh Hall, Nykerk Hall, and the Jack Miller Center. Student recitals were even occasionally held in faculty members' homes.

---

[86] Newspaper clipping (1941), scrapbook, box 4, Cavanaugh Papers.
[87] *Hope College Bulletin* 88 (May 1950).
[88] "Piano recitals among best presented at Hope," Students—newspaper clippings folder, Conway Papers; diary entries, 6-8 June 1930, HC diaries 1929-34, box 1, Schuppert Papers.

Although not a music major, Elton Bruins '50 took enough piano courses to warrant a recital, which took place in December 1949 at piano professor Milton Johnston's home. Performing Schubert's *Impromptu Opus 142, no. 2*, Bruins recalled how thankful he was for the calming atmosphere of Johnson's home. "It was more private . . . it gave us a chance to get our nerves in control . . . yes, you practiced. . . . But when you get in a situation like that, you get very nervous and your hands change."[89]

As the department became more professional, most student performances were faculty initiated. Students like Melissa Johnson, Class of 2015, busily prepared for these required performances and recitals. Responding to a question about her own experiences with making music, Johnson recalled,

> I did require recitals and performances as a soloist, chamber musician, and as part of large ensembles. This in itself was much more than I could have ever anticipated when entering Hope as a freshman. I loved all the performing opportunities I was given; it was just time consuming. I did get connected in a church and was able to eventually work my way into my own music making there. While I only played at church once or twice a month, it was a nice change from all of the required performing I was doing.[90]

Students did, however, find time to initiate their own performances. Greg Phillips '70, presented a concert of his own compositions at Hope Church. The concert—which included works for choir, vocal soloists, violin, trumpet, and organ—featured many Hope music students, including a choir composed of students from the Chapel Choir and the Collegium Musicum. Christopher Turbessi, a 2008 graduate, created as many performance opportunities for himself as possible. These included participating in the concerto competition, auditioning for the Musical Showcase, and one summer performing with his piano trio at a chamber music festival in Fort Worth, Texas. Colin Rensch, Class of 2016, put together a jazz quintet, which performed Chick Corea's *Captain Marvel* at the Musical Showcase and composed *The Frontier*, a three-movement wind suite.[91]

---

[89] Baer and Utting, interview with Elton Bruins, 31 May 2018, Making Music folder.
[90] Melissa Johnson to Marc Baer, email, 13 June 2018, Making Music folder.
[91] *Anchor*, 15 May 1970; Christopher Turbessi and Colin Rensch to Marc Baer, emails, 1 and 6 June 2018, Making Music folder.

Even so, it was often the required performances at Hope College—both good and bad—that were the most meaningful and memorable. Robert Kranendonk '50 could not forget what an honor it was to sing the role of Elijah in the Mount Carmel scene of the oratorio *Elijah* during his time at Hope, while Kim Daelhousen, a 2003 graduate, described her experience singing the *Stabat Mater* with the women's chorus as "transcending."[92] David Lowry '89 recollected his performance at Vespers in 1987:

> If I remember correctly, I had a pitch pipe and started the piece ("I look from afar," by Palestrina), which may have started Vespers that year. As can happen with live music, a bit later in the midst of that piece . . . a disturbance—perhaps a group coming late . . . threw off pitch one of the subsequent voices, which then had a cascading effect upon the starting pitch of the following piece. I cannot now recall how alignment with the instruments was restored, but it was, and with only one cringe-worthy bar of music![93]

Another student, Nannette Olmsted, who had transferred from Hope after her sophomore year, recalled performing at Vespers in a poignant letter to Cavanaugh.

> Every time I think of you and the Chapel Choir, especially singing at Vespers, I realize how much I miss you. . . . All I had to do was close my eyes, and I could see the chapel with all the greenery. In a strange way, that scene always comes to my mind when I hear the word "home." For me, Vespers is a special time of feeling at one with the rest of the choir and with Him in the warmth of His home.[94]

The highlight of the year for the department, and the pinnacle of performing for many students in recent decades, is the Musical Showcase, which had taken place every spring at DeVos Performance Hall in Grand Rapids, but in 2016, it was moved to the new Jack Miller Center. Begun in 1989, the event features nearly every Hope College student musical group in a fast-paced program with seemingly

---

[92] Kranendonk, "Music Maker," Nordstrom and Zuidema, *Hope at the Crossroads*, 240-41; *Milestone* (2001), 94.
[93] David Lowry to Marc Baer, email, 26 June 2018, Making Music folder.
[94] Nannette Olmsted to Cavanaugh (ca. 1971), correspondence 1970-74 folder, box 1, Cavanaugh Papers.

instantaneous transitions between performances. In 2003 then senior Josh Brandenburg performed "Mama Says," from the musical *Footloose*. Brandenburg recalled:

> DeVos was a great experience. You get to walk on stage and give your heart to the audience.... There is no feeling in the world like stepping on stage and knowing that every eye is focused on you, waiting for you to make the night light up. For me, performing is more than just showing what I can do, it is showing who I am and what I am made of.[95]

Faculty as mentors

Student experiences in making music were often defined by the mutually beneficial relationships they formed with faculty members. From the faculty perspective, this was expressed by Nella Meyer in a 1947 communication with John Hollenbach: "We, as faculty members, must have such an enthusiasm for our subjects that this feeling becomes contagious and spreads to those in our charge. If we have not that interest in education and people, we should not be teachers."[96]

In reflecting on their experiences in music, students almost always praised the efforts of a faculty member or two who had made a profound impact on them as both a person and a musician. Filed away in the collections of the Joint Archives of Holland are hundreds of letters sent by students to their music professors, thanking them for their encouragement, high expectations, and Christian influence. A note from Marcia Kay De Graaf '67 to Cavanaugh after returning home from the Chapel Choir's European tour is typical.

> I think you can imagine how I've felt about choir for the past 3 years. But there's more than that. I don't think you realize how much you encouraged me, many times indirectly, to do my best, which was often better than I even thought I could do. For this and much more, I give my heartfelt thanks.... I've been under your Christian direction and influence for four years and have been blessed by it. I'm sure others have and will continue to be blessed by your witness.[97]

[95] *Milestone* (2003), 221.
[96] Meyer to Hollenbach, 20 Oct. 1947, biography 1925-75 folder, Nella Meyer Papers, H88-0105; see also Cavanaugh, "To Search ... and to Find," Music Hope College brochures folder, box 1, MD Papers.
[97] Marcia Kay De Graaf to Cavanaugh, 17 Aug. 1967, correspondence 1965-69 folder, box, 1, Cavanaugh Papers.

Experiencing Resonance

DeVos Musical Showcase

These sentiments hail from sources as far back as the historical record goes. Following the Chapel Choir's performance at the 1933 Baccalaureate service, Professor Snow had them to his home. In gratitude for what was in many cases a four-year-long relationship, choir members presented him this note of thanks:

> We're ready to go.
> But before we depart
> Here's a thought from our heart.
> Your patient work with us so long
> Will ever keep in our souls a song.
> Your winning smile has brought us cheer
> Thru all the days of this past year.
> This little token is rather small
> But it comes with a thought of love from all.[98]

Organ student Ethel Leestma Swets made certain to include a copy of the note in her own hand, revealing just how important Snow's mentoring had been to her during her time at Hope.

Sometimes the relationship spanned decades, even generations. Both John and Harriet Maassen '42, formed a strong bond with Cavanaugh during their time at Hope and were thrilled when their daughter Beth '71 became one of his students.[99] On other occasions, the relationship took form in significant student-faculty collaboration. For his senior recital, Robert Ritsema '57 played in a trio with Wanda Rider, wife of a music professor, and Anthony Kooiker, who taught piano, whereas in 1964, four Music faculty performed solos at a Symphonette concert.[100]

There is a bas-relief in the lobby of the Jack Miller Center titled *Teaching*, which along with six others was moved from Nykerk Hall to Music's new home. Music students understood their professors as teachers. More than that, however, they recognized them as mentors. Referring to Joan Conway, and speaking for several students, Mami Kato '97 said it best: "She's more than just a teacher."[101] Thus, the bas-relief does not begin to do justice to all the ways Music faculty has walked alongside students in their study of music.

---

[98] Scrapbook 1929-36, Ethel Leestma Swets Papers.
[99] John and Harriet Maassen to Cavanaugh, 8 June 1971, correspondence 1970-74 folder, box 1, Cavanaugh Papers.
[100] Baer and Utting interview with Ritsema; *Anchor*, 14 Feb. 1964.
[101] *Holland Sentinel*, 29 Oct. 2000; Mami Kato to Marc Baer, email, 9 Aug. 2018, Making Music folder.

Bas-relief *Teaching*

At almost any hour of the day or night, music may be heard on campus. Whether it is an original single being strummed on the second floor of Wyckoff, a classical melody floating from one of the Jack Miller practice rooms, or a contemporary cover belted from the shower, students at Hope make music. Regardless of the differences in motive, at the root of every student's decision to perform is the chance to showcase a part of themselves. The corporate consequence is resonance, the deep, full, and reverberating quality of sound.

The student experience of making music at Hope has been humorous, nerve wracking, triumphant, embarrassing, educational, relational, life changing, and even deeply spiritual. Despite secular elements of both composition and performance, music at Hope has retained a strong religious dimension. Students reflecting on their musical experience frequently highlight the powerful role music has played in the formation of a mature faith. In the 1920s, Mildred Schuppert went to a friend's Voorhees room, noting that night in her diary, "We had a lovely time—talking and singing hymns."[102] Three decades later, Ann Van Dorp Query '68 candidly stated, "The [Chapel] choir to me was one of the most honest religious experiences I have

---

[102] Diary entry, 11 Nov. 1927, HC diary 1927-, box 1, Schuppert Papers.

ever been a part of."[103] In discussing performing, Frederick Wezeman '64 wrote:

> There is something wonderful and quite intangible that one gains from such an experience that far transcends the satisfaction that one has after that "best concert." The ministry of music is only 50% of it, for the other part I'm sure was what came as inward manifestation, a feeling of the presence of the Almighty, which enabled us in turn to express this feeling through our singing.[104]

But perhaps most revealing, students routinely championed the harmonious blend of the secular and the sacred, and in so doing, making music at Hope taught them about faith. Victoria Longfield, Class of 2015, movingly spoke to this purposeful fusion at the center of Music—and Hope—since the college's beginning:

> For me the most important part of my music experience was the combination of looking at music as a gift from God and growing as a flautist within that context. This combination of faith and music is a rarity among good music schools—in fact, musicians are highly secular, and being a believer within those contexts is often frowned upon. . . . [Hope's Music Department] was a place that all of us could grow as musicians together and grow in our faith together as well. I can remember my freshman and sophomore years primarily when much of my class had Music Theory or Aural Skills and . . . we would all walk across the Pine Grove talking about Diminished 6ths and analysis theories on our way to Chapel together. This combination of faith and music was a deeply embedded part of my experience and something that I cherish greatly to this day.[105]

From performing to joining an ensemble to learning from faculty, many students left Hope acknowledging the powerful role making music could play in their relationship with God. This notion was perpetuated every time they performed, and so, it seems the spiritual dimension of those experiences has made all the difference in the longevity and depth of their impact.

---

[103] Ann Van Dorp Query to Cavanaugh, 19 Sept. 1968, correspondence 1965-69 folder, box 1, Cavanaugh Papers.
[104] Fred Wezeman to Cavanaugh, 14 Feb. 1965, correspondence 1954-64 folder.
[105] Victoria Henry Longfield to Marc Baer, email, 28 June 2018, Making Music folder.

CHAPTER 4

Where Music Dwells

> Where music dwells lingering—and wandering on as loth to die.
> William Wordsworth, *Inside of King's College Chapel, Cambridge*, 1822

> How colorless college life would be without it,
> and how dead Voorhees Hall would be without the trilling and strumming
> that re-echo through its halls and at all hours!
> *Milestone*, 1918

> The department is homeless.
> *The New Hope College Music Hall*, ca. 1956

Come with us through the weathered doors of Dimnent Chapel, over the diagonally tiled floors of the narthex. Take hold of the wood railing and follow us up the stairs to the balcony landing in the south tower. Herein is a forgotten space, empty now, useful either for its access to two wooden doors or as a platform from which to observe a series of small paintings or a few rays of light that stream through a

98 MAKING MUSIC

Mildred Schuppert on practice organ (Milestone, *1932*)

stained-glass window, emblematic of Dimnent Chapel. Every week of the academic year, hundreds of people will pass this way, unaware of the history of this space. If these walls could talk, perhaps they would share the melodies that burst forth from the Kimball organ that Curtis Snow and three students had reassembled here in 1930 after purchasing it second hand in Illinois and on which Roger Rietberg recalled practicing still in the 1940s.[1] Or maybe they would tell stories of students who spent long, frustrating nights here plunking away on the nightmarish old Wurlitzer organ that replaced the Kimball in 1949 and continued to plague organ students with its "bargain-basement-accordion tone" even after it followed them to the Nykerk Hall of Music in 1956.[2]

This little balcony expanse, unused now for over fifty years, is a superfluous space to those who pass through it, but once, it was a place. Geographers suppose there is an important distinction to be made between a space and a place.[3] A space is simply a location, a spot on a map, or a blueprint, devoid of historical meaning. A place, on the other hand, is a space that has been given value and meaning through human experience. The spaces music has occupied at Hope College throughout

[1] *Anchor*, 17 Nov. 1949; Baer interview with Rietberg.
[2] *Anchor*, 14 Nov. 1958.
[3] Yi-Fu Tuan, *Space and Place: The Perspective of Experience* (Minneapolis: University of Minnesota Press, 1977).

the years are great in number and diverse in function. Yet, from stately Van Raalte Memorial Hall in 1903 to the shining Jack Miller Center for Musical Arts, opened in 2015, music has transformed these spaces into vibrant places—successfully at times—and prematurely uprooted from them at other times. It is these spaces and places that help tell the story of music at Hope College. Like a metaphor for music itself, Music's journey toward finding a place to call home on Hope's campus has been dramatic and dynamic. Music was everywhere and nowhere, pushed here and pulled there, tucked away in a chapel tower and showcased on the brightest stage, secure one moment and homeless the next.

This chapter will explore the spaces and places that music has occupied on the campus of Hope College over the years. These include locations where practice rooms, classrooms, and faculty studios existed, and although performance spaces are an important part of music at Hope, this chapter will touch on them only briefly.

Early years, 1866-1907

Most of the early music at Hope was produced for morning chapel, so it should not be surprising that much of the first music performed on campus was found in the college's chapel. Located just east of Van Vleck Hall, the chapel/gymnasium was constructed during the summer of 1862 by Principal Philip Phelps Jr. and his students at what was then called Hope Academy. The chapel featured a stage, furnished with lamps and carpeting in 1883, and enough moveable seating for six hundred people. It also contained an organ used for chapel services, with a new Beatty organ installed in 1882.[4] When Winants Chapel in Graves Hall was dedicated in 1894, and after much lobbying from students, the building was converted into a gymnasium.[5] The Choral Union, a vocal group led by John Nykerk and one of Hope's first student musical organizations, began meeting on Mondays in Winants Chapel shortly after its dedication.

Some of Music's first "courses" were held off campus. In 1882 John Gilmore instructed students in vocal music at a public school near the Hope campus.[6] Five years later, a music class, taught by G. C. Shepard of Grand Rapids, was held in the city's YMCA rooms on Eighth

---

[4] *Excelsiora* 13 (19 Nov. 1882).
[5] Nyenhuis, *Hope College at 150*, 1:216-19; *Anchor*, 1 May and 1 Dec. 1894.
[6] *Excelsiora* 13 (3 Nov. 1882), 31. Presumably this was Froebel school, previously Union and then Central school: Swierenga, *Holland, Michigan*, 1:403.

Chapel in 1862

Street, above Jonkman and Dykstra's clothing store.[7] Other instruction took place on Hope's campus, such as a voice class taught in 1888 by a Holland resident in John Nykerk's room.[8] Just as early music offerings at Hope were inconsistent and scattered, so too were the spaces in which they were held.

With the expansion of the music curriculum at the college in the early 1900s, however, both more space and a more centralized space were needed to host lessons and faculty studios. As a result, Music was moved to the newly opened Van Raalte Memorial Hall, dedicated on September 16, 1903. The college catalog for the 1903-4 academic year states that Music, including faculty studios, was housed, "at present," in a large assembly room on the third floor. At that time, Van Raalte Hall served as the college's primary academic building: in addition to Music, it housed laboratories for the sciences and lecture rooms for courses in humanities disciplines, with a museum located on the third floor.[9]

As the transitory "at present" language above hints, Music's home in Van Raalte was to be short lived. Plans for a new women's dormitory were announced in the 1906-7 catalog, which would include fifty "model, but simple, apartments," along with a dining hall, parlors, and half-a-dozen rooms for the "temporary housing of the School of Music."[10] Increasing college enrollment, combined with the crowded atmosphere of Van Raalte Memorial Hall, most likely contributed to the School of Music being banished from the building. Total student enrollment—at the college, School of Music, and preparatory school—had risen from 292 in 1905 to 335 by 1908, an increase of 15 percent.

[7] *Anchor*, 1 Oct. 1887; Swierenga, *Holland, Michigan*, 1:322.
[8] *Anchor*, 1 Jan. 1888.
[9] *Hope College Catalog* (1903-4), 68.
[10] Ibid. (1906-7), 80.

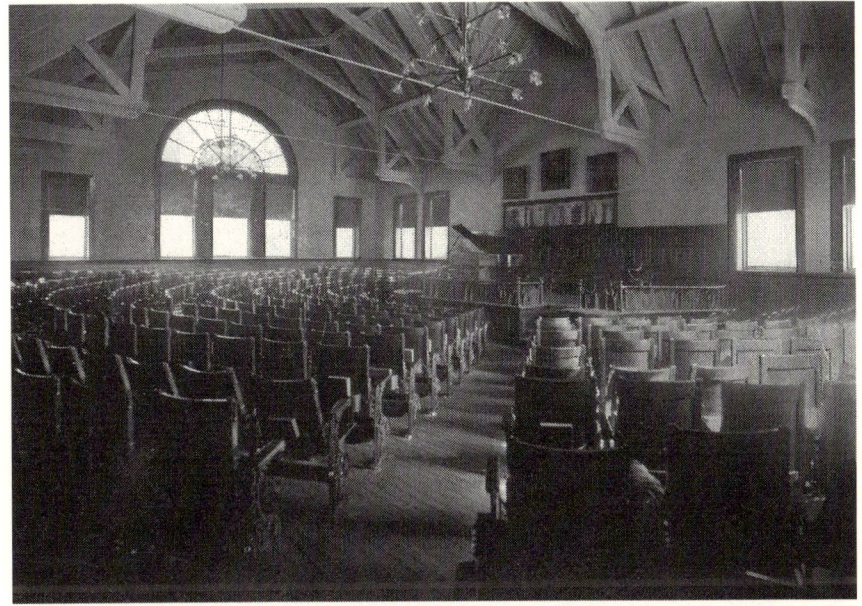

Interior of Winants Chapel

In those same years, enrollment at the School of Music had dropped by more than half, from seventy-six students in 1905 to only thirty-seven in 1908.[11] More space was needed in Van Raalte Hall for lecture rooms, and Music was the chosen sacrifice.[12] Terms such as "at present" and "temporary" reveal the absence of long-range facilities planning, making it unclear where the college intended to move Music following its residency in what came to be named the Elizabeth R. Voorhees dormitory. For decades, college space was constrained: from the completion of Voorhees in 1907 to the new science center in 1941 (later, Lubbers Hall), the only construction at Hope was Dimnent Chapel.

The Voorhees era, 1907-1940

When the Voorhees dormitory opened in fall 1907, it had around seventy rooms, with fifty-four dedicated to students and six set aside for Music.[13] Initially, many rooms were empty, since female enrollment levels remained low, stunted for years by the lack of on-campus housing

[11] Ibid. (1905-6), 71, and (1907-8), 80.
[12] Gerrit John Kollen, *President's Annual Report on Hope College to the Council of Hope College*, 25 Apr. 1906, quoted in Natalie Fulk, "Voorhees Hall: A Symbol of Women's Education at Hope College," *Joint Archives Quarterly* 25 (Winter 2016): 2.
[13] Nyenhuis, *Hope College at 150*, 1:264-75.

Van Raalte Hall

for women. Women were admitted to Hope beginning in 1878 and have enrolled continuously since 1902, but until Voorhees opened its doors, the student population was predominantly male.[14] Thus, although capable of housing over one hundred, only thirteen female students lived in Voorhees during its first year.[15] To further utilize the space and quiet those who questioned the college's decision to build such a large dormitory, rooms were rented out to some of the unmarried faculty members, including John Nykerk, at that time head of the Department of English and secretary of the School of Music. This situation, however, did not last long. In 1916, a short nine years after Voorhees' dedication, seventy-four women participated in Commencement, lending credence to the argument that a female dormitory was critical to promoting women's enrollment at Hope.[16] In 1924 the *Anchor* reported that "Voorhees Hall is, as usual, filled to overflowing" and that Hope "was obliged to refuse twelve applications for admittance because of lack of room."[17] Most of the faculty, in tune with increasing female enrollment, moved out, except for Nykerk, who, despite repeated calls for his departure, refused to leave.

Music studios occupied the west side of the first floor of Voorhees, and what had originally been deemed temporary became

---

[14] Wichers, *Century of Hope*, 89-90.
[15] Lauren Berka, "Legacy of a Landmark: The History of Elizabeth R. Voorhees Hall," *Joint Archives Quarterly* 17 (Fall 2007): 3.
[16] *Hope College Yearbook* (1916-17), 58-62, quoted in Berka, "Legacy of a Landmark," 3.
[17] *Anchor*, 17 Sept. 1924; cf. Nyenhuis, *Hope College at 150*, 1:269.

Serenade in Voorhees courtyard

the department's home for the next thirty-three years. In that time, music helped define the character of the dormitory and its reputation on campus. The 1918 *Milestone* lovingly describes music at Hope in the following way: "How colorless college life would be without it, and how dead Voorhees Hall would be without the trilling and strumming that re-echo thru its halls at all hours!"[18] The *Anchor* also spoke to the unique spirit Music and its students brought to Voorhees: "If the studio at Voorhees dorm could only tell its tales. Swantina, ukulele, Bill, Bones, Rosie, Lue, Janet, and music—bell rings, music stops, and fun's over."[19] So filled with music was Voorhees that it could not avoid becoming the site of musical performances that became rituals performed by collegiate males through the 1960s. On May 12, 1930, the Cosmopolitan Fraternity staged a midnight program from the Voorhees courtyard that awoke their audience slumbering away inside. In an *Anchor* article detailing the event, special credit was given to the "Ford Motor Company, who most accommodatingly manufactured a truck to carry the night."[20] This was one of many serenades to occur over the years in the courtyard to the south of Voorhees.[21]

Studios and practice rooms on the first floor of Voorhees were "furnished in exquisite taste" during the 1925-26 academic year, thanks

[18] *Milestone* (1918), 66.
[19] *Anchor*, 24 Mar. 1920.
[20] Ibid., 21 May 1930.
[21] Ibid., 15 Apr. 1925; HC diaries, 1927- and 1929-34, box 1, Schuppert Papers; 1927-31; scrapbook, Marion De Kuiper Papers, H03-1500.5; *Milestone* (1922), 162, and (1945), 52. In 1931 the Voorhees women turned the tables and serenaded at the fraternity residences: Schuppert diary, 18 Dec. 1931.

to a generous donation by the College Women's League, a group of female students connected with the Reformed Church's Synod of Chicago.²² These first-floor spaces were eventually renamed the Grace Marguerite Browning Studios, after the "generous and inspiring" faculty member who was one of the college's early voice teachers.²³ A new Bush and Lane piano was added to the studios in 1928.²⁴ Instrumental music courses were taught there, as well as voice.²⁵ Proximity to Music secretary John Nykerk's room may have solidified the department's teaching corps.

Once merely a temporary space, Voorhees had now become a meaningful place for many musically inclined students, and in turn, music may have given Voorhees an identity, part of which was spontaneous singing. As a freshman music major living in the dormitory, Mildred Schuppert carefully noted in her diary occasions when, after studying, she joined other women around the lounge's piano to sing, separating these impromptu occasions from her own practicing for piano class.²⁶ Listening to music provided another opportunity to shape a musical character for Voorhees. According to the *Anchor*, "Third floor in Voorhees transformed into a studio—a music studio—perhaps the most unusual ever heard of, the instruments, not piano, violin, or harp, but Victrola; the studies, not classical compositions nor etudes, but jazz."²⁷ A brief history of music at the college given in the September 1940 *Anchor* suggests that Hope students in the first half of the twentieth century struggled to accept jazz on campus: "During the [first] World War, some very shocking changes took place in the music department. . . . In 1918 Hope College had its own JAZZ BAND. We didn't consult the catalogue for that year, but it must have read: 'Hope College offers one of the hottest bands in Western Michigan!'"²⁸ Mockery aside, if the residents of Voorhees were typical, jazz music enjoyed the support of Hope students.

---

²² *Hope College Catalog* 1928-29, *Feb. Bulletin*, 69.
²³ *Anchor*, 18 Sept. 1940.
²⁴ Ibid., 14 Mar. 1928.
²⁵ For voice lessons in Voorhees, see diary entries, 25 Jan. and 1 Feb. 1929, 2 Feb. 1931, HC diaries 1929-34, Schuppert Papers.
²⁶ Diary entries, 8 and 22 Oct., 1 Nov. 1927, 19 Jan. 1928, HC diary 1927-, Schuppert Papers; for another such experience in Voorhees earlier in the decade, see Larry Wagenaar interview with Alice Brower Hoffs, 1999, Alice Hoffs Papers.
²⁷ *Anchor*, 14 Apr. 1920.
²⁸ Ibid., 18 Sept. 1940.

Carnegie Gymnasium interior

New musical spaces

Voorhees provided practice rooms and faculty studios, but it lacked space for recitals and performances. Carnegie Gymnasium, however, did supply such a venue. Built in 1906, with money gifted by the gymnasium's namesake, Carnegie included an auditorium that could seat at least twelve hundred and was frequently used for large events like concerts, lectures, convocations, and commencements; in 1934, for example, the orchestra and the Men's Glee Club staged a two-act operetta, *Don Alonso's Treasure*, in Carnegie.[29] College catalogs repeatedly announced that a pipe organ was to be installed in the auditorium, but apparently, it did not happen. At the same time, Winants Chapel was used for recitals, smaller lectures, concerts, and of course, morning chapel services.[30]

Following the completion of Memorial (hereafter, Dimnent) Chapel in 1929, these arrangements changed. Musical performances, recitals, lectures, concerts, and chapel services gradually migrated from Winants Chapel and Carnegie Gymnasium to Dimnent Chapel.

---

[29] *Holland City News*, 13 Oct. 1927; *Hope College Catalog* (1905-6), 81; *Milestone* (1935), 78.
[30] For a 1923 recital, which included violin and piano professors Karl Wecker and Oscar Cress, see *Anchor*, 14 Nov. 1923.

106   MAKING MUSIC

The new chapel boasted seating for fourteen hundred (over 1,000 on the main floor and another 350 in the balcony) and a fifty-seven-stop organ, built by the E. M. Skinner Organ Company of Boston. President Dimnent was the college organist in 1894-95, his junior year at Hope, which may explain why he expended so much energy securing such a magnificent organ for the new chapel.[31] Often referred to as the Skinner or the chancel organ, in 1929 it was the only such instrument on campus, and as a result, ten organ students were allowed to practice on it.[32] Ethel Leestma was one of these, and in a 2007 interview, she recalled:

> I had the wonderful privilege of playing the beautiful new Skinner organ in the stunning Hope Chapel, with the sun streaming in the late afternoon through the rose window. I was able to practice on that organ three or four hours a day every day for those four years.... I kept my pair of organ shoes on the side of the organ, and I wept when I removed the shoes from the organ on Commencement night.[33]

The absence of a practice organ two years before Dimnent opened caused Mildred Schuppert and Ruth Keppel to walk in the rain to Grace Episcopal Church to practice on their organ.[34] To address this problem, in September 1930, a second-hand Kimball organ was installed in the south tower of Dimnent.[35] Carlyle Neckers '35 remembered the college had two practice organs during his time at Hope, "one in the tower of the chapel, which was an old theatre organ [and] another in the basement of the library, which is Graves building, put up in a soundproof room."[36] In 1949 the Music Department purchased two new practice organs, a Baldwin from the Vahey Music Company of Grand Rapids and a Wurlitzer from Meyer Music House in Holland. The Wurlitzer replaced the Kimball in the south tower of Dimnent, and the Baldwin was installed in an organ studio in the basement of the chapel.[37]

---

[31] See correspondence 1920-29 folder, Dimnent Memorial Chapel Papers.
[32] *Anchor*, 18 Dec. 1929.
[33] *Holland Sentinel*, 15 Apr. 2007.
[34] Diary entry, 1 Nov. 1927, HC diary 1927-, box 1, Schuppert Papers. At the time, the church occupied a building on Ninth Street, now home to the Holland Civic Theatre.
[35] *Anchor*, 8 Oct. 1930.
[36] Aschbrenner interview with Neckers. This space is pictured on the inside cover of the 1942 *Milestone*.
[37] Irwin Lubbers to Harris Meyer, 10 Nov. 1949, facilities—organ 1945-52 folder, box 4, MD Papers; *Anchor*, 17 Nov. 1949; "Hope Memorial Chapel" (n.d.), background

In addition to practice organs and performance space, Dimnent Chapel provided an office for Curtis Snow. According to Ethel Leestma Swets, the office was in a "little closet off the platform of the chapel. The tiny room was so full of music, we had to stand in the hallway to talk to him."[38] Carlyle Neckers remembered, "Mr. Snow's office was right off the platform, the stage, and there was not room for two people in there."[39] As well, the chapel basement provided studio space and classrooms. Looking back on his time as a student, Robert Ritsema recalled, "That's where the music department existed," whereas Nancy Plantenga '56, remembered practicing on a piano there.[40] Music faculty studios were no longer located in Dimnent, but the chapel continued to be used for musical performances. An Easter 1933 program at Dimnent included Curtis and Esther Snow, senior organ student Ethel Leestma, the Chapel Choir, and vocal and violin soloists.[41] In 1942 the Girl's Glee Club held a Dutch *zingen van Psalmen* (singing from Psalms) in Dimnent.[42] And most notably, since 1941, the chapel has been the venue for Christmas Vespers.

Beginning in 1937, the Hope catalog failed to mention Music in its description of Voorhees Hall. Until 1940, however, it did list the Grace Marguerite Browning Studios in the School of Music section, and when Robert Cavanaugh arrived in the fall of 1940 to teach at the college, he was assigned an office in Voorhees, suggesting that between 1937 and 1940, Music had remained in the women's dormitory. It is unclear what finally prompted Music's departure from Voorhees; the ever-increasing female enrollment at the college, however, is sure to have been a factor in that decision. Dimnent Chapel, already being used as a supplementary space for Music during this time, essentially became its home in 1940: a pamphlet published ca. 1940 is the first document to mention Dimnent as the location for Music.[43] Meanwhile, a small music room at the foot of the stairs on the south side of Dimnent, which had served Music

---

material folder, Dimnent Memorial Chapel Papers. The space was probably what is now room 15.

[38] *Holland Sentinel*, 15 Apr. 2007. It is on the south side of the choir loft, which was added later, numbered 27, and now contains cleaning supplies.

[39] Aschbrenner interview with Neckers.

[40] LaBarge interview with Ritsema; Nancy Plantega to Marc Baer, email, 21 Aug. 2018, Making Music folder; "Educational Facilities," Music Building 1956-70 folder, Jantina Holleman Papers; *Milestone* (1940), 91.

[41] Program, scrapbook 1932-35, box 4, Hinkamp Papers.

[42] Concert program, 17 May 1942, vocal ensembles—glee clubs folder.

[43] *A Day at Hope College* (ca. 1940), Wichers' presidency—general brochures and pamphlets, College Advancement Papers, H88-0322.

during the 1930s, was converted into a recording studio for the new Hope College radio program.[44] The Music and Religion Departments shared the classrooms in Dimnent's basement, but it does not appear that this was a suitable arrangement, since Music is not listed under the Dimnent entry in the college catalog for the 1942-43 academic year.

Instead, the first reference to an official music building was made. The September 16, 1942, *Anchor* reported: "The old education building now houses the entire music department. Seven pianos have been moved in, and classrooms and studios for Prof. Robert Cavanaugh and Mrs. Snow have been provided."[45] The former education building, which became known as Columbia Hall and later Columbia Cottage, performed a variety of roles in its time on Hope's campus. Originally built in 1876 on the east side of College Avenue at Eleventh Street, the building first served as the *De Hope* printing office.[46] Beginning in 1887, the *Anchor* was also published there.[47] Then, in 1892, the building was relocated westward to Columbia Avenue and Eleventh Street in order to make way for the construction of Graves Hall.[48] A second floor was added to the structure in 1926-27, as well as eight classrooms, which became the new home for the College High School, until it closed its doors in 1936.[49] Finally, the building was used for teacher education courses before Music moved in.[50] At last, it seemed, Music had found a space of its own. The *Milestone* described the jubilation surrounding the move: "'Now we can make all the noise we want,' sighs Mrs. Snow happily, surveying the new music building." Columbia had space for practice pianos, faculty studios, and a new Victrola, given by the Men's and Women's Glee Clubs.[51]

Unfortunately, before Music could make its mark on the building, its search for a home took yet another dramatic turn. As was happening in colleges across the country, America's involvement in World War II disrupted all aspects of life on Hope's campus. Carnegie Gymnasium was converted into a mess hall, and Western Theological Seminary

---

[44] Aschbrenner interview with Neckers; *Milestone* (1940), 89. This is the room currently numbered 13.
[45] *Anchor*, 16 Sept. 1942.
[46] *Holland City News*, 13 June 1929.
[47] Nyenhuis, *Hope College at 150*, 1:220.
[48] Ibid.
[49] *Anchor*, 13 Apr. 1927; "At the Crossroads: A Campus Map of Hope College in the decade of the 1940s," in *Hope at the Crossroads*, following page xii.
[50] *Milestone* (1942), 40.
[51] Ibid. (1943), 22.

Columbia Hall

lent Zwemer Hall to help house the 252 men in the Army Specialized Training Program (ASTP) after its arrival on campus in October 1943.[52] In addition, the Music Building was sacrificed in order to provide the ASTP with space for administrative offices and an infirmary.[53] After hostilities ended in 1945, the building was converted into a women's dormitory (Columbia Hall) and later, a home for the Knickerbocker fraternity (Columbia Cottage), before it was demolished in 1981 to make room for the Maas Center.[54]

Music may have returned to Columbia Hall after 1945 were it not for the post-secondary enrollment boom that followed the conclusion of World War II. Supported by the GI Bill, millions of young men returning home from the war enrolled in institutions of higher education, and college enrollment numbers across the country skyrocketed. Between 1945 and 1947, student enrollment at Hope increased 400 percent; the student body more than tripled in 1946 alone, growing from 330 to 1207 students.[55] The college, unprepared

[52] Brochure, "We're in the Army Now" (ca. 1943), Wichers presidency—general brochures and pamphlets folder; Nyenhuis, *Hope College at 150*, 1:260.
[53] Myra Berry, "The War Years at Hope," in Nordstrom and Zuidema, *Hope at the Crossroads*, 37; *Milestone* (1944), 19.
[54] Nyenhuis, *Hope College at 150*, 1:413-14.
[55] John Hollenbach, "Coping with the Post War Boom," Nordstrom and Zuidema, *Hope at the Crossroads*, 135.

for the massive influx, scrambled to find space for instruction and for the housing of incoming students.

Retired dean John Hollenbach described the enrollment boom and its impact on the college: "In the half decade following the war, the academic facilities were under great strain. They were reshaped and renovated. They bulged with the growing horde of students. . . . There were no financial resources adequate for new construction."[56] Robert Snow '49 recalled classes being held wherever space could be found, even on campus lawns on warm days.[57] All departments struggled to find time slots and spaces for their courses, but as Hollenbach recalled:

> The Music faculty were the real orphans during the first post-war year (1945-46). . . . music history and theory classes were held in any room of any campus building that was free. There were no private studio-offices. The organ instructor, Mrs. Snow, had the whole Chapel auditorium as her office—or more properly, the Skinner Organ console in the northern corner. Piano students had to find a piano somewhere on campus for practice—in the "Y" rooms, in sorority and fraternity meeting rooms, in the lounges of dormitories.[58]

Other departments at that time also faced similar problems, but the situation for Music was unsustainable.

Space for Music was a problem that could not be fixed, given the physical and financial situation after World War II. President Lubbers and the board of trustees spent a decade trying to solve it on the cheap, until they finally bit the bullet and built Nykerk Hall in the mid-1950s. But in 1946, that solution was still a decade away.

After the turbulence of the war years, it is safe to say that the Music faculty was elated to receive some good news in the summer of 1946. President Lubbers announced that the college had acquired a large house near campus on Ninth Street, the department's new home—Walsh Music Hall.[59] The building provided professors with their own studios, a luxury not yet experienced by Hope's Music faculty.[60] Jantina Holleman's studio included a fireplace, a bay window, and a

[56] Ibid., 154.
[57] Robert Snow, "The Fabulous Forties," *Hope at the Crossroads*, 167.
[58] Hollenbach, "Coping with the Post War Boom," 152.
[59] Ibid.; board minutes, 18 June 1946, 1945-55 folder. As will be evident in what follows, there are contradictory statements about whether the college owned the home or leased it.
[60] Hollenbach, "Coping with the Post War Boom," 152.

Walsh Hall *[handwritten: Saw this in 1955 ... when I visited Hope]*

Bush and Lane grand piano.[61] Walsh Music Hall also supplied practice rooms—helping to augment the classroom space and practice pianos in the basement of Dimnent Chapel and Voorhees Hall—and rooms for student recitals, as well as for classes and visitors.[62]

Walsh Music Hall was not without its tribulations. Constructed in the 1880s by Holland industrialist Heber Walsh, co-owner of the Walsh-DeRoo Milling Company, the building could not be equipped with the technology required to fulfill its new role as Music's home.[63] Hollenbach recalled that the lack of soundproof walls "produced strange medleys" as simultaneous lessons occurred.[64] Connie Klaasen '53 remembered the difficulty of practicing: "I might have been a promising vocalist, but it was so discouraging to practice in Walsh's kitchen where you couldn't tell which voice was yours and which was someone else's in the next room!"[65] Harvey Doorenbos '55 concurred. Responding to plans for Nykerk he stated, "I know how badly it is needed, rather

[61] Aschbrenner interview with Holleman.
[62] *Anchor*, 27 May 1955; *Hope College Catalog* (1947-48), 25; Hollenbach, "Coping with the Post War Boom," 153; Aschbrenner interview with Holleman; Baer and Utting interview with Ritsema.
[63] Nyenhuis, *Hope College at 150*, 1:310.
[64] Hollenbach, "Coping with the Post War Boom," 153.
[65] Connie Klaasen to Cavanaugh, 26 Jan. 1956, correspondence 1954-64 folder, box 1, Cavanaugh Papers.

intimately you might say, having endured, but enjoyed Walsh Music Hall for two years."[66] With several pianos and trilling voices mixing together in imperfect harmony, the strange cacophony that resulted from simultaneous lessons must have been as mesmerizing as it was headache inducing. To add to the noise, various fraternities, including the Cosmopolitans, held their weekly business meetings in Walsh. One *Anchor* article described how "musical strains could he heard issuing forth from Walsh Music Hall," as the Cosmos, alternating from tenor to bass to baritone, practiced for the 1947 All-College Sing.[67] It was also suggested that, given the pressure on campus housing, two male music majors be allowed to live in Walsh Hall.[68]

Walsh Music Hall's structural problems became increasingly ominous. In a 2002 interview, Jantina Holleman recalled a chandelier in Robert Cavanaugh's studio that sank progressively closer and closer to the floor as the ceiling began to sag.[69] Duane Booi, a 1949 graduate and an original member of Holleman's Madrigal Singers, remembers placing bets on when Walsh would collapse from the weight of the practice pianos on both floors.[70]

At the same time, other Music facilities on campus were experiencing stress. In January 1947, President Lubbers sent a letter to First Reformed Church in Holland, then a few blocks west of campus, requesting that the church's organ be made available to college students in need of a practice organ.

> Hope College is having difficulty in providing opportunity for pipe organ students to practice since the chapel organ is occupied all day in the giving of organ lessons. We have two practice organs on the campus, which are in use from 8:20 in the morning until 10:00 in the evening.... We would like to rent the organ for five days a week, Monday-Friday, for eight hours a day.... This favor would be very much appreciated and would be a real help in a very difficult situation.[71]

---

[66] Ibid., Harvey Doorenbos to Cavanaugh, 21 Feb. 1956. See also Larry Siedentop's complaints, *Anchor*, 27 May 1955.
[67] *Anchor*, 27 Mar. 1947.
[68] Music faculty minutes, 31 May 1951. It remains unclear whether this ever happened.
[69] Aschbrenner interview with Holleman.
[70] Duane and P. J. Booi to Marc Baer, 14 July 2018.
[71] Irwin J. Lubbers to Members of the Consistory of First Reformed Church, 28 Jan. 1947, Esther Snow personal file.

Such an arrangement was approved, and the college paid one dollar an hour in addition to ten dollars a week for janitorial services.[72] Elton Bruins '50 remembers having to schedule his practice time at one of the pianos in Walsh, a far cry from earlier days when Ethel Leestma would practice on Dimnent's Skinner Organ for hours, undisturbed.[73] Holleman recalled how the inadequate facilities often forced the Music faculty to get creative:

> We taught in the basement of the chapel, that very first room down the staircase, and there was a closet there and one shelf of that closet had phonograph records, of course 78s. One shelf, that's all I had, and just kind of a catch-as-catch-can cheap record player. How do you teach music history that way . . . you improvise.[74]

Her consternation may be imagined by peeking into the closet on the east side of room 12 in the basement of Dimnent.

Just one year after moving into Walsh Hall, Music had outgrown the facility. Attempting to find a solution, the board of trustees suggested in November 1947 that Van Vleck Hall be "converted into a place to house the rapidly expanding music department."[75] For reasons which remain unclear, this plan was never enacted. The following month, Lubbers was instead instructed to "proceed with negotiations for trading off the Walsh House to Mr. Charles Vander Ven in exchange for his home at 307 College Avenue after obtaining expert appraisals of both parties."[76] No further mention of this is recorded in the board minutes, suggesting the notion came to be seen as disadvantageous for the college. Finally, in 1951, the board proposed the construction of a fine arts building.[77] The timing reflected pressure on the department because of continued post-World War II growth: between 1940 and 1950, the number of Music faculty had doubled, and the number of students taking music courses had tripled.[78]

Hope, in the early 1950s, however, was struggling financially. The Executive Committee minutes from April 12, 1951, report a deficit surpassing $33,000. At the same time, the college's leadership chose to provide financial support for a year to a music faculty member whose

---

[72] Lubbers memorandum, 1947, Esther Snow personal file.
[73] Baer and Utting, interview with Bruins.
[74] Aschbrenner interview with Holleman.
[75] *Anchor*, 13 Nov. 1947.
[76] EC minutes (11 Dec. 1947), 128, board minutes 1945-55 folder, box 3, BOT Papers.
[77] Ibid. (14 June 1951), 261.
[78] *Hope College Bulletin* 88, no. 2 (May 1950), 4.

contract was not being renewed.[79] Planning for a fine arts building amid financial struggles caused by a downturn in enrollment seemed unreasonable—a luxury even—to many. Yet, its proposal at this time spoke precisely to the dire need of Music for not only more but also better space.

The department is homeless

If the need for improved physical resources for Music was dire already in 1951, then by the summer of 1954, a new plan for the department was crucial. The previous fall, it was announced that the college had sold Walsh Music Hall to a local bank and use of the building would conclude after the 1953-54 academic year. Dean Hollenbach expressed his concern for the amount of space needed to house the ever-growing department: "There are six members of the music staff. Besides regular instruction, there are 125 private lessons each week. There should be at least five private studios and ten rooms for practice by the students."[80] In that context, Music's resources were nowhere near what Hollenbach recommended.

To address the problem, in October 1953, the Executive Committee of the board of trustees sought to purchase a property on West Twelfth Street owned by the Duffy family for use as the president's home and convert the current president's home into what would be called the College Music Center.[81] Less than two months later, however, the board authorized the president to "secure preliminary plans for the music wing of the proposed fine arts building," thereby dropping the concept of a dedicated music building and returning to the earlier idea of a fine arts building. The board agreed to "proceed with the building of this wing to house the music department when we must vacate the Walsh Building."[82] In February 1954, Lubbers presented his concept for the music wing of the proposed fine arts building to the board.[83] One month later saw another reversal: the board's building committee decided to pursue preliminary drawings and specifications for a building earmarked for the Music Department.[84]

After years of frustrated hopes, this time a plan would be implemented. It is important to recognize the significance of this

[79] EC minutes (12 Apr. 1951), 168, board minutes 1945-55 folder.
[80] Minutes (16 Oct. 1953), 291, board minutes 1945-55 folder.
[81] Ibid.
[82] EC minutes (18 Dec. 1953), 199, board minutes 1945-55 folder.
[83] Ibid. (5 Feb. 1954), 202.
[84] Building Committee minutes, 30 Mar. 1954, board minutes 1945-55 folder.

juncture. After nearly a century of making music at Hope College, in the early 1950s, the administration recognized not only Music as having the same internal authority as other departments but also the importance of the department in terms of student interest in music courses and faculty opportunities; this led to a commitment to create what amounted to a building devoted to making music.

The *Anchor* first mentioned the future building in spring 1954, stating that preliminary drawings called for a "long, one-story, modernistic building" located in the southwest corner of the athletic field, where the Bultman Center stands today. The main part of the building would "consist of classrooms and studios on the western end and a band room on the eastern end, separated by a small loggia."[85] In July 1954, the board's building committee unanimously recommended that construction on the music building begin as rapidly as funds became available, "because the department of music has no present physical facilities for its activities and because the department of music is an essential part of our curriculum."[86]

To buy the college more time, it appears an agreement was worked out after the July board meeting to keep Music in Walsh Hall for one more academic year. In the Hope College 1954-55 schedule of classes, piano and voice lessons are listed in Walsh Hall, along with a few faculty offices, including that of department head Robert Cavanaugh.[87] It was a temporary solution to a problem that had been festering for years.

As the months passed, the sense of urgency for construction of the music building intensified, as did the need for funds. Approximate building costs initially stood at $170,000, but to expedite the process, the building committee proposed that when $100,000 was in hand, construction should begin.[88] Dean Hollenbach, in his annual report to the board in 1955, admitted, "The music facilities are in the most desperate immediate need (instructionally) of improvement."[89] Yet, Hollenbach simultaneously argued that a new library and gymnasium were of more pressing concern, breaking from his previous championing of Music. When groundbreaking for the Hall of Music finally began on November 23, 1955, a large percentage of the necessary funds

---

[85] *Anchor*, 23 Apr. 1954.
[86] Minutes (11 June 1954), 300, board minutes 1945-55 folder.
[87] Schedule of classes, first semester, 1954-55, Hope College Student Guide, scrapbook, Adelbert Farnsworth Papers, H04-1546.
[88] Minutes, secretary's resource material, 3 June 1955, board minutes 1945-55 folder, box 3, BOT Papers.
[89] Ibid., "Annual Report Dean of the College."

116 MAKING MUSIC

remained to be collected.[90] A brochure published in early 1956 perfectly summarizes Music's need for a new building, as well as the financial obstacles, which were proving difficult to surmount.

> The department is homeless... Walsh Hall, the former Walter [sic] Walsh home on Ninth Street which the estate graciously made available to the college as a music headquarters for a nominal fee, was razed earlier this year to make way for the expansion of Holland's business district. Inadequate as these headquarters were, they did provide at least skeleton facilities for music instruction, rehearsal, and classroom study. Now these are gone. The staff of seven instructors, the band, the orchestra, the choirs and choruses, the hundreds of students, all carry on their work and study when and where they can—if they can. The seminary, despite the distractions it is inviting, has provided classrooms for a minimum music department schedule. But this is strictly an emergency measure that cannot endure. In this critical situation, the college must proceed with construction of the new Music Hall. Against a total building cost of $222,822, the college has received $128,000.[91]

To help raise funds, both the department and the college got creative. In December 1955, President Lubbers called upon his fellow trustees to help fund the music building. Just as he had done with the faculty, Lubbers encouraged all those interested to undertake a personal campaign to raise $500. In addition, the Music faculty had approved a plan initially proposed by Morrette Rider to allow students to sell candy to raise money for the new building.[92] Between candy sales and board members' efforts, the campaign succeeded in funding the new music building.

Home at last, 1956-2015

In September 1956, the Hall of Music opened. At that time in the college's history, half of the student body was either enrolled in a music course, participating in an ensemble, or taking private lessons.[93]

---

[90] Ibid., President Lubbers, 23 Dec. 1955.
[91] *The New Hope College Music Hall* (ca. 1956), facilities—Music Hall, 1956 folder, box 4, MD Papers.
[92] Music faculty minutes, 3 Feb. 1956, box 1, MD Papers.
[93] *Anchor*, 3 Oct. 1958.

Nykerk Hall of Music

A brochure for the new building spoke to the triumph of its opening. "Here, at last, will be the teaching facilities and learning opportunities that our departmental staff and our music students have been denied for so long."[94] On a personal note, Robert Ritsema, a student at the time, spoke for fellow students: "We thought it was incredible, because we had been scattered all over."[95] The first public performance in the new building was held on January 10, 1957; Neil Petty, a vocal student, gave his senior recital, which included a Lieder (a group of German songs), as well as historic English and modern American tunes. Almost all faculty recitals were thereafter held in the music building rather than in Dimnent Chapel.[96]

In December 1962, the Executive Committee of the board approved a motion to name the music building after professor John Nykerk.[97] As far back as 1958, Lubbers had asked the department for their support to name the auditorium after Curtis Snow, the other

---

[94] *The New Hope College Music Hall.*
[95] Baer and Utting interview with Ritsema.
[96] *Anchor*, 18 Dec. 1956; minutes, music faculty meeting, 29 Oct. 1956, box 1, MD Papers; events—recitals (faculty) folder, box 2, MD Papers.
[97] EC minutes, 14 Dec. 1962, board minutes 1959-62 folder.

major figure in Music's early history; in April 1963, this was made official.[98]

Nykerk Hall of Music was not, however, the final answer to Music's space problems. History, which of course never repeats itself, certainly seemed to, for within a few years, there were signs Nykerk Hall was short of space for Music's needs. In 1962 an organ practice room was carved out in the basement of Graves, while in 1963 the department discussed the necessity of a better piano and extra stage space in Winants Auditorium.[99]

A year later, the department began earnest discussion about the possibility of an addition to Nykerk Hall. At a special meeting of department members in fall 1964, the following possibilities for expansion were mentioned: "use of the basement (now used by the maintenance staff), expansion of the east (classroom) wing, expansion of the south (auditorium wing)."[100] The following fall, plans for a significant addition to Nykerk were solidified. These included eliminating the south entrance, and in that space creating an organ practice room; repurposing a maintenance room as a classroom; adding to the music library; and reconfiguring the departmental office.[101]

When the addition was dedicated in October 1970, Nykerk Hall had more than doubled in size.[102] In a letter from Music's chair to the department's alumni, Robert Ritsema stated that, finally, in his opinion, their "crucial and considerable" physical needs had been met: there were eight new teaching studios, eight new practice rooms, conversion of offices into still more performance spaces, adequate room to store instruments, a music library, an electronic music room, a listening room, a staff lounge, and a two-hundred-seat recital hall.[103] Even though the dedication of the Wynand Wichers addition was said to have marked the first time the department was entirely under one roof, Music continued to occupy rooms in Graves Hall and a house on East Tenth Street known as the Music Annex.[104]

[98] *Anchor*, 12 Apr. 1963; minutes, music faculty meeting, 6 Nov. 1958, and 25 Mar. 1963, minutes 1963-67 folder, box 1, MD Papers.
[99] Elton Bruins, *A Step Forward for Hope College: The Building of Graves Hall and Winants Auditorium* (Holland: Hope College, 2009), 9; minutes, music faculty meeting, 18 Sept. 1963, minutes 1963-67 folder, box 1, MD Papers.
[100] Minutes, music faculty meeting, 16 Nov. 1964.
[101] Ibid., 8 and 25 Sept. 1967.
[102] Cavanaugh, Music Department Report for the Year 1968-69, minutes 1967-69 folder.
[103] Robert Ritsema to Fellow Music Alumni, 22 Feb. 1971, Ritsema Papers.
[104] *Anchor*, 19 Oct. 1970, 20 Oct. 1978; *Hope College Catalog* (1970-71), 245.

For the next thirty years, Nykerk Hall faithfully served music students and faculty, as well as the college.[105] As Robert Ritsema recalled, the building provided great practice and listening rooms, and Wichers Auditorium, while "not very beautiful" was regularly filled for faculty recitals. The only space still missing was a large performance hall. In 1994 a draft of the college's facilities master plan stated: "The Music Department does not have satisfactory space for musical performances. Neither the Chapel nor the Knickerbocker theatre are satisfactory, though the department continues, *faute de mieux*, to use the Chapel."[106] Joan Conway, professor of piano from 1969 to 2001, attested that the facilities in Nykerk left much to be desired in terms of rehearsal and performance space.[107] Initially, it was this desire for a large performance hall, rather than the sense that Nykerk at age thirty-eight was too old or no longer worked for the department, that drove Music to begin imagining something more.

In the spring of 1995, Music proposed a set of recommendations for the future improvement of its facilities, a task deemed essential for the continued flourishing of the department. Such improvements would be expensive, and so, in 1999, a new space for organ instruction was added to the north corner of Nykerk Hall.[108] It included a teaching studio, two practice rooms, office space, and a two-thousand-pipe organ.[109] Huw Lewis, organ professor and mastermind of the project, praised the organ's potential as both a teaching and recruiting tool, while also admitting that he hoped it would "one day sit in a new music building."[110] Later that year, in a meeting with a select group of faculty, staff, and community members, a master plan for the physical development of the campus was discussed. Possible ideas included either relocating the Fried International Center and the Delta Phi Cottage and using that area as a connection to the music building or moving the Keppel House and replacing it with a music recital hall.[111] Neither proposal was to be implemented.

---

[105] Jane Klaasen Westerbeke '59, recalled her Sorosis sorority performing *Snow White* on the stage of Snow Auditorium in Nykerk Hall: Westerbeke email to Marc Baer, 29 Aug. 2018, Making Music folder.

[106] Draft of the facilities master plan, prepared by John H. Jacobson, 23 June 1994 (rev. 9/29/94), 7, facilities-recommendations, 1995 folder, box 4, MD Papers.

[107] Baer and Utting interviews with Ritsema and Conway.

[108] Music Department Facilities Recommendations Prepared by Huw R. Lewis, 19 Apr. 1995, facilities- recommendations, 1995 folder; *Anchor*, 30 Aug. 2000.

[109] *Grand Rapids Press*, 18 July 1999; *Anchor*, 30 Aug. 2000.

[110] *Grand Rapids Press*, 14 June 2000.

[111] Minutes, music faculty meeting, 7 Oct. 1999, minutes 1999-2004 folder, box 1, MD Papers.

Jack Miller Center (*courtesy Hope College*)

Every building has a lifespan, and in the minds—and ears—of its occupants, it seemed that Nykerk was nearing its end.[112] Perhaps inspired by the spirit of the dawning of a new millennium, the college's leadership came to the conclusion:

> The Nykerk Hall of Music falls below the College's recent standards of construction. The problem of the Music Department is a major one, because any solution that is satisfactory to the department will come at very high cost. . . . But the Department recognizes that its facilities can be significantly improved: indeed, it feels that they must be improved in order for it to maintain its standing.[113]

Over a decade of planning and fundraising would follow. The fruit of that effort was finally realized in 2015 with the opening of the Jack H. Miller Center for Musical Arts, located on Columbia Avenue between Ninth and Tenth Streets. It is a space that serves Music, as well as the college and community, a space that provides all the facilities necessary to nurture student passion, and a space that has already

---

[112] Baer and Utting interviews with Ritsema and Conway.
[113] Draft of the facilities master plan.

become a *place* for so many individuals—students, faculty, staff, and community members. In the lobby are three bas-reliefs, formerly outside the Twelfth Street entrance to the now-demolished Nykerk Hall, representing the purposes of Music at Hope—teaching, performance, and church music—serving as a testament to the department's past, present, and future.

Music's movement, from Graves to Van Raalte, from Carnegie and Voorhees to Dimnent and Columbia, from Walsh to Nykerk to the Miller Center, is in many ways a window into the physical history of the college.[114] The years following World War II saw growing pains that paralleled flourishing, true of both Hope and its Music Department. The building of Nykerk Hall accomplished spatially what the recognition of Music as a normal department did institutionally, both a result of the professionalization of the faculty (see ch. 2). As a department without a stable home for nearly ninety years of its history, Music at the college had to define what it meant to Hope's students, not by where it was, but by what it did—by the value it brought to campus and community.

---

[114] Many of the spaces Music once occupied either no longer exist, including Carnegie Gymnasium, Columbia Cottage, Walsh Hall, Van Raalte Hall, the Music Annex, and Nykerk Hall, or have been repurposed, such as Graves Hall and Voorhees Dormitory.

122 MAKING MUSIC

CHAPTER 5

The Year in Music

> Nothing less than true, impassioned melody is worthy of
> expressing the affections which we feel for mother Hope.
> *Anchor*, 1888

> School of Music Gives Recital: Audience Listens.
> *Holland City News*, 1917

> Although we do not play a flute or violin,
> does it not make us finer to follow through
> the movements of a great symphony?
> *Anchor*, 1933

The 1888 Hope College graduation was a multiday celebration of student achievement, and without music, such a festivity would have been incomplete. The alumni exercises featured a male quartet—including John Nykerk (then a Hope College student)—singing *In Absence*; followed by a duet performing *Barcarolle*; a soloist, soprano Mrs. G. J. Diekema, singing *Come unto Me*; and the quartet closing the evening with, *Bill of Fare* and *Good Night*. The alumni gathering was followed two days later by the college graduation at Third Reformed Church. Once again, music was woven into the event. There was an overture, *March*; followed by cornet and bass solos, the latter by music instructor G. C. Shepard; and then *Polish National* (which may have been *God Save Poland*), and finally, the graduates sang their class song:

> Now, classmates, raise a rousing song,
> With voices full and clear and strong,
> The song of jubilee!
> Oh, Mother Hope, to thee we sing,
> And thus a grateful tribute bring.
> With happy hearts so free
> Let all our gay and laughing throng
> Sound words of gladness rolled along
> On rich, melodious strains:
> The years of preparation end,
> To other tasks we now can bend,
> For higher work remains.
> For many a day with dripping oars
> We've watched, while moving near the shores;
> Those who the high seas sought;
> But soon we'll likewise spread our sails.
> And swiftly seek through all the gales,
> The sea of deeper thought.

The *Anchor* observed: "The music at the Commencement exercises was excellent and has been much remarked about."[1]

Imagine yourself a senior at Hope College in 1888, or 1941, or 2015. As part of an audience—a partaker and at times a creator of music—what is the rhythm of your year? As the months go by between early fall and graduation, what have you heard, and what significance have you attached to such joyful noise?

A year in music is defined by several forces: the faculty in place with their interests and energies; trends in popular culture, such as ukuleles in the 1920s, or in high musical culture, for example, atonality; the invention or disappearance of college events like Vespers or the All-College Sing; historical context, such as world wars; and, of course, the composition and sensibilities of the student body. Beyond these

---

[1] *Anchor*, June 1888; *Holland City News*, 30 June 1888.

forces, for students, faculty and staff, and the community, there was a well-defined, yet never static, rhythm to the year in music. This chapter addresses the audience perspective, serving as a complement to the student experience.

True impassioned melody, 1866-1941

The fall semester began with an event ushering in a new academic year, initially called the Opening Exercise and subsequently the Convocation. In September 1899, seventy-nine college students and the same number of Hope preparatory school students gathered in Winants Chapel. By tradition, the event began with *Come Thou Almighty King* and closed with the doxology. Convocation moved to Carnegie Hall following the building's opening in 1906. In 1927 two hymns were sung, and between them, voice teacher Beulah Dunwoody sang, *Lead Kindly, Light*, and in 1940 special music was provided by new vocal professor Robert Cavanaugh and new piano professor James Mearns.[2]

Chapel began with the new year: at eight o'clock every weekday morning, music greeted Hope faculty and students, and for the first century of the college's existence, attendance was expected. At chapel everyone present was simultaneously a performer and an audience member. In the early years, a student chorister led singing, while another student played the organ. By the early twentieth century, professors had assumed these roles. After becoming a faculty member, John Nykerk led singing and played the piano in chapel, what one student called "the service of Song," although on some occasions, students took his place.[3]

When Curtis Snow joined the Hope faculty in 1929 as the college organist, the worship service had moved to the newly opened Dimnent Chapel, with its magnificent organ. Snow added organ preludes to chapel services, his own as well as those of students.[4] In the same year he arrived, Snow organized and directed a new ensemble, the sixty-member Chapel Choir. Although the music played on the organ and sung by the choir and audience in chapel was sacred, the Chapel Choir's

---

[2] Hope faculty minutes, 20 Sept. 1899, and 17 Sept. 1927, faculty minutes, 1898-1904 and 1926-28 folders, box 1; *Anchor*, 2 Oct. 1918, and 18 Sept. 1940.

[3] Diary entry, 27 Sept. 1927, HC diary 1927, box 1, Schuppert Papers; James Malcom interview with Gerrit John Van Zoeren, 1976, box 1, Gerrit Van Zoeren Papers; Aschbrenner interview with Neckers; see also Folkert, "Some Recollections About the Hope College Preparatory School."

[4] Diary entries, 3-5, 7, 10, 13-14, 17, 20 Feb. and 4 Nov. 1930; 19 Feb. 1931, HC diaries 1929-34, box 1, Schuppert Papers; *Hope College Bulletin* (Feb. 1931), 63, and (Feb. 1932), 15.

126   MAKING MUSIC

annual end-of-year concert mixed sacred music with classical. In 1931, for example, concert songs included *Praise Ye the Name of the Lord* and *Now is the Month of Maying*.[5] Professor Kenneth Osborne, who succeeded Snow after his death, taught choir members to direct, so that student conductors at chapel services and spring recitals experienced creating music as well as performing.[6]

The first Homecoming was fall 1925, bringing together students, faculty, alumni, and Holland residents for a parade, which included the Hope band wearing orange and blue uniforms.[7] The 1931 Homecoming had a separate music committee made up of student Zella Skillern '32; professor Deckard Ritter, the band director; and Eugene Heeter, who led Holland's American Legion Band.[8] Hope's band preceded the floats in the Friday night parade.

> When the band began to play, the ambling students departed from their role of sedate marchers and became a swirling mass of exuberant collegiates, timing their intricate oscillations to the cadence of the music, providing a novel spectacle to the onlookers that lined the streets, waiting for the appearance of the beautiful floats that followed.

Following the parade, the students and others moved to Carnegie Gymnasium, where cheers "dovetailed with several selections by the band to work up an hilarious spirit."[9] In 1940 a Saturday evening alumni banquet followed the football game, which included chamber music by a student group and songs by a female trio, graduates of the Class of 1939.[10]

A new competition, distinctly for women, originated in the 1930s—the Nykerk Cup Competition. Shortly before he passed away, John Nykerk created what would soon become an enduring tradition—a competition between freshmen and sophomore women, in which, along with teams of actors and an orator from each class, there was a musical number. Nykerk had persuaded several young women attempting to launch a female version of the Pull that such an event would be "too great a strain for the girls," and they should instead compete in oratory,

---

[5]   Program, Chapel Choir folder, box 2, MD Papers; *Anchor*, 27 May 1931.
[6]   Cf. *Milestone* (1938), 86.
[7]   *Anchor*, 18 Nov. 1925.
[8]   1931 Homecoming program, memory book, 1927-31, Marion De Kuiper Papers; see also *Milestone* (1929), 73.
[9]   *Anchor*, 4 Nov. 1931.
[10] Ibid., 16 Oct. 1940.

vocal music, and drama.[11] The first competition was held in Carnegie Gymnasium in March 1936 and won by the freshmen; their trio sang *Giannina Mia*, which triumphed over a piano solo by sophomore Barbara Lampen. Nykerk himself, for his first and last time, awarded the silver cup.[12]

In addition to daily chapel and other recurring musical opportunities, such as Homecoming and the Nykerk Cup, Hope audiences heard music performed by various ensembles. These included glee clubs, orchestra, and band.

The most deeply rooted musical groups in Hope's history are the vocal ensembles: at first, *the* Hope College Glee Club, then subsequently, a Women's (for years Ladies' or Girls') Glee Club and a Men's (sometimes referred to as the Boys') Glee Club. Their performances began in the late fall and continued, both on and off campus—sometimes far removed from Holland—right to the end of the school year.[13] Depending on the venue, the clubs performed both sacred and secular music, which might be understood as the Hope musical paradigm—performing at the highest level no matter the music, or more simply, the best for the best.[14] An early example came in 1896, when the Glee Club gave a concert "in which they rendered the first chorus of *Oedipus Tyrannus*, entirely in the Greek language."[15] To expand the capabilities of vocal music in Holland, after the turn of the twentieth century, Nykerk merged the club with community members into the Choral Union, which he directed.[16] During the decade that followed, Hope students lobbied for a return of the Glee Clubs until, beginning in the 1910s, at least two and sometimes three such ensembles existed at the college.[17]

The Men's Glee Club averaged several dozen members, ranging in size between half that number and fifty.[18] Its revival may have developed out of fraternity singing groups, for example, a Knickerbocker quartet,

---

[11] Ibid., 12 Jan. and 23 Feb. 1938; Mary Good Heuvelhorst, "The Nykerk Cup: How it Began," history folder, Nykerk Cup Competition Papers, H97-1288.
[12] *Anchor*, 18 Mar. 1936; *Milestone* (1936), 85.
[13] Vocal ensembles—glee clubs folder.
[14] Cf. Morrette Rider, "The Challenge of a Good Concert Program," *School Musician* 33 (Oct. 1961): 50-51.
[15] Minutes of the collegiate faculty, 21 Apr. 1896. For the sacred/secular mix in the 1930s Girls' Glee Club concerts, see programs 1928-32, and 1935-37 scrapbooks, boxes 4 and 5, Hinkamp Papers.
[16] Program, Second Annual Hope College Choral Union Concert (1902), vocal ensembles—College Chorus folder, box 2, MD Papers.
[17] *Anchor*, 13 Oct. 1915.
[18] *Hope College Catalog* (1927-28), 22.

which in 1916 shared membership with the Men's Glee Club.[19] For both men and women, there was the issue common to all collegiate student groups—viability over time. Hence the *Anchor*, reporting on a 1916 Men's Glee Club concert, opined that "At the recital, the Men's Glee Club made its real debut into the musical world. Up to this time, there was a question in the minds of many as to the stability of the organization."[20]

Typically, every May, both the Men's and Women's Glee Clubs staged concerts. The Men's Glee Club in 1925 had an international flavor, combining gospel music (*Swing Low, Sweet Chariot*), a Mexican love song (*Marchéta*), the *Volga Boatman's Song*, and a contemporary Australian tune, *God Touched the Rose*.[21] In a 1928 concert, the program was divided into a secular section (e.g., *Croon, Croon Underneath de Moon*, a contemporary southern song) and a sacred section (e.g., *Jerusalem*).[22] During 1938-39, the Men's Glee Club sang in chapel, performed sacred and secular numbers for a Holland Alumni Association Banquet, and sang in Holland-area churches. Every spring, they staged a joint choral concert with the Women's Glee Club and Chapel Choir.[23]

Beginning in 1920, the Women's Glee Club usually comprised about thirty members, although in some years, it was much larger, performing both on and off campus; during a 1925 East coast tour, they met President Calvin Coolidge. That same year saw the formation of a Junior Glee Club, both ensembles' performances mixing classical, sacred, and contemporary music.[24] In late fall 1934, the female ensemble joined the orchestra and the Men's Glee Club to stage a two-act operetta, *Don Alonso's Treasure*, in Carnegie Gymnasium.[25]

Like the Glee Clubs, and reflecting college campuses nationally, other ensembles began to appear, and although some grew, others dissolved. These included a jazz band, a fifteen-member Ladies' Ukulele Orchestra, the Hope Trumpeteers, and the B Natural chorus; the last named was said to "delight the studentry and the churches with their

---

[19] Compare pictures of the two groups in *Milestone* (1916), 86, 88; see also *Anchor*, 26 Jan. 1916.
[20] *Anchor*, 22 Dec. 1916.
[21] Concert program, 20 May 1925, vocal ensembles—glee clubs folder.
[22] Ibid., 1928; for the same division see also Girl's Glee Club program brochure (ca. 1937).
[23] *Milestone* (1939), 106-7; programs, box 2, Curtis Snow Papers, and scrapbook 1935-37, Hinkamp Papers.
[24] *Milestone* (1920), 50; *Anchor*, 3 and 19 Dec. 1924, 9 Feb. 1925, 29 Jan. and 23 Mar. 1927, and 30 May 1928.
[25] *Milestone* (1935), 78.

Women's Glee Club

talent on many occasions."[26] Meantime, although less ephemeral, the band and orchestra reorganized on a regular basis.

From 1915 to 1920, a circa twenty-piece band performed at Hope basketball games and other college events,[27] and when football was allowed by the college authorities, the band played at these games as well—when they could get themselves organized.[28] "During the past season, there was practically no support for this organization," said the 1930 *Milestone*, faulting the absence of financial assistance from the college. "Yet the band carried on, with nothing to motivate the members, except the Hope Spirit and the steadfastness of Edwin Tellman, President of the band."[29] In October 1934, the band was reestablished once again by Curtis Snow, whose goal was to transform it into a symphonic band.[30] Following Snow's death, in 1936 Eugene Heeter assumed leadership of the band. Heeter was director of instrumental music in Holland Public Schools and conducted the Holland Symphony Orchestra and the Holland American Legion band.[31] That he led well was evident when in 1937-38 the band was termed by a Michigan newspaper as "one of the outstanding college musical organizations in this part of the state."

[26] Ibid. (1917), 89, and (1918), 70; *Anchor*, 5 Dec. 1923, 15 Feb. 1928, 18 Sept. 1940; cf. Howe, *Women Music Educators*, 150-51.
[27] *Milestone* (1916), 87; *Anchor*, 11 Oct. 1916; *Holland City News*, 16 Dec. 1920.
[28] *Anchor*, 16 Oct. 1925, 13 Oct. 1932, 5 Oct. 1938.
[29] *Milestone* (1930), 143.
[30] *Anchor*, 10 Oct. 1934; see also Snow, *Musikalisch Frau Schnee*, and *Hope College Bulletin* (Feb. 1935), 18.
[31] *Anchor*, 14 Oct. 1936.

Hope College Trumpeteers (Milestone, *1929*)

Perhaps their new uniforms—funded by Holland merchants—had helped.[32] By 1939 the band numbered over fifty students, performing as a marching band and a symphonic band, playing works such as Schubert's *Ave Maria* at concerts.[33]

Like the band, in the early twentieth century, the orchestra had an intermittent existence. In 1908 the "newly organized Hope College Orchestra" played several times at a fundraiser for the *Anchor*.[34] In the two decades that followed, the orchestra performed for the Ulfilas Club, a Dutch-oriented college organization; at the annual May concert; and at graduation.[35] The 1920 concert featured selections from operas, classical works, lighter pieces, and violin solos and duets.[36] The 1928 concert began with the Grand March from *Aida*, termed "a thrillingly impressive introduction," and concluded with "the rollicking 'Ballet,'" from *Les Millions d'Arlequin*, by Riccardo Drigo.[37]

[32] *Milestone* (1938), 87; *Anchor*, 11 Dec. 1947.
[33] *Milestone* (1939), 105; program, scrapbook 1941-43, box 6, Hinkamp Papers.
[34] *Anchor*, Dec. 1908.
[35] *Holland City News*, 17 June 1915; program for 21 May 1932, scrapbook, Alice Hoffs Papers.
[36] *Anchor*, 12 May 1920.
[37] Ibid., 3 May 1928.

Marching band (Milestone, *1940*)

In addition to performances by student groups, there were throughout the year entertainments provided by either the department or the college. They were staged in Hope's first chapel, opened in 1862, and subsequently in Winants, Carnegie, and Dimnent Chapel.

Early on, the entertainments were systematized by John Nykerk, taking form in what he called the Lyceum Course. Concerts included cantatas, such as William Bradbury's *Esther, the Beautiful Queen* in 1909 and Max Bruch's *Fair Ellen* in 1910.[38] There were longer oratorios as well, such as Handel's *Messiah* and Mendelssohn's *Elijah*, and also lesser-remembered ones, such as Alfred Gaul's *Holy City* and John Stainer's *Crucifixion*.[39]

In the fall of 1927, freshman Mildred Schuppert attended a Lyceum event with three friends, noting in her diary that it was "very, very classical, most reserved," mentioning pieces by Brahms and Dvořák among others.[40] But the music audiences heard over the decades was quite varied. In the years just before World War II, there were performances by the Michigan Symphony Orchestra, the Von

[38] *Holland City News*, 25 Mar. 1909, and 3 Feb. 1910.
[39] *Anchor*, 5 Dec. 1923.
[40] Diary entry, 21 Sept. 1927, HC diary 1927-, box 1, Schuppert Papers.

Hope College Lecture Course

Coleridge-Taylor's "Hiawatha"

By

The CHORAL UNION

Under the Directorship of
Mr. Francis J. Campbell, of the College School of Music

Assisted by the following Chicago Talent:

Madame Ida Burnap Hinshaw, Soprano
Mr. Francis Hughes, Tenor
Mr. Charles La Berge, Baritone

Mrs. E. D. Kremers, Solo Accompanist
Mr. Arthur Heusinkveld, Chorus Accompanist

Carnegie Hall - April 21, 1911
8:15 p. m.

Hiawatha program, 1911

Trapp Family Singers, and the African American tenor Pruth McFarlin (1908-71).[41]

Hope ensembles also performed in musical events. For example, in 1911 the Choral Union staged the cantata *Hiawatha*.[42] Following the path blazed by Nykerk in the 1930s, Curtis Snow combined the Chapel Choir and the Civic Chorus into a new Choral Union, "for the purpose of presenting several musical programs each year at the college," with planning carried out by a Hope faculty committee.[43] Following the deaths of Snow and Nykerk, the Lyceum Series was rebranded as the Choral Union Concert Series when a musical program was offered; see the second segment of this chapter for a sequel.

Beginning in the 1920s, the most significant musical event of the year was the December staging of Handel's *Messiah*. By the 1930s, the performance was as much a midwinter tradition as Christmas Vespers was to become by the late 1970s. In 1932 Curtis Snow directed the University of Michigan Orchestra and the Holland Civic Chorus in a packed Dimnent Chapel performance.[44] Although the musicians varied from year to year, the 1941 *Messiah* was a far larger production than the first Christmas Vespers performed a few days earlier. In front-page coverage, the *Anchor* enumerated a choir of three hundred voices, including the Holland High School a cappella choir and townspeople who had joined the Chapel Choir in the performance. The audience also heard soloists, including a soprano from Detroit, a contralto and a tenor from Chicago, and a bass from Ann Arbor.[45]

Prior to the 1970s, when Christmas Vespers became the mainstay of the year in music, there was an older Vespers, one not anchored in December. Vespers in this earlier era was begun by Curtis Snow as twice-monthly organ recitals, mixing secular and sacred numbers.[46] Snow's first recital, in early September 1929, included works by Beethoven, Saint-Saëns, Bonnet, Schumann, and Bennet.[47] That academic year, Vespers events also took place in late September, October, November, January, March, and April, often including organ recitals in Dimnent

---

[41] Programs, scrapbooks 1938-41 and 1941-43, boxes 5 and 6, Hinkamp Papers; *Anchor*, 2 Oct. 1940.
[42] *Anchor*, 21 Apr. 1911; see also: Apr. 1912, Oct. 1915, 26 Oct. 1916, 26 Feb. 1918, 24 Oct. 1923.
[43] Faculty minutes, 7 and 15 June, 1 Nov. 1935.
[44] *Anchor*, 21 Dec. 1932.
[45] Ibid., 10 Dec. 1941.
[46] Program, events—Vespers (general) 1929-77 folder, box 4, MD Papers; programs, scrapbook 1928-32, box 4, Hinkamp Papers.
[47] Newspaper clipping (1929), scrapbook 1936 folder, box 1, Curtis Snow Papers.

Vesper Recital

Hope Memorial Chapel

April 26, 1931

MISS ETHEL LEESTMA, Organist
Class of 1933

Hymn 1—"Come thou almighty King" —*Giardini*
Scripture
Prayer

"Toccata and Fugue in D Minor" —*Bach*

"Pastorale" —*Franck*

"Fourth Symphony" *Widor*
   Scherzo
   Finale

"Harmonies du Soir" —*Karg-Elert*
"Roulade" —*Bingham*
"O'er Flowery Meads" —*Dunn*

Offertory

"Toccata"—(Suite Gothique) —*Boellman*

Vespers recital program, 1931

Chapel featuring musicians from the University of Michigan School of Music, the Netherlands, France, Austria, and Britain. Hope College was represented as well: Easter Vespers 1933 included Curtis and Esther Snow, senior organ student Ethel Leestma, the Chapel Choir, the Clarion Quartet, and violin soloists.⁴⁸ Having succeeded Snow as college organist and choir director in the fall of 1936, professor Kenneth Osborne announced there would be monthly organ recitals on Sundays. During 1937-38, Osborne himself performed at four of these.

Snow and Osborne were not the only faculty who offered recitals as part of the year in music. Fall faculty recitals in 1922 took place in Winants Chapel, featuring piano, violin, organ, and vocal music.⁴⁹ In 1923 an *Anchor* headline read, "School of Music Delights Public." At the performance the new voice teacher, Anna Michaelson, sang a variety of songs, with violin and piano teachers also performing.⁵⁰

Hope students also gave recitals. In 1907 a local newspaper invited its readers to a concert that evening of "the pupils of the music department of Hope College," who performed works by Schumann, Moszkowski, and Liszt in Winants Chapel; the report went on to state that the recitals had become quite popular.⁵¹ In February 1915, students gave what was termed a new sort of recital, which included *Wedding Day* and *Ich liebe dich* by Grieg, *Meditation* by Massenet, and a Chopin waltz.⁵² The programs point to the Hope paradigm of the best for the best. Some students excelled in their recitals, particularly the graduating seniors, for example, in May 1931, Hazel Paalman, a future Hope music professor, and in December 1937, Barbara Lampen, who performed the *C minor Fantasy* by Mozart, *Vienna Carnival* by Schumann, *G minor Ballade* by Chopin, and *Veils* by Debussy, as well as several other classical pieces.⁵³

During a single semester, spring 1936, the campus community experienced the Salvi Instrumental Quintet, a memorial concert for Curtis Snow, a recital by a Grand Rapids Congregational Church organist, the St. Olaf Lutheran Choir, organ recitals by students Charles Vogan and William Welmers, the Girls' Glee Club, a Hope men's double quartet, the Rink String Quartet, a Soldiers Memorial Service, and pianist Charles Wakefield Cadman, who performed with a vocal quartet. For those who could not get enough organ music, on a Wednesday afternoon in May, they heard a recital by six Hope students and then

---

48 Program, scrapbook 1932-35, box 4, Hinkamp Papers.
49 Program, faculty recital, Hope College School of Music, 6 Oct. 1922, events—recitals (faculty) folder, box 2, MD Papers.
50 *Anchor*, 14 Nov. 1923.
51 *Holland City News*, 6 June 1907.
52 *Anchor*, 3 Feb. 1915.
53 Programs, box 2, Curtis Snow Papers, and scrapbook 1935-37, box 5, Hinkamp Papers; *Anchor*, 1 and 15 Dec. 1937.

that evening a junior recital.[54] These preceded the Hope College High School Commencement, the Holland High and college Baccalaureate services, and the college and Holland High Commencements—all held in Dimnent Chapel over the course of six days in June of that year.[55]

The spring term also saw a series of traditional events that involved music. The Junior-Senior Banquet in March 1927 included violin solos, a male quartet, and the audience singing the *Orange and Blue*.[56] The All-College Day occurred in April. First celebrated in 1930, the event concluded with the All-College Banquet. Depending on the year, banquet attendees could hear any variety of duets, quartets, the Hope band, and faculty performers, but they always concluded with the singing of the *Hope Song*.[57]

The annual Arbor Day Exercises took place in early May, when the Hope community gathered to plant a tree and sing patriotic music. Between the processional and the recessional, the program for 1925 included *America, the Beautiful*, sung by the audience; *The Call*, sung by the senior women; Kipling's *Recessional*, sung by the student body; and the *Star Spangled Banner*, sung by the entire audience.[58] In 1930, after the processional, audiences sang *Marche Triumphale* and *America the Beautiful*, followed by the two Glee Clubs and the Chapel Choir, the *Star Spangled Banner*, and the recessional—Elgar's *Land of Hope and Glory*.[59]

For much of the first two generations of Hope's history, the June Commencement was a week-long affair—with music an important element of each day's events. Making music was memorable: seventy-six years later, Alice Hoffs recalled performing Beethoven's *Larghetto, 2nd Symphony* on the piano at her 1923 graduation in Carnegie Gymnasium.[60]

In 1927 Baccalaureate began with a Handel anthem performed by the Men's Glee Club, concluding with Haydn's *The Heavens Are Telling*,

---

[54] Programs, scrapbook 1935-37, box 5, Hinkamp Papers.
[55] Ibid.
[56] Program, memory book 1923-27, Susanne (Dragt) Vander Borgh Papers; *Hope College Song Book*, 2-3.
[57] Programs, scrapbook, Ethel Leestma Swets Papers and scrapbook 1932-35, box 4, Hinkamp Papers; *Hope College Song Book*, 4-5.
[58] Arbor Day Exercises program, 1 May 1925, box 2, Adelaide and Geraldine Dykhuizen Papers, H88-0046.
[59] Program, 9 May 1930, box 2, Curtis Snow Papers; faculty minutes, 1915-26, loose leaf, 9 May 1930.
[60] Larry Wagenaar interview with Alice Hoffs, 1999, Alice (Brower) Hoffs Papers; program, 1920-24 folder, box 2, Commencement and Baccalaureate collection.

Pageant of Hope

sung by the Girl's Glee Club.[61] Tuesday was the alumni gathering. In 1885 music for the alumni was provided by "local talent." *The Days We Love*, composed by professor W. A. Shields, was sung by the entire alumni, led by a quartet.[62] Finally, there was the college Commencement. In 1867 this included a festival held the evening of June 24 in the chapel, interspersing music and orations. Everyone sang *Great is the Lord*; a quintet, a quartet, a trio, and duets performed; a chorus sang *Columbia's Call*, a Civil War song; and the program ended with the doxology.[63] At subsequent graduations, the entertainment varied but always included both choral and instrumental music.[64]

An unusual aspect of Commencement in 1916 was a semicentennial pageant, which provided a template for similar events every decade through 1966. The pageants were a three-day-long affair prior to the June Commencement, with the pinnacle of each pageant being a production that often included several hundred Hope faculty and students. A faculty committee worked with the senior class to stage the two performances of the 1916 Pageant of Hope.[65] The event recalled the history of Holland and Hope College from Van Raalte

---

[61] Program, vocal ensembles—glee clubs folder, box 2, MD Papers.
[62] *Holland City News*, 27 June 1885.
[63] *Intercalary Exhibition of Hope College* (1867), inside cover Hinkamp scrapbook 1932-35, box 4, Hinkamp Papers.
[64] *Holland City News*, 19 June 1903, 17 June 1909; faculty minutes, 12 June 1920, 12 June 1921, 15 June 1923.
[65] Faculty minutes, 4 Feb. 1916; *Alumni Magazine* (Oct. 1966), 10; see also Wichers, *Century of Hope*, 150-53, and Songs of Hope College, 1865-1993.

and his followers leaving the Netherlands through 1916; songs were interspersed throughout the dramatic narrative.[66]

In this first era, students and other audience members experienced other special events—all of which heard the making of music. The laying of the Graves Hall cornerstone on October 12, 1892, began with a chorus by students; John Nykerk then led a choir singing *Praise Ye the Father*, and the ceremony concluded with the doxology.[67] An 1896 fundraising concert for remodeling the college gymnasium featured the Glee Club, a female quartet, a duet, and a John Nykerk solo, whereas a similar event for the *Anchor* featured the orchestra, a quartet, and various solos.[68] There was music at events honoring faculty and friends of the college who had passed away, for important political and Christian visitors, as well as celebrating George Washington and the YMCA.[69] Perhaps the most interesting was the Hope College Society Festival of 1906, organized by the Athletic Association as a fundraiser for sports teams. Held on the third floor of Van Raalte Hall, the festival included Holland's Apollo Orchestra performing and various other events in between their numbers, including "Take a Shot at the Faculty!!!," wherein "The likenesses of the various faculty members, painted on revolving boards, gave the students excellent opportunities for settling some old scores."[70]

By World War II, some musical traditions had become deeply rooted in the soil of Hope: daily chapel with its choir; Homecoming; vocal groups, especially the Glee Clubs; Choral Union concerts, most notably the *Messiah*; recitals by students and faculty, in particular, organ recitals; and at the end of the academic year, the Commencement exercises. We turn now to the modern era and how some musical traditions were refashioned and others were invented.

"The music you have made," 1941-2015

Helen Voogd, a freshman vocalist at the time recalled "We were just getting ready to sing at the 4:00 p.m. service when we heard of the attack [Pearl Harbor]. It all hit us hard." Jantina Holleman remembered years

---

[66] *Grand Rapids News*, 8 May 1916.
[67] *Holland City News*, 13 Oct. 1927.
[68] Program, vocal ensembles–glee clubs folder; *Anchor*, Dec. 1908.
[69] Programs and clippings, 1933-63 folder, box 1, Curtis Snow Papers; scrapbooks 1928-32 and 1932-35, box 4, Hinkamp Papers; faculty minutes, 8 Dec. 1928.
[70] Program, Hope College Student Years of Wynand Wichers and Alyda [Mae DePree '09] 1904-9 folder, Wynand Wichers Papers, H88-200; *Anchor*, 1 Feb. 1906; Swierenga, *Holland, Michigan*, 3:2067.

The Year in Music 139

later that students "were in quite an emotional state at the program." Barbara Folensbee Timmer, then a junior accompanist, looked back at December 7, 1941: "That was the day that we did our first Vespers at Hope College. I played the piano for that." After the performance, she returned to her dorm, turned on the radio and learned that Pearl Harbor had been attacked.[71]

That very first Christmas Vespers included student organists and pianists, the Girls' and Men's Glee Clubs, a sextet, a string trio, and the Chapel Choir, who sang the *Hallelujah Chorus*. Other vocal music included traditional seasonal pieces, *O, Come, All Ye Faithful* and *O Holy Night*, as well as pieces by Handel and Beethoven.[72] Approximately five hundred people were in the audience that afternoon.[73]

In December 1941, it would have been impossible to predict that the first Christmas Vespers would, in half a generation, become enormously popular on the campus and in the community. This segment of the chapter revisits the year in music, examining the era since 1941.

The Music Department began sponsoring its own convocation in 1993, which followed the college's opening event of the academic year. Held that year on a Wednesday afternoon in Dimnent Chapel, it included vocal music as well as piano, violin, and organ performances.[74]

A decade earlier, the college began holding arts and humanities fairs, which included performances by music students. Between 1989 and when the event ended in 2005, the music segment was known as the Collage Concert, featuring various instrumental ensembles and choirs and functioning as a prequel to the spring Musical Showcase. The October 1992 Collage Concert included music by the Hope Chapel Choir, College Chorus, Collegium Musicum, the Symphonette, and the Jazz and Wind Ensembles, and in 2001, it again featured all the major music ensembles.[75]

Homecoming continued as a traditional event, music being interspersed with athletics and other activities. Beginning in 1952,

---

[71] *Milestone* (1992), 24; *Holland Sentinel*, 28 Nov. 1996; Geoffrey Reynolds interview with Barbara Timmer, 13 July 2001, Hope College Living Heritage Oral History Project; Timmer, "The War Years," in Nordstrom and Zuidema, *Hope at the Crossroads*, 16-17.
[72] Program, scrapbook 1941-43, box 6, Hinkamp Papers.
[73] Press release, 27 Nov. 2006, Vespers (Christmas) 1991-present folder, box 3, MD Papers.
[74] Program, Hope College Music Department Fall Convocation, events folder, box 2, MD Papers.
[75] *Anchor*, 21 Oct. 1992; press release 28 Sept. 2001, events—collage concert folder, box 2, MD Papers.

and thereafter, depending on the year, parades, banquets, pep rallies, bonfires, and, of course, football games all preceded Sunday afternoon Vespers programs.[76] By the late 1960s, the program was no longer called Vespers; from 1973 it was instead billed as the Homecoming Recital. During the college's centennial year of 1966, there was a special Homecoming concert, where Anthony Kooiker performed a recital at the dedication of the newly acquired Steinway concert grand piano. Beginning in the early 1970s, the department staged a Kletz concert during Homecoming, featuring the concert and stage bands performing a mix of Broadway show tunes, classical music, and "oldies but goodies," as a press release termed it.[77]

Shortly after Homecoming, there came a new event, Parents' Weekend. In 1970 there was a special Sunday service in Dimnent Chapel, starring the College Chorus and Roger Davis on the organ.[78] The year 1990 saw a combined orchestra and wind ensemble concert as part of the event. Musical numbers included Rossini's *Tancredi Overture*, William Schuman's *Chester*, "Jupiter" from Holst's *The Planets*, and songs from *My Fair Lady*. The orchestra played *Night on Bald Mountain* by Mussorgsky, as well as works by Gounod, Elgar, and Prokofiev.[79]

Another new fall event came with the 1997 addition of Linda Dykstra to the faculty. Beginning the following year, she introduced the Liederabend, a concert of German art songs. Through 2016, when Dykstra retired, students replicated nineteenth-century performance venues for the event, singing works by Schubert, Schumann, Mendelssohn, Wolf, and Strauss.[80]

Through the 1960s, the college set aside an hour on Tuesday mornings to devote to assemblies, many of which were focused on music. In 1948-49, for example, the student body heard the American Male Chorus (made up of 24 World War II veterans), a cello-piano recital, the Concert Band, the University of Michigan Symphony Orchestra, a special Christmas program, the Glee Clubs, and a string quartet. In January 1967, touring pianist David Renner performed works by Beethoven and Schumann at one of the year's all-college assemblies.[81]

[76] *Milestone* (1942), 111, (1943), 71, (1945), 53, (1949), 179; *Anchor*, 30 Oct. 1953, and 20 Nov. 1962; clipping, news releases and clippings folder, Jantina Holleman Papers.
[77] Events—recitals (Homecoming), 1952-75 folder, box 3, MD Papers.
[78] *Anchor*, 4 Nov. 1970.
[79] Program, 2 Nov. 1990, instrumental ensembles–combined concerts, 1956- folder, box 1, MD Papers.
[80] Linda Dykstra to Marc Baer, email, 8 Oct. 2018, Making Music folder.
[81] Assembly programs topical file; *Anchor*, 21 Apr. 1949, 6 Jan. 1967.

Christmas Vespers has continued throughout the years, but the *Messiah* was a far larger production and for Nancy Lummen Plantenga '56 the highlight of her time at Hope.[82] Harley Brown '59, recalled that "During my era, the Vespers was nothing. . . . A little Christmas concert, that's about it."[83] Faculty and students on campus in the late 1940s and early 1950s recalled the decline of Vespers audiences. What saved the event was its reinvention by Music faculty Jantina Holleman and Anthony Kooiker, who transformed a patriotic remembrance into an Advent celebration.[84] As a tradition that connected campus and community and reflected the creativity of the Music Department, Vespers was transformed once again in the 1960s by organ professor Roger Davis.[85] When faculty member Robert Ritsema came to Hope in 1967, he noticed that instrumental music in Vespers was an afterthought. Davis asked him to have a small string group play, and Vespers took off.[86]

Over the decades since 1941, Vespers has mixed tradition and invention. Innovations included organ solos in 1944, a brass choir in 1957, the tower chimes and a harpsichord in 1961, and a handbell choir in 1999.[87] The traditional opening of Vespers was John Joubert's *Torches*, sung by a procession that included the College Chorus and Chapel Choir, generating, according to the *Anchor*, "tremendous excitement."[88] By the 1970s, hundreds of Hope students were participating and performing before audiences that, over the four Vespers concerts, would number in the thousands.

As participants, students experienced Vespers as a transformative event. David Lowry '89, recalled being both terrified and fully alive performing a solo for the 1987 Vespers: "In Chapel Choir under Roger Rietberg, we created something beautiful, worshipped, and collaborated in a (for me) short-lived community."[89] Audience members experienced similar emotions. One professor told Cavanaugh, "I was so choked up

[82] Nancy Plantenga to Marc Baer email, 21 Aug. 2018, Making Music folder. Compare the 1944 programs for each, both in terms of form and content: scrapbook 1943-52, box 6, Hinkamp Papers. In the 1950s, the *Milestone* covered the *Messiah* production, while failing to mention Christmas Vespers.
[83] Marc Baer interview with Harley Brown, 30 Aug. 2018, Making Music folder.
[84] Program, 1946, events—Vespers (Christmas) 1944-71 folder, box 3, MD Papers; Aschbrenner interview with Holleman; *Holland Sentinel*, 28 Nov. 1996.
[85] Press release, 28 Nov 1989, Vespers (Christmas) 1981-90 folder, box 3, MD Papers.
[86] Baer and Utting interview with Ritsema; Aschbrenner interview Holleman.
[87] *Anchor*, 17 Dec. 1944, 8 Dec. 1957, 3 Dec. 1961; *Milestone* (1997), 27.
[88] *Anchor*, 3 Dec. 1981.
[89] David Lowry to Marc Baer, email, 26 June 2018, Making Music folder.

that I couldn't sing the hymn. This is Christmas music and worship in its most effective form."[90] Community members also participated; Alice Hoffs '23 played the organ at Vespers for several decades.[91]

Until the late 1970s, the *Messiah* followed on the heels of Vespers, bringing together the Chancel Choir, the Chapel Choir, and other interested students and faculty, with hundreds of participants practicing for months.[92] In 1956 Roger Rietberg accompanied the chorus on the organ, with Anthony Kooiker on the piano, and the orchestra, directed by Morrette Rider, also performed. As in the past, professional soloists made appearances.[93] By the 1960s, the *Messiah* was performed every other year, most likely due to the rising popularity of Christmas Vespers, and beginning in 1971, every three years, until its final performance in 1977. Before then, those unable to attend the two-and-a-half-hour concert could hear it on a Holland radio station.[94]

Other musical events in December included an orchestra pops concert in the Kletz and the Madrigal Dinner, first offered in 1977, under the leadership of department chair Stuart Sharp. The event included medieval music and brass fanfares, dancers, and theatre professor George Ralph playing the part of the Lord of Misrule. Somewhat prophetically, Sharp stated: "It is something we may want to establish as a tradition." And the early December dinner continued into the twenty-first century.[95] The Madrigal Singers were formed in 1947 as an a cappella group by professor Jantina Holleman.[96] They gave concerts, for example in spring 1949, when they presented traditional English songs, including *Summer Is A Coming In* and *Now Is the Month of Maying*, and participated in Vespers in December.[97] The group went out of existence in 1951, but its music has resurfaced on several occasions thanks to the efforts of new faculty. In the mid-1960s, the music was taken up by the Motet Choir, from 1969 entitled the Collegium Musicum—performing madrigals and motets, vocal and instrumental music from the era between the Middle Ages and the eighteenth century.[98] A decade later,

---

[90] Henry Ten Hoor to Cavanaugh, 9 Dec. (ca. 1966), correspondence, 1965-69 folder, box 1, Cavanaugh Papers.
[91] Larry Wagenaar interview with Alice Brower Hoffs, 1999, Alice Hoffs Papers.
[92] *Anchor*, 18 Dec. 1951, 13 Dec. 1963, 10 Dec. 1965.
[93] Ibid., 18 Dec. 1956.
[94] Ibid., 12 Dec. 1950.
[95] Ibid., 9 Dec. 1977; events—Madrigal Dinner folder, box 2, MD Papers.
[96] *Anchor*, 16 Oct. 1947.
[97] Ibid., 21 Apr. 1949; *Milestone* (1949), 144.
[98] *Anchor*, 14 Nov. 1969, 8 May 1970.

Madrigal Singers

the Collegium Musicum was rebranded as a select ensemble of singers, appearing at the Madrigal Dinner.

On Hope's campus, spring semester, like fall, was filled with student and faculty recitals, as well as guest performers and concerts by departmental ensembles, including several new ones formed in the post-1941 era, one of which was the Chancel Choir, which in later years was renamed the College Chorus. Founded in 1949 by Jantina Holleman, and subsequently directed by Roger Rietberg, the one-hundred-member choir performed a mix of secular and sacred music on its own, as well as jointly with other ensembles. A performance in 1959 included Haydn's *Great Is the Lord Our Maker* and Mozart's *Horn Quintet in E Flat Major*.[99]

The Hope Symphonette made its first appearance in 1953, performing works of Sibelius, Khachaturian, and Billings.[100] Composed of nineteen members selected by audition from the orchestra, the Symphonette played on several Sunday afternoons in Dimnent Chapel. In February 1954, they performed pieces composed by Schubert, Khachaturian, Carleton Kelch, and Mozart.[101] By the mid-1960s, the

---

[99] Ibid., 6 May 1953, 8 May 1959.
[100] Ibid., 22 Nov. 1953.
[101] Ibid., 16 Oct. 1953; program, instrumental ensembles—Symphonette 1953-74 folder, box 1, MD Papers.

Chancel Choir

Symphonette had held two hundred concerts. A Hope graduate and former concertmaster of the orchestra who had heard the Symphonette perform wrote President Lubbers: "I was amazed at the group's technical skill and artistic interpretation."[102]

Still another new group, the Jazz Ensemble, was formed in 1974 by music professor Robert Cecil. In a 1984 concert in the Kletz, they played *Easy Street* by A. R. Jones, Gordon Goodwin's *Hot Monkey Love*, and Victor Young's *Stella by Starlight*.[103] Another jazz concert was held in DeWitt Theatre in 1986, when two student combos played works by Benny Golson, Thelonious Monk, John Coltrane, Rogers and Hammerstein, and McCartney and Lennon.[104]

Cecil rebranded the Concert Band, which took the stage in 1976 as the Wind Ensemble. Typically, between October and March, the group staged four concerts. Composed of from forty to fifty wind and percussion students, the Wind Ensemble presented audiences with a remarkable variety of music, from *West Side Story* to works by Sousa, Handel, and Wagner, to the music of *Lord of the Rings*.[105]

---

[102] Jeffrey Wiersum to Irwin Lubbers, 26 Apr. 1955, Symphonette tours folder, box 5, Rider Papers.
[103] *Anchor*, 15 Mar. 1984; press release, 16 Mar. 1984, instrumental ensembles—Jazz Ensemble, 1974- folder.
[104] *Anchor*, 16 Apr. 1986; program, 22 Apr. 1986, instrumental ensembles—Jazz Ensemble, 1974- folder.
[105] *Anchor*, 2 Mar. 1988, 24 Feb. 2010.

Symphonette

Until 1954 March typically saw Glee Club concerts, whereupon the ensembles were folded into the Chapel Choir. Upon returning from their spring break tour, the choir gave a home concert, for example, in 1970, performing sacred works by Mendelssohn, Rachmaninoff, and Tallis.[106] The orchestra staged a concert prior to its tours. When they were not preparing to hit the road, the orchestra played chamber music, including Bach's *Brandenburg Concerto No. 5* in 1951 and in 1973 Mendelssohn's *Concerto in E Minor*.[107]

One might say Hope's band was heard all over the place. In the 1960s, the Pep Band played at home basketball games. As with other groups, from time to time, it would disappear, due to lack of student interest. The Concert Band had a steadier existence, performing an Under the Pines concert regularly from the late 1940s. In 1949, under the conductorship of Morrette Rider, concert audiences heard twentieth-century music, such as Louis Ganne's *Father of Victory* and Rider's own *Anchor of Hope*, while playing pops concerts on other occasions—including P.D.Q. Bach's *Grand Serenade for an Awful Lot of Winds and Percussion*.[108] From the early 1960s, in late May, the band

---

[106] Press release, 14 May 1970, and program, 1970 spring concert tour, vocal ensembles—Chapel Choir, 1970- folder.
[107] *Anchor*, 15 Mar. 1951; program, 6 Mar. 1973, instrumental ensembles—orchestra, 1973-84 folder.
[108] *Milestone* (1949), 145; program, scrapbook 1943-52, box 6, Hinkamp Papers; *Anchor*, 24 Mar. 1949, and 30 Nov. 1953.

Jazz Ensemble (Anchor, *1977*)

staged annual Kletz and Pine Grove concerts; in some instances, senior members of the band served as conductors. Appropriately, in May 1965, the band's concert in the Pine Grove opened with Aaron Copland's *An Outdoor Overture*.[109]

Creativity consistently characterized the music faculty. For Hope audiences, this frequently took form when directors combined ensembles. In November 1981, for example, the band and the Collegium Musicum joined in a concert in Dimnent Chapel. The Collegium performed two selections accompanied by a brass choir, while the band played sacred arrangements by Brahms, Charles Ives, Norman Dello Joio, and Gordon Jacob; a week later, the Chapel Choir and Symphonette presented a concert, with Honegger's *King David* as a featured number.[110] A November 1989 celebration of the music of Aaron Copland featured the brass ensemble, orchestra, Chapel Choir, and College Chorus—a total of two hundred and fifty students.[111] In April 1995, a student chamber music concert was offered to audiences, featuring a percussion ensemble, saxophone and French horn quartets, and a woodwind quintet.[112]

[109] *Anchor*, 8 Feb. 1963, and 21 May 1965; news release, 21 May 1971, ensembles, instrumental, band 1926-82 folder.
[110] *Anchor*, 5 and 12 Nov. 1981.
[111] Ibid., 8 Nov. 1989.
[112] Ibid., 5 Apr. 1995.

Pine Grove concert

The year 1950 saw another new opportunity for audiences to experience music. The college held its first Fine Arts Festival in April of that year in the Little Theatre, housed on the fourth floor of what is today Lubbers Hall. The chamber orchestra performed music by American composers.[113] By the early 1960s, additional venues were added, including Dimnent Chapel, where audiences heard *A German Requiem*, by the combined Chapel Choir and College Chorus, with Joyce Morrison performing as a soprano soloist. The theme of the 1965 festival was the Negro and American culture, and featured Ethel Waters as vocalist and composer Ulysses Kay. The final year of the festival's existence was 1966, when audiences experienced Dutch church music.[114]

In terms of both duration and significance, the addition of the Musical Showcase permanently altered the year in music. In 1987 Music chair Robert Ritsema organized a joint concert by the Chapel Choir and the Symphonette in Grand Rapids' DeVos Performance Hall. The following year, Ritsema added other ensembles.[115] Then, in April 1989, hundreds of students participated as vocal and instrumental soloists

[113] Program, First Annual Fine Arts Festival, events—Fine Arts Festival 1950-66 folder, box 2, MD Papers.
[114] Events—Fine Arts Festival folder; *Anchor*, 23 Apr. 1965, 25 Mar. 1966.
[115] *Grand Rapids Press*, 11 Mar. 1999.

and members of twelve ensembles in the first-ever Musical Showcase.[116] By 1992 the event had attracted an audience of well over one thousand. At the "fast-moving, no-nonsense-pace" performance that year, there were eight soloists, all the major ensembles, Collegium Musicum, the Woodwind Quintet, the Brass Quintet, the Percussion Ensemble, the Opera Workshop, and a group called the Creative Arts Collective.[117]

Since 1937, at the end of every spring semester, students have anticipated a traditional event, May Day, previously All-College Day.[118] In 1949 the college band provided music for the first-year Hope women, who on May 13 marched to the Pine Grove for the coronation of the May Queen.[119] Initially, May Day music was classical—in 1941 the orchestra performed works by Mozart, Shubert, and Elgar, and in 1955, Hope student Robert Ritsema played a cello solo—but by the late 1980s, Dave Wopat, described as a "high-tech, pop-rock performer," and the Jazz Band played in the Pine Grove over the noon hour.[120] By then the name of the event had changed, first to Spring Festival and then subsequently to Spring Fling.

One final event, the All-College Sing, was held just prior to graduation, and although not sponsored by the Music Department, it was intimately connected to it. This was the premiere student vocal event at Hope College.[121] It was initiated by music professor Robert Cavanaugh and dean of women Elizabeth Lichty, as a means of encouraging more students to remain after finals for the graduation exercises.[122] The initial All-College Sing took place on the steps of Graves Hall in June 1940, with the college orchestra leading off by playing several pieces.[123] Fraternities and sororities competed, with the women of Sigma Sigma taking home a silver cup with their rendition of *Sylvia*.[124]

---

[116] *Anchor*, 5 and 12 Apr. 1989; program, Hope College Musical Showcase, 5 Apr. 1989, events—Musical Showcase folder.

[117] Press release, 18 Feb. 1992, events—Musical Showcase folder.

[118] For music at the first May Day, see program, scrapbook 1935-37, box 5, Hinkamp Papers. See also *Anchor*, 8 Feb. 1979, 1 May 1980. The event evolved from a yearly celebration of the birthday of Elizabeth Voorhees, after whom Voorhees Hall was named; buildings and grounds—Voorhees Hall topical file.

[119] *Anchor*, 19 May 1949; program, May Day Coronation (1949), Spring Fling topical file.

[120] *Milestone* (1941), 82, 111, and (1983), 53; *Anchor*, 29 Apr. 1982; program, *Salute to Spring* (1955) and Social Activities Committee memorandum, 18 Apr. 1989, Spring Fling topical file.

[121] *Milestone* (1958), 64; Wichers, *Century of Hope*, 214.

[122] *Anchor*, 20 Mar. 1959.

[123] Ibid., 5 June 1940; *Milestone* (1941), 122.

[124] *Milestone* (1941), 122.

In 1941 rain forced the event to move from the Pine Grove to Dimnent, and it continued there until the late 1950s. The 1941 Sing began with a string trio, followed by audience singing. Each fraternity and sorority then sang one number and its own society's song, and while judges tabulated the results, the audience again sang.[125] In the late 1940s, the event was moved to March. By then, the student newspaper understood that the purpose of the All-College Sing was "to promote music on the campus and provide an enjoyable evening for students, faculty, and town people." In 1949 the Hop-ives, a group of student wives, sang at the close of the competition, while the judges determined the winners.[126] The Delphis won the cup for sororities, singing the African American spiritual *Steal Away*, arranged by Roy Ringwald, with the Arcadians beating out the other fraternities with their rendition of Frederic Bullard's *Winter Song*.[127]

By 1955 the student newspaper dubbed the All-College Sing a "classic."[128] Robert Ritsema recalled that when he was a student at Hope, "Every fraternity and sorority was required to be in it, and every member of the fraternity and sorority had to sing . . . no matter if you couldn't sing." Rehearsals went on for weeks prior to the event. "We'd get together and rehearse at night," according to Ritsema. Music faculty were often chosen as judges, while others served as advisors for the event. Subsequently, Ritsema avowed, "I think we . . . not necessarily pushed it but accepted it as being a part of what was going on at the college."[129]

The 1950s represented the event's zenith, and in 1958, it moved to the Holland Civic Center. That year, the Delphis, dressed in red polka-dot bonnets, with matching white blouses and skirts, won the sorority competition with *Cindy*. The Fraternal Society, wearing light gray trousers and dark sport coats, won with their rendition of *Wonderful Copenhagen*. An added feature that year was the appearance of the Durfee Hall waiters, dressed in jackets. They first rendered a version of *Sixteen Tons* and then sang *Sugartime*. Following the performance, the audience sang while the judges deliberated. At the end, the directors from the victorious Delphis and Fraters led the audience in the *Alma Mater Hymn*.[130]

---

[125] Ibid. (1942), 113; program, scrapbook 1941-43, box 6, Hinkamp Papers.
[126] *Anchor*, 10 Mar. 1949.
[127] Ibid., 24 Mar. 1949.
[128] Ibid., 25 Feb. 1955; 1955 program in scrapbook, Adelbert Farnsworth Papers.
[129] Baer and Utting interview with Ritsema.
[130] *Anchor*, 14 Mar. 1958.

Arcadians practicing for All-College Sing, 1959
Harley Brown, directing

Following the late 1950s, the All-College Sing was reformulated several times and then cancelled in 1967 because of a protest by the Arcadian and Knickerbocker fraternities due to "dissention within and among the various fraternities and sororities."[131] The event returned in 1975, much altered, died for a second time in 1998, and was briefly revived in the new millennium and held in the Knickerbocker Theatre with individuals rather than organizations performing; it disappeared for good in 2002.[132]

The final event of the year in music was graduation, held in either May or June. In 1946 the Music department presented a Commencement concert, whose focus was singing by the Women's Glee Club. In subsequent years, there were musicales. For the 1963 graduation, the department planned the music, including soloists and an accompanist.[133]

---

[131] Ibid., 6 Mar. 1959, 17 Feb. and 3 Mar. 1967; "History of the All-College Sing," All-College Sing Topical File.

[132] *Anchor*, 28 Feb. and 21 Mar. 1975, 29 Sept. 1983, 11 and 18 Nov. 1987; *Milestone* (2000), 20, and (2001), 34.

[133] Program, Hope College Commencement concert, events folder, and Music Department minutes, 23 Apr. 1963, boxes 1 and 2, MD Papers; program, scrapbook 1943-52, box 6, Hinkamp Papers.

As in the first era, so in the second, between Convocation and Commencement, music was everywhere, and what was heard varied by the year. The World War II era was one stimulus. The Army Specialized Training Program soldiers at Hope sponsored a musical program in March 1944, which included the Women's Glee Club, whereas during one week in May 1945, audiences listened to music at a memorial service for the twenty-seven Hope men killed in action during World War II, a program celebrating V-E Day, and an event commemorating the liberation of the Netherlands.[134]

Following the war, the department continued to perform at special events. Institutional festivities served as stimuli: for example, presidential inaugurations. The audience at the inauguration of Wynand Wichers in October 1931 heard an organ prelude, a musical processional and recessional, and in between, a choral response, solos, and an anthem by the Chapel Choir. The 1945 inauguration of Irwin Lubbers was limited to organ music. The Chapel Choir performed at Calvin VanderWerf's inauguration in November 1963, at Gordon Van Wylen's in October 1972, at John Jacobson's in October 1987 (singing the first verse of Psalm 42 in Dutch), and at James Bultman's in October 1999. The latter included an original work, *Wings of Hope*, by composer-in-residence Ray Shattenkirk.[135]

Music was also performed at the dedication of new buildings, beginning in 1942 with the Science Building (now Lubbers Hall).[136] The Chapel Choir sang at the October 1961 dedication of Van Zoeren Library, whereas the choir and orchestra performed at the 1978 dedication of the Dow Center.[137] The Wichers addition to Nykerk Hall of Music was of course celebrated with music in October 1970, including Pergolesi's *Stabat Mater*.[138] The college orchestra performed in DeWitt Theatre in fall 1971, soon after the building opened, while in 1986, the Jazz Ensemble "jammed" in the new Maas Center auditorium, the *Anchor* reporting: "The pieces ranged in style from the Big Band Style of the forties to some very modern bebop pieces and some beautiful blues style."[139]

[134] Programs, scrapbook 1943-52, box 6, Hinkamp Papers.
[135] Programs, box 2, Curtis Snow Papers, and box 6, Hinkamp Papers; *Anchor*, 8 Nov. 1963, 13 and 27 Oct. 1999.
[136] Programs, scrapbook 1941-43, Hinkamp Papers.
[137] Ibid., 1961-63; *Anchor*, 27 Oct. 1978.
[138] *Anchor*, 19 Oct. 1970; program, events—dedications 1929-2000 folder, box 2, MD Papers.
[139] *Anchor*, 22 Oct. 1986; program, 28 Oct. 1986, instrumental ensembles—Jazz Ensemble, 1974- folder.

Perhaps the most unusual musical event of any year came in 1992, with a concert featuring the music of John Cage. The orchestra began with Cage's *4'33"*; then made a milkshake with a blender, followed by a performer meandering through the audience with a leaf blower; and finished with *Solo for Voice 72*—which included screaming. The *Anchor*'s take on the evening was: "The utter strangeness of the concert was freeing in a way. It served to let one experience things without preconceptions, forcing one to fully experience everything in its own right."[140] You, reader, may be the judge.

One measure of the vitality of music on Hope's campus comes from examining the front page of the student newspaper. The *Anchor* issue of March 24, 1949, had articles on the Women's Glee Club spring tour, listing the songs for both the secular and sacred programs, and the Men's and Women's Glee Clubs' Easter concert, which took up a fourth of the front page. Fifty years later, there was not a single mention of music on Hope's campus.[141] Comparing the later with the earlier era reveals fewer occasions for those who were not music majors or faculty to perform either instrumental or vocal music. And although Arbor Day and the All-College Sing had disappeared, Christmas Vespers frequently attracted audiences in the thousands.

What, then, was the musical experience of the years between 1866 and 2015 at Hope College? Audiences throughout these years heard plenty of music, but the musical experience in the decades since the first graduation was quite varied. No two years were the same; perhaps the singular "year" in the title of this chapter is misleading, but at the same time, the rhythm's core was stable. Considering new buildings and presidents, as well as traditional events, such as graduation and occasional pageants, music was part of the warp and woof of the college. By the early twenty-first century, the *Messiah* concert, once vital, was a distant memory. In contrast, audiences in 2005 experienced between seventy and one hundred concerts and recitals given by the Department of Music's students, faculty, and guests.[142]

A second realm of significance was the international—or multicultural—bent of music heard by audiences. An early 1930s Girls' Glee Club program included *Deep River* and *I'm Gwine to Sing*," identified in the program as Negro Spirituals, whereas an early 1950s Men's Glee Club concert, "Songs of Other Lands," included music from

---

[140] *Anchor*, 25 Nov 1992.
[141] Ibid., 24 Mar. 1949, 17 Mar. 1999.
[142] Compare *Hope College Catalog*, 2004-5, and *Milestone*, 2005.

Wales, Russia, Yugoslavia, and Arabia.[143] During World War II, a spring concert of the Girls' Glee Club included *Thou God of All Nations*, as well as Russian, Chinese, and English songs "dedicated to the allies."[144]

Finally, in a back-to-the-future moment, 2014 saw the formation of the Chapel String Quartet, which joined the Chapel Band for worship services.[145] This brings us full circle, from 1866 to the end of our story, when once again music and chapel are blended. Musical performances, in particular, Christmas Vespers, touch audiences deeply, perhaps like no other experience. A former student reflected, in the context of Vespers: "I do have a deep love for God. The only way I can really express it is in music. There is no group that is such a part of that experience as the Chapel Choir." And a faculty colleague, having just heard the *Messiah* program, said to Robert Cavanaugh: "It was the first time I have ever listened to it with a tear in the eye. . . . In my many years at Hope College, the most deeply religious and spiritual experiences I have had have been evoked by the music you have made."[146]

---

[143] Concert programs, vocal ensembles—glee clubs folder.
[144] Spring Concert of the Hope College Girls' Glee Club, glee clubs folder.
[145] *Anchor*, 12 and 19 Nov. 2014.
[146] Nannette Olmsted to Cavanaugh (ca.1971), Henry ten Hoor to Cavanaugh, 17 Dec. 1971, correspondence 1970-74 folder, box 1, Cavanaugh Papers.

154 MAKING MUSIC

CHAPTER 6

Finding Its Tune: A Musical Community

> The [Choral Union] concerts in the past have been of such
> a high order that they have the reputation of
> being the musical event of the year.
> *Holland City News*, 1908

> It is said that the Dutchman has a reputation for vocal talent.
> *Anchor*, 1915

> There is in Holland twice as much real musical talent
> as in any other city in the state five times Holland's
> size, and I know what I'm talking about.
> John Nykerk, 1925

Following an all-day open house at the Netherlands Museum, twelve hundred people gathered in Dimnent Chapel on the night of February 9, 1938, to commemorate the anniversary of the settlement of Holland, Michigan, by Dutch immigrants. Nearly filling the chapel, the large crowd was treated to a musical program courtesy of Hope College and the Holland community, presided over by Hope president Wynand Wichers. Preceding the service, faculty member Esther Snow played the organ prelude, *Adagio Espressivo*, by Arthur Goodhart. Two numbers, *Now Let Every Tongue Adore Thee*, by Bach, and *Now Thank We All Our God*, by Johann Crueger, were then rendered by the Holland Civic Chorus. Snow accompanied on the piano, while her colleague Kenneth Osborne conducted. A trumpet quartet composed of four Hope College students followed with the playing of *The Nederlands Volkslied* and *Wilhelmus*.[1]

At first glance, such an event may seem unique and perhaps inconsequential, but it was neither. Although the content was distinctive, the style was not.[2] Rather, what took place that evening in 1938 was emblematic of musical events occurring throughout that year and in other years, before and after, and its format was far from insignificant. In fact, a closer dissection of its participants underscores an important discovery and in turn raises some questions. It turns out there was a close relationship between town and gown that music helped foster. In other words, the commemoration in 1938 was an event for the community, held at Hope College, led by Hope music professors, and featuring college faculty and students, as well as the premiere community chorus. This discovery begs three questions: When and why did such a partnership begin between the college and the community? What has been the nature of the relationship and its evolution over time? And what has collaboration regarding music meant for both the college and the community? Each question will be explored in the course of this chapter.

The answer to the first question requires a brief review of the musical landscape of pre-1900 Holland. Although an 1888 *Anchor* article encouraged students to procure college songbooks, practice singing, and shout to their heart's content in order to "astonish all the quiet Hollanders," there were plenty of "music-loving citizens" to be found in the West Michigan community.[3] The first record of a musical event in Holland is of a sacred concert in 1858 by a mixed sextet from Allegan, presented in Van Vleck Hall.[4] In 1875 the Holland Musical Association was formed, at first directed by Cornelis Van Oostenbrugge, Class of

---

[1] *Holland City News*, 10 Feb. 1938; *Commemorative Exercises on the Ninety-First Anniversary of the Colonization of Western Michigan by the Netherlands People*, program, scrapbook 1938-41, box 5, Hinkamp Papers.
[2] The 90th anniversary event the year before was constructed differently, for which, see program, scrapbook 1938-41, Hinkamp Papers.
[3] *Anchor*, 1 May 1888; *Holland City News*, 30 June 1888.
[4] Swierenga, *Holland, Michigan*, 3:2051.

1876 and music tutor, 1871-77.⁵ He was succeeded by Neil Downie, superintendent of Holland Public Schools. In 1897 Hope professor John Nykerk assembled a 315-voice choir for Holland's semicentennial celebration. Skillfully drilled, the ensemble's performance inspired an audience of thousands at the ceremonies in Centennial Park. Among the choir members were many leading citizens of Holland. By 1900 most of the city's Reformed churches supported vocal ensembles, which sang not only in Sunday worship services but also in concerts, including Christmas and Easter cantatas.⁶

In these vignettes, the community's connection to the college is apparent, and clearly, this relationship was reciprocal. What is less clear is in sorting out cause and effect. Was the vitality of the musical scene in Holland due to the inherent musicality of its citizenry or to the presence of a vibrant music program at Hope College? The success of music, both at Hope and in the community, seems to have been the result of a partnership best understood as *mutualism*, which developed out of necessity on some occasions, with a burst of creativity on others. For analytical purposes, this chapter tells the story by separating community and college. It must be remembered, however, that the answer to the question just posed lies in that area of overlap between what, in most settings, would be seen as distinct and, in other settings, antagonistic—thus the phrase, "town *versus* gown." Mutualism is witnessed in the anecdote above and in recalling that both Holland and Hope College were founded within a few years of each other by the same Dutch settlers.⁷ The result is that there have been countless occasions large and small where Dutchness has brought town and gown together on the same stage.

Consider the decade 1931-41. On either side of the 1938 commemoration, there were related events. January 1931 saw the funeral service for Gerrit Diekema, Class of 1881, Michigan politician, and ambassador to the Netherlands. The service was held in Dimnent Chapel, and Hope College professors John Nykerk and Curtis Snow oversaw the musical element of the occasion.⁸ Next, in 1933, there was a program held in Dimnent Chapel commemorating the four hundredth anniversary of the birth of Prince William of Orange, including an organ prelude, a male chorus, and a solo; audience and chorus sang the

---

⁵ Ibid., 3:2054; *Hope College Catalog* (1876-77), 22, 44.
⁶ Swierenga, *Holland, Michigan*, 3:2054.
⁷ Cf. *Holland City News*, 30 June 1888.
⁸ Program, scrapbook 1928-32, box 4, Hinkamp Papers.

Program for Prince William of Orange 1933 event

Dutch national anthem.⁹ In May 1935, there was a special convocation to honor the Dutch ambassador, who was awarded an honorary degree by the college. Curtis Snow played the organ, including a processional, *God of Our Fathers*, by Daniel Roberts and George Warren, and other pieces by Rachmaninoff and Gericke, and a song of blessing was sung in Dutch by the choir and audience.¹⁰ In January 1940, a convocation was held to confer an honorary degree on a Dutch ambassador. On this occasion, Hope professor Kenneth Osborne played the organ, whereas the Chapel Choir rendered several songs a cappella.¹¹ Then, in June 1941, to celebrate a visit to West Michigan by Princess Juliana of the Netherlands, Esther Snow performed on the Dimnent Chapel organ; a Hope trombone quartet played the Dutch national anthem; the Chapel Choir sang two songs, the *Old Netherlands Melody* and *Onward Ye People*, by Jean Sibelius; and choir and audience together sang *De Zegenbede* (the blessing).¹²

9   Program, scrapbook, 1929-36, box 2, Curtis Snow Papers; diary entry, 25 Apr. 1933, HC diaries 1929-34, box 1, Schuppert Papers.
10   Program, scrapbook 1935-37, box 5, Hinkamp Papers.
11   Ibid., 1938-41.
12   Ibid., 1941-43, box 6. For similar occasions in 1928 and 1949, see scrapbooks

If the "when and why" question takes us back to the mid-nineteenth-century origins of college and community, then what follows is an investigation into how the collaboration grew beyond its origins to arrive at the meaning of music for both town and gown. The nature and evolution of this relationship can be explored using two distinct approaches. The first is to consider how the Holland community and Hope College supported each other in making music.

Town for gown

At Hope College, music often drew on local community members. Until the late 1890s, music instruction at Hope was the responsibility not only of faculty and students at the college and its private high school but also "outsiders." These included tutors and musicians from Holland and nearby cities, particularly Grand Rapids. For example, in 1888, a singing school directed by a Holland resident was held on Wednesday evenings.[13] In 1894 the college catalog advertised opportunities for instruction in voice and piano with two well-regarded Grand Rapids musicians.[14] But the local community provided what was soon to be called the Hope College School of Music with more than just instructors. Well into the twentieth century, nonmatriculated local community members were music students at Hope. The 1926 college catalog states: "Students of all grades are admitted into the School of Music." Although the *Anchor* reported in 1925 that half of the 104 students in the School of Music were townspeople, the actual proportion for that year was more like a third; of these, fourteen were in the Preparatory School, and nine were Hope alumni, leaving sixteen others. Having said that, for most years—barring the World War I and Great Depression eras—townspeople outnumbered Hope College and Preparatory School students.[15]

Many of Hope's early ceremonial occasions would have had no music but for the music supplied by talent from Holland and the surrounding communities. The college's decision to enhance such events with professional musicians was greatly admired by residents, for as Robert Swierenga has noted, "Hollanders appreciate good

---

  1928-32 and 1941-52, boxes 4 and 6; faculty minutes, 8 Dec. 1928.
[13] *Anchor*, 1 Jan. 1888.
[14] *Hope College Catalog* (1894-95), 37.
[15] Ibid., 1926 (May Bulletin), 156; *Anchor*, 14 Oct. 1925; Corcoran, "Who Were the School of Music students?"

music."[16] In particular, members of the local community frequently supplied the music at Hope's pre-1900 Commencement exercises. In 1885 Commencement was held at Hope Church with music furnished this time by talent from the greater Grand Rapids area. Thanks to a viola solo by Frank Lawson of Grand Rapids, a trombone solo by Frank Holton, and a vocal duet by G. C. Shepard and the wife of Frank Lawson, both of Grand Rapids, the music was judged the "finest ever produced" at a Hope Commencement.[17]

During the first century of Hope's existence, collegiate ensembles struggled with inconsistent interest and leadership, which was addressed with the arrival of John Nykerk, who joined the faculty in 1895. By the turn of the century, he was merging townspeople, college students, and faculty into groups capable of joint productions. In 1902, under Nykerk's direction, the Choral Union—which included townspeople—performed its second annual concert. Junior—and future Hope professor—Thomas Welmers served as pianist, joining Breyman's Orchestra, a "Ladies' Quartet," and a double quartet, which included Hope students, alumni, and townspeople.[18] The following year's concert, "David, the Shepherd Boy," billed as a sacred cantata, included Chicago singer Gerard Dinkeloo, Class of 1900. Nykerk played both Samuel and Jonathan, in addition to directing the event.[19]

The majority of early student musical groups at Hope did not begin, much less solidify, until after the turn of the twentieth century.[20] Meanwhile, the 1883 general Commencement was again held at Hope Church, with music furnished by Gee's Orchestra of Holland.[21] The group—formed in 1877 by Dr. D. M. Gee, a local dentist considered a "musical mastermind"—consisted in fact of only five instruments.[22]

To enhance Hope College ensembles, community members were often included. Before the college was even chartered in 1866, an early singing society, Euphemia, was formed with the purpose of conducting the singing at the Sunday service at Hope Church, then meeting in

---

[16] *Holland City News*, 28 June 1879; Swierenga, *Holland, Michigan*, 3:2055.
[17] *Holland City News*, 27 June 1885.
[18] Program, vocal ensembles—College Chorus folder, box 2, MD Papers. Breyman's was one of two such groups in Holland, although in Swierenga's opinion, calling either of the six- to ten-member ensembles an orchestra might be generous: Swierenga, *Holland, Michigan*, 3:2067.
[19] Program, vocal ensembles—College Chorus folder.
[20] See chs. 3 and 5.
[21] *Holland City News*, 30 June 1883. For Gee, see Swierenga, *Holland, Michigan*, 2:1320, 3:2060.
[22] Swierenga, *Holland, Michigan*, 3:2060.

the old district schoolhouse. According to the *Anchor*, "To this society belonged not only most of the [Hope Academy] students but also a sprinkling of the fair daughters of Holland."[23] At times, the Hope band and orchestra clearly depended on community members to "fill-out the ensemble."[24]

In the meantime, community groups extended an invitation to college students to join their organizations. The 1939-40 catalog offered students the following opportunities: "The Holland Civic Chorus, under the direction of [Hope professor] Kenneth Osborne, and the Holland Symphony Orchestra, under the direction of Eugene Heeter, are available for membership to those students who wish to study the larger oratorio and symphonic forms of music."[25] Heeter was town plus gown personified, for in addition to his other duties, he directed instrumental music for the Holland Public Schools and the Hope College and American Legion bands, and he served on the Tulip Time music committee. In addition to the city's Civic Chorus and Symphony, the Holland Musicians Club also welcomed students, including Ethel Leestma and Mildred Schuppert.[26]

Community groups also took the initiative in staging performances. Examples include the May 1941 concert at Dimnent Chapel, sponsored by the Holland Rotary and Kiwanis clubs. The event included the University of Michigan Symphony Orchestra, organist Esther Snow, the Holland High School a cappella choir, and the college's Chapel Choir.[27] The Chapel Choir sang at a Thanksgiving service held three years later in the Holland Armory.

Even as Hope's enrollment continued to increase, especially following World War II, and college ensembles became better established, local talent was not pushed to the side. Instead, joint concerts were scheduled, and local performers continued to support college-sponsored events. One example is a 1940 Hope chapel service, when Robert Cavanaugh sang *Ballad of America*, accompanied by the Holland High School orchestra and a cappella choir. Another came in 1965, when

---

[23] *Anchor*, 1 Sept. 1888.
[24] Ibid., 14 Dec. 1921; see also 1922 program, instrumental ensembles—orchestra, 1921-72 folder, box 1, MD Papers; *Milestone* (1945), 73; Aschbrenner interview with Holleman.
[25] *Hope College Catalog* (1939-40), 65. Heeter's effort to improve the orchestra by including college students led some Holland members to complain: Swierenga, *Holland, Michigan*, 3:2009, 2070-71.
[26] Scrapbook, Ethel Leestma Swets Papers; diary entries, 11 and 25 Feb. 1931, HC diaries 1929-34, box 1, Schuppert Papers.
[27] Program, scrapbook 1941-43, box 6, Hinkamp Papers.

162   MAKING MUSIC

Vespers 1958 (*courtesy Holland Photography, Ted Jungblut*)

Larrie Clark, director of vocal music at Holland Public Schools, was a soloist in the Hope Chapel Choir and orchestra's rendition of Gabriel Fauré's *Requiem*.[28] The partnership with local schools continued, and in the 1970s, Hope held joint concerts with Holland High School.[29]

The most important example of local talent being used in a college event is Christmas Vespers. To this day, the production, performed as much for the enjoyment of the community as the college, showcases the musical prowess of the Music faculty, other faculty and staff, students, and community members. In the 1958 Christmas Vespers service, community members served on the Vespers committee and as vocal soloists and organists.[30] Christmas Vespers is also a testament to enthusiastic audiences that the Holland community has provided college productions for decades.

Gown for town

The key to mutualism is reciprocity of benefits, that is, such relationships profit both participants. Thus, the second way to explore

[28] *Anchor*, 13 Nov. 1940, and 5 Mar. 1965.
[29] Ibid., 23 Apr. 1976; program, instrumental ensembles-orchestra 1921-72 folder.
[30] Brochure, 1958, events—Vespers 1944-71 folder.

Finding Its Tune   163

Poster for performance at Forest Grove

COLLEGIAN QUARTET
—OF—
HOLLAND
—IN—
Harmony and Humor
Y. M. C. A. HALL
Forest Grove
TUES., APRIL 18
Eight o'clock   Admission 15c

the nature of the connection between town and gown is through college initiatives on behalf of the community. Just as the community had done for the college before 1900, in the new century, the college would help furnish music for important community events. This was through student initiatives and faculty resourcefulness that sometimes drew in students and by programs promoted by college leaders.

According to an entry in the 1943 *Milestone*, "Hope music students, performing for churches, clubs, and other organizations, contribute much of the musical life of the community."[31] Evidence to support this claim abounds, particularly in the era before the Second World War. In 1915-16 the Knickerbocker Quartet performed in several West Michigan communities, while the student-organized Prins-Baker Quartet helped provide the music for an eighth grade production of *Rip Van Winkle* in the high school auditorium and then three years later sang at Bethany Reformed Church.[32] Also known as the Collegian Quartet, the group had a vaudevillian quality, evident in photographs and in a poster for a performance in Jamestown, just east of Holland.

Throughout the diaries of Mildred Schuppert, Class of 1931, there are glimpses of Hope music majors participating in the musical life of Holland churches. Schuppert faithfully recorded in her diary

---
[31] *Milestone* (1943), 22.
[32] *Anchor*, 26 Jan. 1916, 19 Nov. 1919; brochure, 9 June 1916, scrapbook, Peter G. Baker Papers.

Twelfth Street Harmony

each of the occasions when either she or other music majors performed, most often her friends Hazel Paalman '31 and Ethel Leestma '33. Schuppert herself played the organ for First Reformed Church, Hope Church, Third Reformed Church, and the Methodist Church on more than a dozen occasions between February 1929 and January 1931.[33] Two decades later, Harley Brown '59, sang in Hope Church's choir; subsequently, in his senior year, he served as choir director for Fourth Reformed Church.[34]

Beyond churches, clubs, and organizations, Hope College students performed for larger audiences. The Musical Arts Club organized the Sunday afternoon Vespers series,[35] which included student and faculty recitals, as well as other performances. Looking backward, the most significant contribution of the club was the Christmas program on that fateful afternoon of December 7, 1941.[36] Student initiatives for making music for the community go back to that small orchestra organized at the turn of the twentieth century and the Collegian Quartet of the

---

[33] HC diary 1927- and HC diaries 1929-34, box 1, Schuppert Papers. On 21 Feb. 1931, she and Leestma went to Hope Church to help Curtis Snow tune the organ.
[34] Scrapbook, Harley D. Brown Papers, H18-1999.
[35] The organization planned three events during the 1944-45 year; *Milestone* (1945), 61.
[36] See ch. 5.

World War I era. And they continue to the present day in the form of student-led a cappella groups, like Luminescence and Twelfth Street Harmony, which for several years have sung the national anthem at Hope College basketball games.

Students making music paralleled initiatives by faculty, especially in churches and at related religious events. At the thirteenth annual Praise Service in 1932, sponsored by the Federation of Women's Societies of the Churches of Holland and Vicinity, Curtis Snow played the organ prelude, the Chapel Choir sang Handel's *Holy Art Thou*, and Hope students performed solos, including Ethel Leestma on the piano.[37] In the 1940s, Hope ensembles, including the Girls' Glee Club, provided music for area churches, as well as for a luncheon at the General Synod of the Reformed Church in America. In that same decade, the Women's and Men's Glee Clubs joined area church leaders, the Hope YWCA and YMCA, and the Holland Christian Endeavor Union in both Good Friday afternoon and Easter sunrise services in Dimnent Chapel.[38] The Chapel Choir, along with professor Roger Rietberg on the organ, provided music for a 1951 Reformation Day Service sponsored by Classis Holland.[39] In 1981 and again in 1987, the Chapel Choir, Symphonette, and Third Reformed Church choir combined to stage Arthur Honegger's *King David* in Dimnent Chapel.

The Chapel Choir and various Hope instrumental ensembles presented numerous concerts aimed at community audiences, and some of these would not have been staged without the college sponsoring them. The 1957 Tulip Time audience benefitted from the contributions of the Music and Speech Departments, who collaborated on staging the American folk-opera, *Down in the Valley*, performed at the relatively new (1954) Civic Center. The following year, the Music and Theatre Departments offered Tulip Time viewers *The Red Mill*, a popular operetta.[40]

There is a long history of the music faculty staging events for local students. The earliest example was in 1926, billed as an "educational concert," a partnership of Hope's orchestra and the Holland Public

---

[37] Program, scrapbook 1932-35, box 4, Hinkamp Papers.
[38] *Anchor*, 24 Mar. 1949.
[39] *Milestone* (1945), 60; programs, 1941-43 and 1943-52 scrapbooks, box 6, Hinkamp Papers.
[40] Programs, American Folk Opera and the Red Mill, events—Tulip Time and municipal programs 1936-95 folder, box 3, MD Papers; news clipping, scrapbook box 2, Cavanaugh Papers; *Anchor*, 10 May 1957, 16 May 1958.

Harley Brown, *The Red Mill*, 1958

not the right outfit for the production

Schools music program.⁴¹ This was followed four years later by a collaboration between Curtis Snow and Eugene Heeter. Together, they organized a four-day music festival during Tulip Time, "the like of which Holland has never before had the privilege of sponsoring," which included Hope's Glee Clubs, high school bands from Holland and Grand Rapids, and the Holland Civic Chorus.⁴²

From the 1950s through the 1970s, Hope faculty brought their music to West Michigan schools. There were Young People's Concerts in the early 1950s, sponsored by the Holland chapter of the American Association of University Women and featuring the Hope orchestra, and conducted by Morrette Rider. The Chapel Choir performed at the 1958 Westshore Music Clinic at Grand Haven High School, when the Hope students played for an audience of West Michigan high school choirs; there were similar events for schools in Wyoming Park, Hamilton, Grand Haven, and Ludington.⁴³ Conductor Robert Ritsema continued what Rider had begun; thus, the early 1970s saw joint orchestral concerts, including Hope College and high schools in West Ottawa, Holland, and Muskegon.⁴⁴

⁴¹ Program, instrumental ensembles—orchestra, 1921-72 folder.
⁴² *Anchor*, 7 May 1930.
⁴³ Ibid., 14 Nov. 1958; programs, instrumental ensembles—orchestra, 1921-72, and instrumental ensembles—Symphonette, 1953-74 folders.
⁴⁴ Press release, 2 Mar. 1972, and programs, instrumental ensembles—orchestra, 1921-72 folder; *Anchor*, 6 Mar. 1972, 30 Sept. 1977.

It is impossible to ignore the theme of gown-inspired music for a local audience, which through the 1950s was overwhelmingly Dutch, both ethnically and culturally. The Chapel Choir performed in 1965 for the Dutch prince when he visited Holland to help dedicate the De Zwaan windmill.[45] In 1982 the Music Department presented a "Music of the Netherlands" concert as part of the celebrations of the Bicentennial of the Treaty of Amity and Commerce between the Netherlands and the United States. In addition to a faculty brass ensemble, the Collegium Musicum, directed by Richard Carlson; the Symphonette, led by Robert Ritsema; and the Chapel Choir, guided by Roger Rietberg, all performed.[46]

Along these lines, perhaps the most important community event at which college students, faculty, alumni, and ensembles regularly perform has already been mentioned—Holland's annual Tulip Time festival. From early in the history of the event, which began in 1929, the gown for town theme has remained important. For example, May 1931, the third iteration of the festival, saw two events at Dimnent Chapel: a Dutch psalm sing on Sunday evening, with Curtis Snow as organist and John Nykerk leading the audience, and on the following day, the Holland Civic Chorus performing Haydn's *Spring*.[47] In 1939 Esther Snow helped produce and direct *Tulip Tales*, a play for Tulip Time, whereas Hope's marching band performed in the parade, as it continued to do in the years following.[48] Several times in the 1940s, the Chapel Choir and the Hope Glee Clubs participated in Tulip Time.[49] In 1951 Tulip Time enlisted Hope College to cosponsor a performance of Haydn's oratorio *The Creation*. The event included the college's Oratorio Chorus and Orchestra, Hope junior Dorothy Ten Brink, alumnus Paul Kranendonk '50, and several faculty members, including Robert Cavanaugh and Harvey Davis, who served as director.[50]

In the decade of the 1950s, Anthony Kooiker regularly presented Tulip Time concerts.[51] His colleague Roger Davis initiated the Tulip Time organ recital series in 1971, using the occasion of the dedication

---

[45] Press release, 11 May 1965, events—Tulip Time and municipal programs 1936-95 folder.
[46] *Anchor*, 7 Oct. 1982.
[47] Program, scrapbook 1929-36, box 2, Curtis Snow Papers.
[48] *Milestone* (1939), 105, and (1941), 83; *Anchor*, 19 May 1948, and 7 May 1949; Swierenga, *Holland, Michigan*, 3:2013.
[49] *Milestone* (1941), 80, 85; *Anchor*, 19 May 1948, 7 May 1949.
[50] Scrapbook 1943-52, box 6, Hinkamp Papers.
[51] *Anchor*, 14 May 1953; *Holland Evening Sentinel*, 11 May 1964.

> HOPE
> HOSTS
> HOLLAND
>
> The students of Hope College take pleasure in welcoming you, the citizens of its mother community, to a campus open house, projected as a tribute to each of you, designed to acquaint you with ourselves and with our College, intended to strengthen the ties of friendship and goodwill which befit our common traditions.

"Hope Hosts Holland" program

of the Dutch Pels and Van Leeuwen organ in the balcony of Dimnent Chapel. In 1974 Davis estimated that around two thousand people attended the recitals during that year's festival.[52] Davis managed the recitals until 1988, and to this day, Hope faculty, students, alumni, and professionals provide twenty-minute organ programs for Tulip Time.[53]

The Chapel Choir was one of the ensembles represented at the annual home concert, which in the past ended the Tulip Time festival.[54] Other Hope ensembles in the celebration included the Women's Glee Club and the Hope College Symphony Orchestra, which in 1963 presented Liszt's *Second Concerto*, with Anthony Kooiker as pianist.[55]

All-College Reviews in 1939 and 1940 introduced hundreds of high school students to Hope through music provided by the college band, a women's instrumental trio, the Men's and Women's Glee Clubs, and the Chapel Choir.[56] A decade later, intending to further strengthen the ties of friendship and goodwill, Hope hosted Holland in an evening

---

[52] *Hope College Alumni Magazine* 27 (Summer 1974): 34.
[53] Tulip Time organ recital brochures, events—Tulip Time and municipal programs 1936-95 folder.
[54] *Anchor*, 16 May 1958; press release, 11 May 1965, events—Tulip Time and municipal programs 1936-95 folder.
[55] "Tulip Time in Holland, Michigan," brochure, 1963, events—Tulip Time and municipal programs 1936-95 folder.
[56] *Anchor*, 24 May 1939; programs, scrapbook 1938-41, box 5, Hinkamp Papers.

open house just after the 1951 Tulip Time festival. The event was designed to acquaint the community with the college and featured several numbers by the Music Department.[57]

In addition to individuals from Hope performing at community events, the college regularly offered musical occasions for the community, Christmas Vespers representing the most successful example. Over the course of the last century, there have been numerous such events. Seeing an opportunity to expand music's audience beyond the campus and into the community, John Nykerk founded, and for two decades organized, the Lyceum Course, an annual series of musical events and lectures held in Winants Chapel and Carnegie Hall. This was later called the College Lecture Course and later still the Hope College Concert Series and represented a prequel to the community's Cooperative Concert Association and the college's Great Performance Series.[58] Proceeds from Nykerk's Lyceum Course generated funds for purchasing musical instruments, including a Steinway piano for the chapel and books for the library.[59]

Nykerk recruited significant acts, including a Bavarian orchestra and singers in 1915, a piano trio in 1916, a Dutch violinist and singers from Chicago in 1918 and 1923, violinist Harry Frabman and the Royal Hungarian Orchestra in 1928, and the Welsh Imperial Singers in 1931. Songs for the 1931 event included *March of the Men of Harlech* and a dozen others, a local newspaper commenting that the fourteen-member group "fulfilled every promise of excellency that preceded their coming."[60]

Beginning in the early twentieth century, Holland was not the only West Michigan community to benefit from Hope College–sponsored events. In 1917 the Glee Club gave concerts in Grand Haven as well as Holland.[61] Six years later, the B Natural Chorus toured nearby towns with Hope president Edward Dimnent, while the college orchestra arranged performances in Grand Haven, Muskegon, and Grand Rapids; these were an early form of the ensemble tours discussed in chapter 3.[62] "Busy Year for Hope Songsters," declared an *Anchor*

---

[57] "Hope Hosts Holland," program, scrapbook 1943-52, box 6, Hinkamp Papers.
[58] *Anchor*, 2 Oct. 1940, 28 May 1953; programs, scrapbook 1941-43, box 6, Hinkamp Papers.
[59] Wichers, *Century of Hope*, 167.
[60] *Holland City News*, 19 Feb. 1931. Mildred Schuppert noted in her diary that she attended the concert, adding "!!!": diary entry 13 Feb. 1931, HC diaries 1929-34, box 1, Schuppert Papers.
[61] *Anchor*, 3 Oct. 1917.
[62] Ibid., 14 Feb. 1923; *Milestone* (1923), 99-100.

Brown Bag Concert, 2016

headline in 1924. The accompanying article reported that the Girl's Glee Club had performed some eight concerts in the Holland area, as well as a Thanksgiving trip to Kalamazoo and Detroit.[63] Although the Men's Glee Club also performed off campus, for example, in Zeeland, in 1949, on occasion, the two Glee Clubs performed together, as they did in 1931 in Grand Rapids.[64] The Chapel Choir regularly sang at area choral festivals, including December 1935 in Kalamazoo, December 1944 and February 1954 in Grand Rapids, and in 1993 in Holland at the March Festival. In February 1954, the Symphonette presented concerts around West Michigan. Another community-centered event, the Brown Bag Concert Series, was founded in 2008 by Hope College piano professor Andrew Le. Based on the premise that classical music should be universally accessible, the series requires performers to dress casually and encourages audience members of all ages to "come and go as they please, and ... bring a brown bag lunch and make as much or as little noise as they wish."[65]

Much of Hope College's interaction with the community has been initiated by impassioned Music faculty who, instead of operating solely within collegiate confines, have routinely given their time and talent to local communities. This chapter would be incomplete without discussing the impact individual faculty members have had on their

[63] *Anchor*, 3 Dec. 1924.
[64] Ibid., 27 May 1931, and 21 Apr. 1949.
[65] https://hope.edu/academics/music/special-programs-opportunities/index.html.

neighbors. Over the years, Hope music faculty have been instrumental in generating the people, resources, and talent necessary to bring more music to West Michigan. They have produced and performed in concerts, created ensembles, served on their boards, played in local churches, and mentored other teachers.

In addition to creating the Lyceum series and directing a large chorus for the city's semicentennial in 1897, John Nykerk in 1905 led the Hope College Choral Union in a production of Holland's first-ever oratorio, Mendelssohn's *Elijah*. Prominent soloists from West Michigan also aided the student chorus in the production. Following the performance, the *Anchor* claimed, "It was the greatest thing ever attempted by the Union and also its greatest achievement," while a local newspaper termed it "the most daring and ambitious undertaking in the musical history of Holland."[66]

Curtis Snow provides yet another early model. He served Hope Church as organist and youth choir director. In October 1929, Snow launched Vespers, a series of bimonthly Sunday afternoon performances and organized occasional events such as a performance of Haydn's *Creation* in spring 1934 for a town as well as a gown audience.[67]

Snow's most significant contribution to the community, however, was the founding of the Holland Civic Chorus and particularly its production of Handel's *Messiah*, perhaps the most important musical event staged in the pre-World War II era and first performed by Hope College's Choral Union on the eve of the 1910 Commencement. Francis Campbell, who taught voice at Hope from 1907 to 1924, and also sang in the quartet, directed the performance. Other featured vocalists included Mr. and Mrs. W. J. Fenton and Elizabeth Wickstrom.[68] The oratorio was performed several times before the Choral Union disbanded in 1915. Then in 1929, a group of Holland-area teachers, members of the Teachers Choral Club, invited Curtis Snow to direct them in performing Handel's *Messiah* that December.[69] Sponsored by the Holland Musicians Club, the group assumed the name Holland Civic Chorus and became Holland's first community chorale.[70] The sixty-voice chorus presented the Christmas section of Handel's *Messiah*, including the *Hallelujah Chorus*, in Dimnent Chapel on December 18,

---

[66] *Anchor*, 1 Apr. and 1 July 1905; *Holland City News*, 9 June 1905; *Milestone* (1905), 151.
[67] Program, scrapbook 1928-32, box 4, Hinkamp Papers.
[68] Program, vocal ensembles—College Chorus folder, box 2, MD Papers.
[69] Holland Civic Chorus record book, 1930-38 folder, box 1, Curtis Snow Papers.
[70] Swierenga, *Holland, Michigan*, 3:2054; *Holland City News*, 12 Dec. 1929.

"THE MESSIAH"

AN ORATORIO BY GEORGE FREDERICK HANDEL

—Presented By—

Holland Civic Chorus

MR. W. CURTIS SNOW, Conductor

Hope College Memorial Chapel
Monday Evening, December 14, 8:00 p. m.

ACCOMPANIED BY

MISS SARAH LACEY	at the Piano
MRS. W. CURTIS SNOW	at the Organ

SOLOISTS

MRS. J. VAN DONGEN	Soprano
MRS. H. DOTTERWEICH	Contralto
MR. HARRY FRIESEMA	Tenor
MR. LYNN CLARK	Basso

(This epoch-making composition was improvised in twenty-four days and first presented in Dublin, April 13, 1742, for the benefit of the Society for Relieving Prisoners, the Charitable Infirmary, and the Mercer's Hospital. The following year it was performed under the composer's direction in London. The audience was deeply affected, and at the "Hallelujah Chorus" the King rose to his feet, his court following his example, and this evidence of devotion and respect has remained the rule at all subsequent performances.)

Messiah program, 1931

1929, the end of Snow's first semester at the college.[71] Following a successful first performance, the chorus extended an invitation to Hope students, and by October 1931, the group boasted 140 members.[72] From this beginning, the *Messiah* performance became a yearly event, a Christmas tradition, and a midwinter cultural anchor comparable to Christmas Vespers today. Snow also united gown and town groups for other occasions, for example, a concert in Dimnent Chapel in May 1933 that combined the Holland Civic Chorus, directed by Snow, and the Holland Civic Orchestra.[73]

In 1934 the Civic Chorus and the Chapel Choir, another of Snow's creations, combined to form the board of directors of the Choral Union of Holland. Three chorus members joined with an equal number of representatives from Hope and Holland, along with Snow and student Kathleen Donahue, president of the Chapel Choir.[74] The combining of the two organizations was said to be a longtime dream of Snow, who "worked unceasingly to bring the highest type of performance to the public."[75]

As was true for her husband, Esther Snow was also deeply involved in the Hope and Holland musical communities. In 1930-31 she served as vice president and as a member of the program committee of the five-year-old Holland Musicians Club, which promoted the "musical interests of the community." She drew many impressive performers to Holland, helping to quench the thirst of Hollanders for quality music.[76] Snow served as director of music at Hope Reformed Church for a quarter century and as organist for the *Messiah* productions and regularly performed in Vespers programs, beginning with the first Christmas Vespers in 1941. The previous spring, she had composed and directed the music for the 1941 Pageant of Hope, performed four times at the Ottawa County Fairgrounds.[77] The pageant, *The Pilgrim—A Pageant in Eight Episodes*, was written by Hope president, Edward Dimnent.[78] Included in the performance was a children's choir and the Hope Men's

---

[71] *Holland City News*, 12 Dec. 1929.
[72] Holland Civic Chorus record book, 13 Oct. 1930.
[73] Program, scrapbook 1932-35, box 4, Hinkamp Papers.
[74] Holland Civic Chorus record book, 7 Oct. 1935.
[75] Ibid.; faculty minutes, 7 and 15 June 1935, Faculty of Hope College Papers.
[76] Snow spoke at the 25 Feb. 1931 meeting of the club on the topic, "Church Music": HC diaries 1929-34, box 1, Schuppert Papers.
[77] G. Keith Gingles to Gordon Van Wylen, 14 Feb. 1983, 1941—*The Pilgrim: A Pageant in Eight Episodes* folder, box 2, Anniversaries of Hope College. See also ch. 5.
[78] Flyer, scrapbook 1941-43, box 6, Hinkamp Papers.

Glee Club, with musical leads by professor Robert Cavanaugh and student Gertrude Bolema '44.[79]

Cavanaugh joined the music faculty the year prior to the 1941 pageant. Over a career that would span nearly four decades, the contributions he made to further the involvement of Hope's Music Department with the local community were arguably as important as his internal role at the college. During Cavanaugh's first fall at Hope, he began training a two-hundred-member chorus to perform Handel's *Messiah*. Cavanaugh directed the 1940 presentation of the *Messiah*, the first to be under the auspices of Hope College. The Holland Civic Chorus could no longer occupy Dimnent Chapel together with the Chapel Choir; the Civic Chorus subsequently passed out of existence. Despite this, the *Messiah* performance was still far from an all-Hope event. In 1946, in spite of terrible weather, Holland music lovers turned out in droves to hear Cavanaugh's three-hundred-voice chorus, one of the largest in *Messiah* history, which included Hope College's Chapel Choir, Hope alumna Trixie Moore's Holland High School a cappella choir, and approximately sixty-five local singers.[80] Esther Snow performed the organ throughout, and Hope junior Alma Vander Hill '48 accompanied on the piano.[81] As was tradition by then, professional soloists were also recruited to further enhance the production. That year, Nancy Carr, a soprano from Chicago; Helene Hekman, a contralto originally from Grand Rapids; Ralph Lear, a tenor from New York City; and David Austin, a bass from Chicago, performed at the event.[82]

The community-focused careers of Nykerk, the Snows, and Cavanaugh served as templates for their successors. Jantina Holleman coordinated Christmas Vespers and led the effort to publicize the event.[83] She was professionally active throughout West Michigan, working with the Holland Piano Forum to mentor piano teachers, conducting workshops for teachers, and directing not one but three church choirs.[84] In the early 1960s, Morrette Rider hosted two series of fifteen programs each on Grand Rapids' WOOD-TV: *The Symphony Orchestra* and *Music Since 1900*.[85] Roger Rietberg served Third Reformed

[79] *Milestone* (1942), 109.
[80] *Holland City News*, 19 Dec. 1946.
[81] Ibid.
[82] Ibid.
[83] Ritsema to Holleman, 23 Aug. 1972, correspondence 1968-92 folder, Holleman Papers; *Hope College Magazine* 31 (Spring 1978): 9.
[84] *Hope College Magazine* 31 (Spring 1978): 10.
[85] *Anchor*, 22 Sept. 1961, 18 Sept. 1964; *Holland Evening Sentinel*, 12 Oct. 1961; *Alumni Magazine*, Oct. 1964; Outline of Program Content for Music since 1900,

Finding Its Tune 175

Faculty Trio

Church as organist and choir director, and he directed the Western Theological Seminary men's choir.

With cellist Robert Ritsema and violinist Harrison Ryker (on the faculty 1968-73), Anthony Kooiker formed the Faculty Trio, which in 1971-72 performed in Holland and Grand Rapids on six occasions. Ritsema was the long-time orchestra director at Christmas Vespers. He played cello for the Kalamazoo Symphony Orchestra and was a member of the Early Music Ensemble of West Michigan, performing on medieval and Renaissance instruments.[86] For two decades, Ritsema conducted the Kalamazoo Junior Symphony and worked with the Blue Lake Fine Arts Camp, whereas Russell Floyd (on the faculty 1985-99) served as director of the West Shore Youth Symphony, Joan Conway served as artistic director of Saugatuck's Chamber Music Festival, and Charles Aschbrenner served as pianist for the Grand Rapids Ballet.[87]

Each of these cases points to the benefit to both the college and the community of cultural appreciation. Besides talent, the college

correspondence 1953-68 folder, Rider Papers; Rider, "Television for Education," *MSBOA Journal* 23 (Nov. 1962): 18-24.
[86] *Grand Rapids Press*, 1 Feb. 1996; biographical folder, Ritsema Papers.
[87] *Holland Sentinel*, 29 Oct. 2000; see also Baer and Utting interview with Ritsema.

often provided community ensembles with needed rehearsal and performance space. When Kenyon Hall, Holland's first opera house, located on the southwest corner of River Avenue at Eighth Street burned down in 1877, the city was left without a suitable indoor music venue. That is until 1879, when Hope's administration stepped in and allowed Dallas Gee's band to play a concert in the college chapel, and 1913, when the college hosted the well-known Dutch pianist Paul Van Katwijk in Winants Chapel.[88]

Community orchestral groups were invited to perform in Carnegie Gymnasium, and Dimnent Chapel was made available to the Holland Civic Chorus for *Messiah* rehearsals. Yet space was a precious commodity for Music (see ch. 4). So when outside groups attempted to utilize Music's spaces, their efforts could be passionately rebuked. The Music faculty minutes for October 31, 1950, reveal one such conflict over the use of Dimnent Chapel:

> Complaints of several students were presented. These were in the nature of a protest at being asked to give up their scheduled practice time in the Chapel because of outside groups using the Chapel. They are all most willing to cooperate when the building is used for college functions.... The Music faculty unanimously agreed that this matter should receive careful consideration by the administration.[89]

Even with the occasional tension, it seems that what has been gained is far greater than what has been given up. This is evident in joint ventures such as the Cooperative Concert Association's annual series, held in Dimnent Chapel, and the similar Community Concerts, which in 1971 merged with Hope's Great Performance Series.[90]

The final question is: What has such collaboration meant for both the college and the community? In a letter to a potential donor in 1925, President Dimnent understood the new chapel would exist for the community as well as for the college, "a building for Community Religious Gatherings and Social Service Organizations," as he put it, including "Community Choral Work" and music: "The musical equipment will be such that large choruses capable of rendering

---

[88] Swierenga, *Holland, Michigan*, 3:2060; *Holland City News*, 15 May 1913.
[89] Music faculty minutes, 31 Oct. 1950.
[90] *Anchor*, 2 Oct. 1940; *Milestone* (1945), 55.

standard programs, pageants, and such entertainments may be accommodated."[91]

In a 1999 letter to the *Anchor*, two members of Hope's Class of 2000, Paula Champion and Jessica Loomis, offered their perspective on the department's contributions to the community.

> For a small town, Holland is one of the most culturally rich cities in Michigan. The contributions that the music department makes to our community are vital to the continuation of this unique arts experience. For example, the Collage Concert that was held on October 14 drew crowds that filled the main floor of the chapel—twice in one day. The 55th annual Vespers that will take place in December will, as always, sell out in two hours. People have been calling the music office for months asking when those tickets go on sale. Every week, at least two concerts are performed by music students or are sponsored by the department. Members of the Holland community regularly attend these programs. There are certain people who come to every single event and know us by name. They genuinely care about what we do and who we are.[92]

Years earlier, Alfred Fedak '75, lamented: "And how I long for those days when I could walk across the street and hear a free concert or recital almost every night!"[93] These three perspectives—one from a Hope College president, the second from two students, and the third from an alumnus—point to a partnership, neither formal nor legal but all the more significant because it was organic. The Hope College Community Council sought to strengthen what it perceived to be a weakened partnership by sponsoring an event in 1959, "The Church, the Community, and the College," which brought Stanley Kresge and Norman Vincent Peale as speakers and included performances by Hope's Symphonette and Chapel Choir. The organization proved to be short lived, perhaps because the town-gown relationship did not need a formal organization for it to flourish.[94]

---

[91] "The Purposes Underlying the Building of a Chapel," attachment, President Edward Dimnent to August H. Landwehr, 17 July 1925, correspondence 1920-29 folder, Dimnent Memorial Chapel Papers.

[92] *Anchor*, 27 Oct. 1999.

[93] *The Arts: News from Hope College Arts Division*, Feb. 1978, arts newsletter folder, box 1, MD Papers.

[94] Program, Community Council topical file; cf. Swierenga, *Holland, Michigan*, 3: ch. 30, esp. 2086.

The last word in this regard goes to Robert Ritsema, who stated in the context of the support by the local community for music at Hope: "I really always did enjoy my performances here on campus." When asked by an interviewer in 2000 whether music had provided an opportunity for cooperation between Holland and Hope, Ritsema replied, "Well, it has, and we are so blessed. People who come here are always so amazed at the crowds we draw for our concerts. And this faithful group that attends here. It's the real rapport built up, I think, with the people of the community."[95]

---

[95] Baer and Utting interview with Ritsema and LaBarge interview with Ritsema.

CONCLUSION

> The man that hath no music in himself,
> Nor is not moved with concord of sweet sounds,
> Is fit for treasons, stratagems, and spoils....
> Let no such man be trusted.
> William Shakespeare, *The Merchant of Venice*, 1599

> As a nation we are beginning to place greater emphasis
> upon the study of music in our schools and colleges,
> for the comprehension and appreciation of aesthetics
> is a distinct spiritual asset, which must be made a
> lawful heritage of every American.
> *Hope College Bulletin*, 1919

The October 2013 *News from Hope College* included a two-page article, "On the Shoulders of Giants," which detailed plans for the Jack H. Miller Center for Musical Arts, anticipated to become the home of the Department of Music in fall 2015. In honoring faculty from Robert Cavanaugh through Charles Aschbrenner, and by providing for the first time in Hope's history a permanent home with spectacular performance venues, the Miller Center represents a powerful statement to campus and community about the place of music at Hope from the days of John Nykerk, Curtis Snow, Ethel Leestma and Millie Schuppert to the present.

Readers bring their own personal worldviews to books, worldviews that define how we make sense of life. There are two views one may take in reading *Making Music*, and both are based on how we are to understand the sacred and the secular at Hope College, from its earliest days to the present. For example, is Dimnent Chapel a sacred space whose rules are defined spiritually and applied to every event that occurs within its walls? Was the Commencement music for a Christian college, when the occasion took place in First Church, appropriate when an older hymn was sung but inappropriate when modern secular music was played? When the Chapel Choir toured, should it have confined its repertoire to sacred music? These and related topics have found their way to the leadership of Hope College and the Music Department.

One view is that the secular is destined to devour the sacred because they are at war, and the secular is, as the saying goes, "on the right side of history." Thus, evidence of secular music as Hope moved from its mid-nineteenth-century origins to the early twenty-first century may reflect—or perhaps even helped cause—the college's shift away from its Christian heritage.[1] The inevitable triumph of secularization is, however, an old-fashioned theory, born in the 1960s, but since then, debunked by historians.[2] And in the Hope College context, such an approach does not seem to align with the preponderance of evidence to the contrary as presented in this volume, for instance, concert programs listing sacred and secular music side by side and even the words of Robert Cavanaugh's *Alma Mater Hymn*.

The other view is that the categories—sacred and secular—overlap. Indeed, if we think about our own lives, they too are often symbiotic, for instance, the overlap of a choral recital and a basketball game in Carnegie Gymnasium on the same day. This approach does seem to align with the weight of the evidence from the college's history. This was evident early on in a touching communication from the Class of 1896, thanking the faculty not only for promoting their intellectual

---

[1] There are hints of such thinking in James Kennedy and Caroline Simon, *Can Hope Endure: A Historical Case Study in Christian Higher Education* (Grand Rapids: Eerdmans, 2005).

[2] Recently, Michael Saler, "Modernity and Disenchantment: A Historiographic Review," *American Historical Review* 111 (June 2006): 692-716.

development but also "for our progress toward a higher and fully developed moral manhood in affording us advice, teaching and worthy example."[3] It was also evident—as documented in a mid-twentieth-century *Milestone*—in what the arts at Hope College aimed to teach: "IN ART AND MUSIC: Of the holiness of beauty but also of the beauty of holiness."[4]

What then is the purpose of music at Hope College? The answer, from early in the history of the college, has been to produce the best performance possible with the best music from across all genres. Thomas Folkert pointed this out when he remembered Roger Rietberg as a professor who embodied this spirit, but Rietberg is only one of many who have made this point throughout the decades.[5] And then, on the other hand, alumni, students, and faculty have also recognized that this can happen through the One who holds all things together.

There are, in closing, these prescient words from Dorothy Sayers, the early twentieth-century British novelist, essayist, poet, and lay theologian. When asked what work was Christian, she replied, with her usual aplomb, "The only Christian work is good work, well done."[6] To a large degree, that characterizes Music, from before there was a department with that name to the most recent student recital—being the best for the best.

---

[3] Faculty minutes, 1 May 1896, minutes of the collegiate faculty.
[4] *Milestone* (1950), 2; see also "Sacred Music" (n.d.), manuscripts folder, box 1, Cavanaugh Papers, and Anthony Kooiker, "Some Thoughts on the Contemporary Musical Scene," *Opus* (1957), 1-5.
[5] Thomas Folkert to Marc Baer, email, 21 Aug. 2018, Making Music folder; cf. Harper, "Music in Liberal Arts," 271.
[6] Dorothy Sayers, *Creed or Chaos?* (Manchester, NH: Sophia Institute, 1996), 108.

APPENDIX

Hope College Music Faculty, 1866-2016[1]

Jacob E. Nyenhuis and Marc Baer

Part-time teachers, accompanists, and instructors, 1866-1929

1862
Gilmore, **William**, 1862-69: tutor in music.

1878
Kommers, **Tinis J.**, 1878-82: teacher of vocal music, 1878-79, 1881-82.

1881
Van Hees, **John George**, **Jr.**, 1881-82: in charge of vocal music.

1881
Kleinheksel, **John H.**, **Jr.**, 1881-82: in charge of vocal music; professor of Greek, English, and Algebra.

---

[1] This list of faculty was constructed from appendix 3 of Jacob E. Nyenhuis *et alii*, *Hope College at 150: Anchored in Faith, Educating for Leadership and Service in a Global Society*, 2 vols. (Holland, MI: Van Raalte Press, 2019), 2:911-1042. Published with permission. In creating this list, the authors relied on college catalogs, *Milestones*, the *Anchor*, and music department records deposited in the Hope College Collection in the Joint Archives of Holland.

1882
Gilmore, John, 1882-83: in charge of vocal music.

1883
Peeke, Harmon V. S., 1883-84: in charge of vocal music.

1884
Shepard, G. C., 1884-85: instructor in vocal music and voice.

1885
Nykerk, John B., 1885-1936: (**Holland Academy**) instructor in vocal music, 1885-90; professor of music, 1891-95; assistant professor of English, 1891-95; English and music, 1903-4; director of the Choral Union, 1904-9; (**Hope College**) professor of music, 1893-95; assistant professor of English, 1893-95; professor of the English language and literature, 1895-1905, 1916-36; in charge of vocal music, 1895-96, 1897-1904; in charge of vocal music, and geology, 1896-97; professor of the English language and literature and elocution, 1905-11; on leave in England at Oxford University, 1906-7; professor of the English language and literature and public speaking, 1911-16; public speaking, 1925-29; public speaking and forensics, 1929-31; professor of English literature, 1928-31; speech and forensics, 1931-36; secretary, 1909-36; secretary of the music department, 1909-36; dean, 1922-23; dean of men, 1923-31.

1894
Heeren, J. J., 1894-96: instructor in theory and sight-singing.

1903
Bistline, Josef, 1903-5: violin and viola.
Post, Henry C., 1903-13: instructor in piano, 1903-4, 1909-10; piano, harmony, and composition, 1904-9; on leave, 1911-13.
Van Hasselt, Herman, 1903-4: violin.

1904
Kolyn, Andrew Judson, 1904-6: rudiments and sight singing.
Pease, Clarence E., 1904-7: voice.
Raiguel, Dorothy, 1904-7: accompanist.
Yates, Amy (*also* **Kremers, Amy Yates**), 1904-9: piano.

1905
Conlon, Katherine (*also* **Johnson, Katherine Conlon**), 1905-13: violin and viola.

Appendix: Hope College Music Faculty, 1866–2016   185

1907
Campbell, Francis, 1907-24: voice, 1907-13; director of oratorio, 1922-24.

1909
Bennett, C. Bess, 1909-13: harmony and composition, 1909-11; harmony, 1911-13.
Schuelke, Ann S., 1909-11: accompanist.

1911
Heusinkveld, Arthur H., 1911-19: instructor in sight singing, 1911-12; accompanist, 1911-12; instructor in English and German, 1915-16; assistant professor of English, 1916-19; accompanist and assistant secretary, 1915-19.
Lamale, William P., 1911-12: pipe organ, theory, and composition.
Wing, Hazel, 1911-14: piano.

1912
Hartley, Walter, 1912-16: pipe organ, theory, and composition. *not the one when I was at Hope*
Meyer, Harris, 1912-16: accompanist.

1913
Browning, Grace M., 1913-16: voice.
Coleman, Clara, 1913-17: violin.

1914
Cress, Oscar, 1914-29: instructor in piano, 1914-16; in piano and harmony, 1916-27; in piano, 1927-29.
Wilkins, W. W., 1914-16: instructor in orchestral instruments.

1915
Deacon, Stanley, 1915-18: instructor in voice.

1917
Meinecke, Bruno, 1917-22: professor of Latin, 1917-18; Rodman Professor of the Latin Language and Literature, 1918-20, 1921-22; on leave, 1920-21; violin, 1917-22.

1918
Andersch, Arthur, 1918: instructor in piano.
Andersch, Carl, 1918: instructor in voice.
Fenton, Grace Dudley, 1918-40: instructor in voice and singing, 1918-24; in voice culture and singing and directress (director) of men's and women's glee clubs, 1924-34; instructor in voice and diction; glee clubs, 1934-40.

Marble, Mabel, 1918-19: part-time instructor in piano.
Robbins, Martha C., 1918-32: accompanist in Voice Department, 1918-22; accompanist, 1929-32.

1919
Hamelink, Susanna, 1919-22: accompanist.
Tower, Harold, 1919-22: instructor in pipe organ and harmony, director of glee clubs.
Vander Werp, Jeannette, 1919-24: accompanist, 1919-20; instructor in Latin, 1923-24.

1920
Weid, Perry P., 1920-21: special instructor in violin.

1921
Metz, Ethelyn, 1921-22: instructor in interpretation.

1922
Kots, George, 1922-23: chapel accompanist.
Pellegrom, Ruth, 1922-23: accompanist in Voice Department.
Tuller, Sherman, 1922-23: special instructor in violin and director of orchestra.
Warnshuis, Henrietta, 1922-23: accompanist in Voice Department.

1923
Barkema, Martha, 1923-29: instructor in singing, 1923-29; in French and music, 1927-29.
Kingsbury, Ronald, 1923-24: special instructor in violin and director of orchestra, assistant.
Le Mere, George, 1923-27: special instructor in cello.
Meyer, Nella, 1923-65: instructor in French, 1923-25, 1929-37; instructor in piano, 1929-37; on leave, 1937-40; instructor in French and piano, 1945-46; associate professor of French, 1946-55; professor of French, 1955-65; professor emerita, 1965.
Michaelson, Anna, 1923-31: part-time instructor in voice and singing, 1923-24; in voice, 1924-27; in voice culture and singing, 1929-31.
Wecker, Karl, 1923-24: part-time instructor in violin.

1924
Dok, George, 1924-27: special instructor in pipe organ.
Fairbanks, Harvey, 1924-26: special instructor in violin and director of orchestra, 1924-25; in violin, 1925-26.

1925

De Pree, **Mrs. Edward**, 1925-29: pianist, 1925-26; accompanist, 1926-29.

Dunham, **Rowland W.**, 1925-26: harmony, composition, and musical appreciation, 1925-26.

Kollen, **John Lloyd**, 1925-27: director of college orchestra, 1925-27; special instructor in musical history and appreciation, 1926-27; accompanist, 1926-27.

1926

Johnson, **Herman C.**, 1926-27: conductor of college band.

Lokker, **Hazel**, 1926-27: accompanist.

Ritter, **Walter**, 1926-29: special instructor in violin, 1926-29; director of orchestra, 1927-29.

Webb, **Christine Augusta**, 1926-29: special instructor in public school music, 1926-29; accompanist, 1926-29.

1927

Dunwoody, **Beulah Harper**, 1927-29: special instructor in voice culture and singing.

Handelink, **Margaret**, 1927-30: instructor in brass.

Loomis, **Mrs. W. H.**, 1927-28: special instructor in theory, history, and appreciation of music.

Nienhuis, **Hazel D.**, 1927-28: accompanist.

1928

Karsten, **Helene Prisman** (**Mrs. Harold J.**), 1928-63: instructor in theory, history, and appreciation of music, 1928-30; in piano, 1929-34, 1940-45, 1952-63; in piano, composition, and methods and children's classes in piano, 1934-40; part-time instructor in piano, 1946-52. *She was at Hope when I was there*

1929

Boughter, **Esther**, 1929-30: special instructor in public school music.

Full-time faculty, 1929-2016

1929

Snow, **W. Curtis**, 1929-35: instructor in organ and theory and in piano, 1929-31; in theory, history, and appreciation of music and in pipe organ, theory, and harmony, 1929-30; in pipe organ, theory, history,

188 MAKING MUSIC

and appreciation of music and director of chapel choir, 1930-34; professor of organ and piano, 1931-35.

1934
Beach, Evelyn M., 1934-37: instructor in piano, trumpet, and theory.
Lacey, Sarah E., 1934-36: instructor in piano, history of music, and theory.

1936
Osborne, Kenneth, 1936-40: instructor in organ and piano, 1936-40; director of Music Department, 1936-40.

1937
Snow, Esther MacFarlane (Mrs. W. Curtis Snow), 1937-65: instructor in piano and theory, 1937-40; instructor in piano, organ, and theory of music, 1940-45; instructor in music theory and pipe organ, 1945-46; assistant professor of music theory and pipe organ, 1946-47; assistant professor of organ and piano, 1947-54; assistant professor of German, 1954-65; assistant in Vienna Summer School, 1956-63; assistant professor emerita, 1965.

[handwritten: my German Professor]

1940
Cavanaugh, Robert William, 1940-76: instructor in voice and theory of music, 1940-45; on leave, 1943-44; associate professor of music theory and voice, 1945-53; on leave, 1949-50; head of department of music, 1950-59, 1961-62; professor of music theory and voice, 1953-59, 1961-62, 1963-67; professor of music, 1959-61, 1962-63, 1967-76; chairman of the department of music, 1963-69.
Mearns, James, 1940-42: instructor in English and in public school music theory and piano.
Vogan, Charles, 1940-41: instructor in organ.

1945
Gomez-Loerch, Winifred, 1945-47: instructor in public school music.

1946
Holleman, Jantina Wilhelmina, 1946-87: instructor in music theory and piano, 1946-48; assistant professor of music theory and piano, 1948-60; on leave, 1953-54; associate professor of music, 1960-83, of music theory and piano, 1961-62, 1963-67; professor of music, 1983-87; professor emerita, 1987.

Johnston, Milton Urban, 1946-50: instructor in music theory and piano, 1946-48; assistant professor of music theory and piano, 1948-50.

1947

Baughman, Norma H., 1947-68: instructor in voice, 1947-60; assistant professor of voice, 1960-62; assistant professor emerita, 1962; assistant in music, 1967-68.

[handwritten: my voice instructor]

Paalman, Hazel M., 1947-49: assistant professor of music theory and voice.

Rider, Morrette L., 1947-75: assistant professor of music theory and instruments, 1947-50; on leave, 1950-51; associate professor of music theory and instrument(s), 1951-59, 1961-62, 1963-65; associate professor of music, 1959-60; professor of music theory and instrument, 1965-67; professor of music, 1967-75; dean of academic affairs, 1967-74.

1949

Davis, Harvey Owen, 1949-52: instructor in music theory and voice.

1950

Druckenmiller, William H., 1950-51: instructor in music theory and string instruments.

Kooiker, Anthony, 1950-87: associate professor of music theory and piano, 1950-57; on leave, 1957-59; associate professor of music, 1959-61; on leave, 1961-62; professor of music, 1962-63, 1965-66, 1967-87; professor of music theory and piano, 1963-64; on leave, 1964-65, 1966-67; chairman/chairperson of the department, 1973-77; professor emeritus, 1987.

1954

Rietberg, Roger J., 1954-90: instructor in music theory and organ, 1954-58; assistant professor of music theory and organ, 1958-59; assistant professor of music, 1959-68; associate director of admissions, 1964; director of admissions, 1964-68; associate professor of music, 1968-78; professor of music, 1978-90; professor emeritus, 1990.

1957

Hartly, Walter, 1957-58: instructor in music.

1959

Schaberg, Albert Roy, 1959-62: instructor in music.

1962
Cecil, Robert M., 1962-85: assistant professor of music, 1962-66; associate professor of music, 1966-78; on leave, 1971-72; professor of music, 1978-85; on leave, 1978-79; professor emeritus, 1985.

Morrison, Joyce M., 1962-97: instructor in music, 1962-67; assistant professor of music, 1967-76; associate professor of music, 1976-97; on leave, spring semester 1983; associate professor emerita, 1997.

1963
Aschbrenner, Charles C., 1963-2008: instructor in music, 1963-67; assistant professor of music, 1967-72; on leave, spring semester 1971; associate professor of music, 1972-83; on leave, 1977-78; professor of music, 1983-2008; professor emeritus, 2008.

Davis, Roger E., 1963-90: instructor in music, 1963-67; assistant professor of music, 1967-73; associate professor of music, 1973-85; on leave, fall semester 1982; professor of music, 1985-90.

1964
Tallis, James H., 1964-68: assistant professor of music.

1966
Mathis, William S., 1966-67: dean of academic affairs and professor of music.

1967
Ritsema, Robert A., 1967-99: assistant professor of music, 1967-69; associate professor of music, 1969-75; chairman/chairperson of the department, 1969-73, 1988-94; on leave, 1973-74; professor of music, 1975-99; acting chairperson of the department, spring semester 1997; professor emeritus, 1999.

Thompson, Robert, 1967-68: instructor in music.

1968
Jennings, Norman L., 1968-70: assistant professor of music.

Ryker, Harrison, 1968-73: assistant professor of music.

1969
Conway, Joan C., 1969-2001: assistant professor of music, 1969-77; associate professor of music, 1977-86; professor of music, 1986-2001; professor emerita, 2001.

1970
Lehman, Carroll, 1970-75: assistant professor of music, 1970-75; on leave, spring semester 1975.

1972
Greenberg, Phillip B., 1972-75: assistant professor of music.

1975
Berman, Deborah, 1975-76: visiting instructor in music.
Moore, Terry L., 1975-82: assistant professor of music.
Sharp, Stuart W., 1975-2005: associate professor of music, 1975-85; on leave, fall semester 1982; chairman/chairperson of the department, 1977-88, 2002-5; professor of music, 1985-2005; professor emeritus, 2005.

1982
Carlson, Richard R., 1982-83: visiting instructor in music.
Natvig, Mary, 1982-84: visiting assistant professor of music.
Votta, Michael, Jr., 1982-84: assistant professor of music.

1984
Gray, Charles K., 1984-86: assistant professor of music.

1985
Floyd, Samuel Russell, III, 1985-99: assistant professor of music, 1985-90; associate professor of music, 1990-99.

1986
Gilbert, John H., 1986-91: assistant professor of music.
Thompson, Robert F., 1986-93: assistant professor of music.

1987
Frederickson, Karen B., 1987-91: associate professor of music.

1988
Strouf, Linda Kay, 1988-present: part time, music and interdisciplinary studies (IDS), 1988-93; adjunct assistant professor of music and IDS, 1993-present; divisional recruitment coordinator in the fine arts, 1991-2007.

1989
Leenhouts, Margaret, 1989-92: visiting instructor in music.

1990

Ferguson, J. Scott, 1990-94: assistant professor of music, 1990-93; associate professor of music, 1993-94.

Lewis, Huw R., 1990-present: associate professor of music, 1990-99; chairperson of the department, 1994-97; professor of music, 1999-present; on sabbatical leave, spring semester 2004.

1991

Stalf, Denise H., 1991-92: visiting professor of music.

1992

Ball, Wesley A., 1992-2002: associate professor of music, 1992-2002; chairperson of the department, 1997-2002.

Craioveanu, Mihai D., 1992-present: associate professor of music, 1992-2001; professor of music, 2001-present; on sabbatical leave, spring semesters 2007 and 2014.

1993

Coyle, Brian R., 1993-2019: assistant professor of music, 1993-99; associate professor of music, 1999-2007; professor of music, 2007-2019; on sabbatical leave, spring semesters 2008 and 2015; chairperson of the department, 2008-11; director of jazz studies, 2008-2018.

1994

Morrow, James, 1994-97: assistant professor of music and director of choral activities.

1997

Dykstra, Linda L., 1997-2017: assistant professor of music, 1998-2005; associate professor of music, 2005-17; associate professor emerita.

Jermihov, Peter, 1997-98: visiting associate professor and director of choral activities.

Kennedy-Dygas, Margaret A., 1997-2009: professor of music, 1997-2009; chairperson of the department, 2005-8.

1998

Richmond, Brad W., 1998-2019: associate professor of music, 1998-2008; on sabbatical leave, spring semester 2006; director of choral activities, 1998-2018; professor of music, 2008-19; on sabbatical leave, spring semester 2014.

Sanborn, Timothy, 1998-2002: visiting assistant professor of music, 1998-99; part-time lecturer in music, 1999-2002.

Wolfe, Jennifer, 1998-2018: part-time lecturer in music, 2002-4; adjunct assistant professor of music, 2004-11; leave of absence, spring semester 2006; assistant professor of music, 2012-18; on sabbatical leave, spring semester 2014.

1999
Piippo, Richard G., 1999-2014: associate professor of music, 1999-2014; on sabbatical leave, spring 2008; associate professor emeritus, 2014.

Ward, Steven D., 1999-2006: assistant professor of music.

2000
Savaglio, Paula C., 2000-2002: visiting assistant professor of music.

2001
Claar, Elizabeth O. (*also* **West, Elizabeth O.**), 2001-present: part-time lecturer in music (staff accompanist), 2001-6, and fall 2010; assistant professor of music, 2011-14; part-time lecturer, 2014-present.

Han, Mansoon (Kim), 2001-4: assistant professor of music.

2002
Hodson, Robert, 2002-2019: assistant professor of music, 2002-6; associate professor of music, 2006-12; on sabbatical leave, fall semester 2008; professor of music, 2012-19; chairperson of the department, 2011-14.

Kolean, Lora L., 2002-present: part-time lecturer in music, 2002-12; adjunct assistant professor of music, 2013-present.

2004
Martin, Blair L., 2004-7: assistant professor of music.

Park, Soyeon, 2004-5: visiting instructor in music.

2005
Le, Andrew, 2005-19: assistant professor of music, 2005-11; associate professor of music, 2011-19; on sabbatical leave, spring semester 2012.

Leach, Jimmy, 2005-17: part-time lecturer in music, 2005-6; visiting assistant professor of music, 2006-7; part-time lecturer in music, 2014-17.

Randel, Julia Phillips, 2005-17: assistant professor of music, 2005-11; associate professor of music, 2011-17; on sabbatical leave, spring semester 2012; chairperson of the department, 2014-17.

2007

Hornbach, Christina M., 2007-present: assistant professor of music, 2007-13; director of the music education program, 2007-present; associate professor of music, 2013-17; professor of music, 2017-present.

Southard, Robert G. (Gabe), 2007-present: assistant professor of music, 2007-13; associate professor of music, 2013-present; on sabbatical leave, fall semester 2014.

2008

Clark, Adam L., 2008-15: assistant professor of music.

Schouest, Scott J., 2008-9: visiting assistant professor of music.

2010

Kim, Jung Woo, 2010-present: assistant professor of music, 2010-16; associate professor of music, 2016-present.

2014

Lestrud, Ingrid, 2014-15: visiting assistant professor of music.

2015

Fashun, Christopher, 2015-present: assistant professor of music.

Part-time faculty: 1929-2016

1931

Van Antwerp, Lucille, 1931-32: instructor in violin, viola, cello, and orchestration and director of college orchestra.

1936

Heeter, Eugene, 1936: director of band.

Zwemer, Daniel, 1936-40: director of band.

1943

Baughman, Stanley, 1943-46: special instructor in voice.

Burrows, Reba, 1943-45: special instructor in public school music and theory.

1944

Quackenbush, Palmer, 1944-46: special instructor in stringed instruments and orchestra, 1944-45; instructor in stringed instruments and director of orchestra, 1945-46.

1946
Cook, Helen M., 1946-47: part-time instructor in music theory and voice.
Kisinger, Everett, 1946: director of bands.

1949
Guild, Maurice Alvin, 1949-50: special instructor in music.

1952
Cutler, Granville, 1952-54: instructor in brass instruments.
Everett, Ransome, Jr., 1952-59: instructor in percussion instruments, 1952-53; part-time instructor, music—percussion instruments, 1958-59.
Hills, Arthur C., 1952-58: instructor in clarinet and bassoon, 1952-55; part-time instructor in music—clarinet and bassoon, 1955-58.
Vanderheuvel, Kenneth, 1952-59: instructor in oboe and saxophone, 1952-55; part-time instructor in oboe and saxophone, 1955-59.

1953
Kelch, Betty Lindberg, 1953-55: special instructor in violin, cello, and music education.

1954
Roth, Raymond, 1954-59: instructor in brass instruments, 1954-55; part-time instructor in music—brass instruments, 1955-59.
Smith, Marjorie H., 1954-56: instructor in cello.

1955
Kleynenberg, Peter A., 1955-65: instructor in cello, faculty quartet, 1955-59; part-time instructor in music, 1959-65.

1958
MacFarland, William, 1958-59: part-time instructor in music—bass instruments.

1959
Langejans, Calvin, 1959-96: part-time instructor in music, 1959-63, 1985-96; assistant in music, 1963-96.
Martin, Leroy, 1959-71: part-time instructor in music, 1959-63; assistant in music, 1963-71.

1960
Robbert, Iris, 1960-64: part-time instructor in music.
Schaberg, Gail, 1960-62: part-time instructor in music.

1961
King, Charles, 1961: part-time instructor in music, 1961.
Rider, Wanda N., 1961-75: part-time instructor in music, 1961-63, 1972-75.

1963
Mitchell, Dwain, 1963-68: part-time instructor in music, 1963-65; assistant in music, 1965-68.

1964
Mitchell, Deana, 1964-68: assistant in music.
Tallis, Joan, 1964-68: part-time instructor in music, 1964-65; assistant in music, 1965-68.
Ter Molen, Edna, 1964-66: part-time, music, 1964-65; assistant in music, 1965-66.

1965
Warnaar, Gail L., 1965-97: assistant in music, 1965-85; part-time lecturer in music, 1985-86; adjunct assistant professor of music, 1986-97; adjunct associate professor emerita, 1997.

1966
Viswat, Alma, 1966-70: assistant in music.

1967
Barlow, Dulcie, 1967-68: assistant in music.
Halik, Glen, 1967-68: assistant in music.
Palma, Eleanor J., 1967-86: assistant in music, 1967-68; part-time teaching associate, 1973-85; part-time lecturer, music, fall 1985; adjunct assistant professor of music, spring 1986.
Vande Mark, Ray, 1967-71: assistant in music.

1968
Dauser, Helen, 1968-88: assistant in music, 1968-69, 1971-72; part-time teaching associate, music, 1972-85; part-time lecturer, music, 1985-88.
Nelson, Joseph, 1968-69: assistant in music.

1970
Martin, Leroy, 1970-71: assistant in music.

1971
Jackson, John, 1971-2000: assistant in music, 1971-72; part-time teaching associate, 1972-73, 1974-85; part-time lecturer, 1985-2000.

Kraft, Roberta, 1971-2009: assistant in music, 1971-74, 1976-85; part-time lecturer, music, 1985-90; adjunct assistant professor of music, 1990-2002; adjunct associate professor of music, 2002-9; adjunct associate professor emerita, 2009.
Warnaar, Donald, 1971-72: assistant in music.
Working, Thomas, 1971-2004: assistant in music, 1971-72; part-time lecturer, music, 1989-2004.

1972
Hopper, Francis H., 1972-78: assistant in music.

1973
Sherman, Margaret, 1973-80: part-time teaching associate in music.
Working, Julie, 1973-80: part-time teaching associate in music.

1974
Formsma, Bruce, 1974-89: part-time teaching associate in music, 1974-89; part-time lecturer in music, 1985-89.
Malfroid, Larry, 1974-2015: part-time teaching associate in music, 1974-82; part-time lecturer in music, 1985-86; adjunct assistant professor of music, 1986-2001; adjunct associate professor of music, 2001-15.
Minor, Brian, 1974-78: part-time teaching associate in music.
Spring, Peter, 1974-80: part-time teaching associate in music.
Woshakiwsky, George, 1974-78: part-time teaching associate in music.

1977
Brannen, Linda, 1977-79: part-time teaching associate in music.
Swieringa, Mary, 1977-80: part-time teaching associate in music.

1978
Engstrom, Mary, 1978-85: part-time teaching associate in music.

1980
Erickson, Thomas, 1980-2004: part-time teaching associate in music, 1980-85; part-time lecturer, music, 1985-2004.
Speaker, Robert, 1980-84: part-time teaching associate in music (voice).

1984
Langejans, Thomas, 1984-96: teaching associate in music.

1985
Brown, Jill, 1985-94: teaching associate in music, 1985-89; part-time lecturer, music in 1989-94.

1987
Klein, Lonnie D., 1987-88: intern in music.

1991
Hoats, Charlie, 1991-2018: part-time lecturer in music, 1991-2001; instructor in jazz bass, 2001-18.

Ross, Jimmy, 1991-2004: percussionist, 1991-93; percussionist for dance, 1993-98; part-time lecturer and percussionist for dance, 1998-2004.

1995
Snyder, Donel, 1995-2000: part-time instructor in music.

1996
Erskine, John, 1996-2015: part-time instructor in music.
Heger, Avis, 1996-2001: part-time instructor in harp.
Secor, Greg, 1996-2018: part-time instructor in percussion.

1998
Lea, Charlie, 1998-2004: part-time instructor in music.
Mallett, Edward, 1998-99: visiting assistant professor of music.
Okada, Jun, 1998-2001: instructor in piano.
Scholten, John, 1998-2005: instructor in music.
Talaga, Stephen C. (Steve), 1998-2020: part-time lecturer in music, 1998-2008; instructor in music, 2008-13; adjunct assistant professor of music, 2013-20.

1999
Ward, Kristin, 1999-2006: teaching associate.

2000
Craioveanu, Deborah, 2000-2011: part-time instructor in violin.
Lunn, Robert, 2000-2007: part-time lecturer in music.

2001
Martin, David, 2001-present: part-time lecturer in music, 2001-15; adjunct assistant professor of music, 2015-present.
Pilon, Sherri, 2001-19: part-time lecturer in music, 2001-15; adjunct assistant professor of music, 2015-19.

2002
DeBoer, James R., 2002-present: part-time lecturer in music, 2002-7; adjunct associate professor of music, 2007-present.

2003
Alberts, Lorraine, 2003-06: part-time lecturer in music.
Janus, Ryan, 2003-8: visiting instructor in music, 2003-4; part-time lecturer in music, 2005-8.
Sooy, Julie, 2003-19: part-time lecturer in music, 2003-9; adjunct assistant professor of music, 2009-19.

2004
Corbató, Barbara, 2004-present: part-time instructor of viola.
Hoyer, John, 2004-15: part-time instructor.
Hyde, Michael, 2004-18: part-time instructor of jazz guitar.
LaGrande, Elizabeth, 1998-2005: part-time instructor.
Mattson, David, 2004-08: part-time lecturer in music.
Oonk, James, 2004-07: part-time lecturer in music.
Smitter-Baker, Pamela, 2004-07: part-time instructor.
VanDeWalker, Rebecca, 2004-07: part-time instructor of flute.
Van Lente, Michael, 2004-16: part-time instructor of percussion.

2005
Phillips, Harvey, 2005-06: part-time instructor of voice.

2006
Clapp, John, 2006-15: instructor in music.
Lockwood, Tom, 2006-present: part-time lecturer in music.
Norris, Sylvia, 2006-07: part-time instructor of voice.
Peterson, Erich, 2006-15: part-time instructor of horn.

2007
Holden, Jonathan, 2007-09: part-time lecturer in music.
Hyde, Edye Evans, 2007-18: part-time instructor in jazz vocals.
Southard, Sarah, 2007-present: part-time lecturer in music, instructor of oboe.

2008
Puccini, Dorival, 2008-15: part-time instructor in trumpet.
Spencer, Daniel, 2008-12: part-time instructor in trombone.

2009

Schekman, Joel, 2009-18: part-time instructor in clarinet.
Straus, Melissa, 2009-18: part-time instructor in bass.
Waldvogel-Warren, Martha, 2009-present: part-time instructor in harp.

2015

Graham, Adam, 2015-present: part-time lecturer in music, instructor of low brass.

Index

A

Alberts, Lorraine, 199
Alcott, Mary E., 73
Alcott, Sarah Gertrude, 72, 73
Anchor, The (student newspaper), xiv, 7, 11, 17-19, 21-23, 30, 37, 47, 53, 72, 75-76, 79, 82-84, 86, 102-4, 108, 112, 115, 124, 128, 130, 133, 135, 138, 141, 151-52
Andersch, Arthur, 185
Andersch, Carl, 185
Arne, Thomas, 48
Aschbrenner, Charles C., ix, 56-57, 57, 58, 63-64, 175, 179, 190
Austin, David, 174

B

Bach, Johann Sebastian (German composer), 52-53, 69, 145, 156
Bach, P.D.Q. (Peter Schickele), 145
Baker, Peter G., 76
Baker, Tunis, 76
Ball, Wesley A., 192
Barkema, Martha, 35, 186
Barlow, Dulcie, 196
Bast, David, 61
Baughman, Norma H., 189
Baughman, Stanley, 194
Beach, Evelyn M., 188
Beethoven, Ludwig van (German composer), 52-53, 60, 78, 133, 136, 139-40
Bennet, John, 133
Bennett, C. Bess, 185
Bergen, John, 15
Berman, Deborah, 191
Bernstein, Leonard, 60
Billings, William, 143

202　MAKING MUSIC

Bistline, Josef, 184
Bloch, Ernest, 52
board of trustees, 15, 19, 24, 28, 34, 110, 113-17, 173
Boccherini, Luigi (Italian composer), 78
Boers, Henry, 34
Bolema, Gertrude, 174
Bonnet, Joseph, 133
Booi, Duane, 48, 112
Boughter, Esther, 187
Bradbury, William (American composer), 131
Brahms, Johannes (German composer), 52-53, 131, 146
Brandenburg, Josh, 92
Brannen, Linda, 197
Breyman, William, 83
Broek, Albertus, 72
Brower, Alice M., 76
Brown, Harley, 141, 164, *166*
Browning, Grace Marguerite, 185; studios, 104, 107
Bruch, Max, 131
Bruins, Elton, 90, 113
buildings. *See* separate entries
Bullard, Frederic, 149
Bultman, James (Hope president), 151
Burrows, Reba, 194

C

Cadman, Charles Wakefield (American composer), 135
Cage, John, 152
Campbell, Francis, 9, 13, 171, 185
Carlson, Richard R., 167, 191
Carnegie Gymnasium, 17, 105, 108, 121n, 125-28, 131, 136, 169, 176, 180

Carr, Nancy, 174
Cavanaugh, Robert William, 21, 23-24, *24*, 25, 27-29, 36, 43-45, *45*, 46, 48, 52, 54, 60-62, 65, 79-80, 82, 86-88, 91, 94, 107-8, 112, 115, 125, 141, 148, 153, 161, 167, 174, 179-80, 188
Cecil, Robert M., 144, 190
Champion, Paula, 177
chapel (gymnasium) (1862), 1, 99, 100
chapel services, 1, 3, 7, 10, 38n19, 39, 41, 47, 54, 68, 71-74, 79, 82, 88, 96, 99, 105, 125-28, 138, 153, 161
Chopin, Frédéric (Polish composer), 57, 135
churches (Holland, MI):
Bethany Reformed, 163;
Fellowship Reformed, 61;
First Reformed, 2, 112, 164, 180; Fourth Reformed, 164;
Grace Episcopal, 106; Hope Reformed, 43, 90, 160, 164, 171, 173; Methodist, 164;
Third Reformed, 2, 48, 53-54, 124, 164-65, 174-75
Claar, Elizabeth O., 193
Clapp, John, 199
Clark, Adam L., 194
Clark, Larrie, 162
Cloetingh, Arthur, 77
Coleman, Clara, 185
Coleridge-Taylor, Samuel (English composer), 82
College High School: xi; 20, 108, 136, 159; as Hope Academy, xi, 5-6, 8, 10, 37, 99, 161; as Pioneer School, xi; as Preparatory School: xi, 1-2,

4-5, 8, 10, 16-17, 34, 35n9, 37n15, 66, 72, 74, 100, 125, 159
Coltrane, John (American jazz saxophonist), 144
Columbia Hall, 21, 108-9, 121n
Colyer, H. E., 6
commencement. *See* events: graduation
concerts. *See* performances
Conlon, Katherine, 184
Conway, Joan C., 45, 52, 56, 61-62, 62, 63-65, 94, 119, 175, 190
Cook, Helen M., 195
Coolidge, Calvin (US president), 128
Copland, Aaron (American composer), 63, 146
Corbató, Barbara, 199
Corea, Chick, 90
Coyle, Brian R., 192
Craioveanu, Deborah, 198
Craioveanu, Mihai D., 192
Cress, Oscar, 185
Crueger, Johann, 156
Cutler, Granville, 195

D

Daelhousen, Kim, 91
Dauser, Helen, 196
Davis, Harvey Owen, 27, 167, 189
Davis, Roger E., 54-55, 55, 56, 64, 140-41, 167-68, 190
Deacon, Stanley, 82, 185
DeBoer, James R., 199
Debussy, Claude (French composer), 52, 135
De Graaf, Marcia Kay, 92
Department of Music: accreditation of, 25, 29-30, 45, 50;
curriculum, 4, 8-9, 11n45, 13, 15-18, 20, 22, 25-29, 30, 43, 47, 57, 60, 99, 100, 104; degrees, 9-10, 13, 15-21, 25, 27-30, 41, 44, 50, 53, 65, 69, 104, 112, 163-64; founding of, xiv
De Pree, Mrs. Edward, 187
Diekema, Gerrit, 157
Diekema, G. J., 123
Dimnent, Edward D., 16, 18, 23, 106, 169, 173, 176
Dimnent (formerly Memorial) Chapel, 18, 39-40, 49, 68-69, 78, 97-98, 101, 105-7, 111, 117, 125, 131, 133, 136, 139-40, 143, 146-47, 155, 157-58, 161, 165, 167-68, 172-74, 176, 180
Dinkeloo, Ger[h]ard John, 72, 160
Dok, George, 186
Donahue, Kathleen, 173
Doorenbos, Harvey, 111
Downie, Neil, 157
Drigo, Riccardo (Italian composer), 130
Druckenmiller, William H., 189
Dunham, Rowland W., 187
Dunwoody, Beulah Harper, 125, 187
Duruflé, Maurice (French composer), 55
Dvořák, Antonín (Czech composer), 131
Dykema, Anno, 72
Dykstra, Linda L., 140, 192

E

Eenigenburg, Susan, 80
Elgar, Edward, 136, 140, 148
Emerson, Luther, 4

Enesco, Georges, 60
Engstrom, Mary, 197
ensembles: a cappella, 78, 142; band, 17, 20, 22, 26, 31, 40-41, 49-50, 59-60, 70, 84-85, 116, 126-27, 129-31, 136, 140, 144-46, 148, 161, 167-68; B Natural Chorus, 128-29, 169; Chapel Choir, 20, 22, 25, 40-41, 43-46, 52-54, 61, 68, 70, 73, 80, 82-83, 85-88, 90-92, 94-95, 107, 125-26, 128, 133-34, 136, 139, 141-42, 145-47, 151, 153, 158, 161-62, 165-68, 170, 173-74, 177, 180; Choral Union, 11, 44, 81-82, 99, 127, 133, 138, 160, 171, 173; College Chorus (Chancel Choir), 48, 53-55, 70, 83, 139, 144, 146-47; Collegium Musicum, 90, 139, 142-43, 146, 148, 167; Glee Clubs, 3, 8, 10-14, 19, 23, 25, 31, 37, 44, 73, 75-77, 82, 85-86, 127-28, 136, 138-40, 145, 166-67, 169, Men's (Boys'), 22, 44-45, 52, 71, 80, 82, 86, 88-89, 105, 108, 127-28, 136, 152, 165, 168, 170, 173-74, Women's (Girls', Ladies'), 22, 43-44, 74, 86, 88, 107-8, 127-29, 135-37, 139, 150-53, 165, 168, 170; Hope Trumpeteers, 128, 130; jazz (band)ensemble, 79, 90, 104, 128, 139, 144, 146, 148, 151; Ladies' Ukulele Orchestra (Girl's Ukulele Club), 14, 79, 128; Luminescence, 78, 165; Madrigal Singers, 22, 47-48, 79-80, 112, 142-43; Oratorio Chorus, 167; Orchestra (Symphony), 7, 8, 17, 19, 22-23, 37, 49-50, 55, 60-61, 68, 70, 83-85, 105, 116, 127, 129-30, 138, 140, 142-48, 151-52, 161, 164-67, 168-69, 175; quartets, 4, 49, 73, 76, 123-24, 135-38, 140, 146, 153, 156, 158, 160, 171, Clarion, 135, College, 7, 72, Knickerbocker, 79, 127, 163, Prins-Baker (Collegian, Hope College), 76-77, 163-64; Symphonette, 47, 49, 54, 59-61, 70, 85, 94, 139, 143-47, 165, 167, 170, 177; Twelfth Street Harmony, 78, 165; Wind Ensemble, 31, 85, 139-40, 144; Women's Choir, 51
Erickson, Thomas, 197
Erskine, John, 198
events: All-College Banquet, 136; All-College Day, 136, 148; All-College Review, 168; All-College Sing, 27, 78, 112, 148-50; Alumni Association Banquet, 126, 128; Arbor Day, 136; Arts and Humanities Fair, 139; assemblies, 1, 140; Christmas Vespers, 27-28, 51, 55, 78, 107, 133, 139, 141-42, 153, 162, 169, 173-75, 177; commemorations and celebrations, 155-58, 167; convocations: college, 125, other, 139, 158; Day of Prayer, 3; dedication: of Dimnent Chapel organs, 40, 167-68, of Dow Center, 151, of Graves Hall, 99, 138, of Wichers addition to Nykerk, 118, 151,

of Science Building (Lubbers Hall), 151, of Van Zoeren Library, 151, of Voorhees Hall, 14; Fine Arts Festival, 27, 147; graduation, 1-4, 6, 81, 83, 102, 106, 123-25, 180; Homecoming, 27, 78, 126, 139-40; Hope College Society Festival, 138; Junior exhibition, 3; Junior-Senior Banquet, 138; Lyceum Course, 131, 133, 169, 171; Madrigal Dinner, 142-43; May Day, 148; Messiah production, 27, 43-44, 131, 133, 138, 141-42, 153, 171-74, 176; Musical Showcase, 54, 61, 90-93, 139, 147-48; Nykerk Cup competition, 126-27; pageants, 77, 137, 173, 176; Parents' Weekend, 140; presidential inaugurations, 14, 68, 151; sporting, 85, 129, 145, 165; Spring Festival, 148; Spring Fling, 148; Vespers series, 40-41, 44, 48, 78-79, 91, 133-35, 140, 164, 171

Everett, Ransome, Jr., 195

F

faculty, xiii; and chapel participation, xi, 38, 125; and collaboration, 3-4, 6, 21, 28, 39, 69-70, 72, 73, 77, 79, 83, 89-90, 94, 137-38, 141-42, 149, 156, 160, 163, 165-67, 170; early, 2, 5-6, 10, 15-17, 19-20, 23, 25, 34-36, 66, 113; female, 42-44, 46, 121; list of, 1866-2015, 183-200; nonmusic, 22; as mentors, 92, 96; and performance, 60-64, 133, 135, 186; professionalization of, 28, 30-31, 34, 65-66

faith, religion, 70, 74, 95-96, 153, 165, 167, 180-81

Fashun, Christopher, 194

Fauré, Gabriel (French composer), 54, 162

Fedak, Alfred, 177

Federlein, Gottlieb, 74

Fenton, Grace Dudley, 44, 185

Fenton, W. J., 171

Ferguson, J. Scott, 192

Floyd, Russell, 63, 175

Floyd, Samuel Russell, III, 191

Folkert, Thomas, 58, 181

Formsma, Bruce, 197

Frabman, Harry, 169

Franck, César (French composer), 68

Frederickson, Karen B., 191

Fried, Paul, 44

G

Ganne, Louis, 145

Gaul, Alfred, 131

Gay, John, 61

Gee, Dallas M., 160, 176

General Synod of the Reformed Church in America, 165

Gericke, Wilhelm, 158

Gershwin, George (American composer), 56

Gilbert, John H., 191

Gilmore, John, 4-5, 33-35, 99, 184

Gilmore, William, 3-5, 33, 183

Golson, Benny (American jazz composer), 144

Gomez-Loerch, Winifred, 188

Goodhart, Arthur, 156
Goodwin, Gordon, 144
Gounod, Charles (French composer), 140
Graham, Adam, 200
Graves Hall, 99, 106, 108, 118, 138, 148
Gray, Charles K., 52, 191
Greenberg, Phillip B., 191
Guild, Maurice Alvin, 195
Guilmant, Félix-Alexandre (French composer), 69

H

Halik, Glen, 196
Hamelink, Susanna, 186
Hammerstein, Oscar, II (American lyricist), 144
Handel, George Frideric (German composer), xv, 131, 133, 136, 139, 144, 171, 174
Handelink, Margaret, 187
Hartley, Walter, 185
Hartly, Walter, 189
Haydn, Joseph (Austrian composer), 27, 136, 143, 171
Heeren, J. J., 9, 184
Heeter, Eugene, 126, 129, 161, 166, 194
Heger, Avis, 198
Hekman, Helene, 174
Heusinkveld, Arthur H., 185
Hills, Arthur C., 195
Hinga, Milton, 88
Hoats, Charlie, 198
Hodson, Robert, 193
Hoffman, Harvey, 87
Hoffs, Alice, 38, 136, 142
Hoffs, Marinus A., 76
Holden, Jonathan, 199
Holleman, Jantina Wilhelmina, 23, 25-27, 31, 46, 47, 47, 48, 51, 53, 60, 65-66, 79-80, 82, 89, 110, 112, 138, 141-43, 174. 188
Hollenbach, John, 92, 110-11, 114-15
Holst, Gustav (English composer), 140
Holton, Frank, 160
Honegger, Arthur, 146, 165
Hopper, Francis H., 197
Hornbach, Christina M., 194
Hoyer, John, 199
Huizenga, Philip, 87
Hyde, Edye Evans, 199
Hyde, Michael, 199

I

Ihrman, Pieter, 72
Ives, Charles (American composer), 146

J

Jack H. Miller Center for Musical Arts, xiii, 31, 42, 46, 52, 54, 58, 61, 64, 89, 91, 94-95, 99, 120-21, 179-80
Jackson, John, 196
Jacob, Gordon (English composer), 146
Jacobson, John (Hope president), 151
Janus, Ryan, 199
Jennings, Norman L., 190
Jermihov, Peter, 192
Johnson, Elizabeth, 57
Johnson, Herman C., 187
Johnson, Katherine Conlon, 184
Johnson, Melissa, 90

Index 207

Johnston, Milton, 29, 90, 189
Joio, Norman Dello (American composer), 146
Jones, A. R., 144
Jones, Sarah L., 72
Joubert, John P. (British composer), 141
Juliana, Princess (Netherlands), 158

K

Karsten, Helene Prisman, 44, 56, 187
Kato, Mami, 94
Kay, Ulysses (American composer), 147
Kelch, Betty Lindberg, 195
Kelch, Carleton, 143
Kennedy-Dygas, Margaret A., 192
Keppel, Ruth, 106
Khachaturian, Aram (Soviet Armenian composer), 143
Kim, Jung Woo, 194
King, Charles, 196
Kingsbury, Ronald, 186
Kipling, Rudyard (English author), 136
Kisinger, Everett, 195
Klaasen, Connie, 111
Kleinheksel, John, 34
Kleinheksel, John H., Jr., 5, 183
Klein, Lonnie D., 198
Kleynenberg, Peter A., 195
Kolean, Lora L., 193
Kollen, Gerrit (Hope president), 13-15, 25, 31-32
Kollen, John Lloyd, 187
Kolyn, Andrew Judson, 184
Kommers, Tunis (or Tinis) J., 5, 183

Kooiker, Anthony, 50-51, *51*, 52, 62, 94, 140-42, 167-68, 175, 189
Kots, George, 186
Kraft, Roberta, 197
Kranendonk, Paul, 167
Kranendonk, Robert, 80, 91
Kremers, Amy Yates, 184
Kresge, Stanley, 177

L

Lacey, Sarah E., 43, 188
LaGrande, Elizabeth, 199
Lamale, William P., 185
Lamar, John, 74
Lampen, Barbara, 127, 135
Langejans, Calvin, 195
Langejans, Thomas, 197
Lawson, Frank, 160
Lea, Charlie, 198
Leach, Jimmy, 193
Lear, Ralph, 174
Leenhouts, Margaret, 191
Leestma, Ethel, 67-68, *68*, 69, 72, 75, 80, 106, 113, 134, 161, 164-65, 180
Lehman, Carroll, 191
Le Mere, George, 186
Lennon, John (founder of the Beatles), 144
Lestrud, Ingrid, 194
Lewis, Huw R., 119, 192
Lichty, Elizabeth, 148
Liszt, Franz (Hungarian composer), 52, 135, 168
Lockwood, Tom, 199
Lokker, Hazel, 187
Longfield, Victoria, 96
Loomis, Jessica, 177
Loomis, Mrs. W. H., 38, 187
Lowry, David, 91, 141

208 MAKING MUSIC

Lubbers, Irwin L. (Hope president), 25, 29, 31, 45-46, 50, 86-87, 110, 112-14, 116-17, 144, 151
Lunn, Robert, 198

M

Maassen, Beth, 94
Maassen, Harriet, 94
Maassen, John, 94
MacFarland, William, 195
Mac Farlane, Esther, 40
Malfroid, Larry, 197
Mallett, Edward, 198
Marble, Mabel, 186
Martin, Blair L., 193
Martin, David, 198
Martin, Leroy, 195-96
Marx, Groucho (American comedian), 61
Massenet, Jules (French composer), 135
Mathis, William S., 190
Mattson, David, 199
McCall, Carolyn, 78
McCartney, Paul (Beatles guitarist), 144
McFarlin, Pruth, 133
Mearns, James, 45, 125, 188
Meinecke, Bruno, 185
Mendelssohn, Felix (German composer), 2, 62, 72, 81, 131, 140, 145, 171
Metz, Ethelyn, 186
Meyerbeer, Giacomo, 2
Meyer, Harris, 77, 185
Meyer, Nella, 35, 92, 186
Michael, Del, 63
Michaelson, Anna, 135, 186
Michel, Delbert, 63

Milestone, The (yearbook), 16-17, 35, 39, 84-85, 103, 108, 129, 141n82, 163, 181, 183n
Minor, Brian, 197
Mitchell, Deana, 196
Mitchell, Dwain, 196
Monk, Thelonious (American jazz composer), 144
Moore, Terry L., 191
Moore, Trixie, 174
Morrison, Joyce M., 147, 190
Morrow, James, 192
Moszkowski, Moritz (German composer), 135
Mozart, Wolfgang Amadeus (Austrian composer), 4, 135, 143, 148
Muilenburg, Teunis, 6, 74
Mulder, Beverly, 55
Music Annex, 118, 121n
Music Committee. *See* Department of Music
musical groups and organizations (Holland, MI): Apollo Orchestra, 138; Breyman's Orchestra, 160; Cooperative Concert Association, 176; Euphemia, 160; Gee's Orchestra, 160, 176; Holland Civic Chorus, 156, 161, 171, 176; Holland Musical Association, 156; Holland Musician's Club, 161, 176; Holland Symphony Orchestra, 129, 161; Teachers Choral Club, 171
Mussorgsky, Modest (Russian composer), 140

N

Natvig, Mary, 191

Neckers, Carlyle, 106-7
Nelson, Joseph, 196
Nettinga, Cornelia, 14, 18, *19*
Nienhuis, Hazel D., 187
Nies, Helenus, 74
Niessink, Richard, 41
Nixon, Richard (US president), 87
Nixon, Pat (First Lady), 87
Noetzel, Lauren, 80
Norris, Sylvia, 199
Nykerk, J. D., 13
Nykerk, John B., xiv, 6-7, *7*, 8-11, 13-15, 17-19, 24-25, 35-36, *36*, 37-40, 58, 63, 65-66, 72-73, 76, 81, *81*, 84, 88, 99-100, 102, 104, 111, 117, 123, 125-27, 131, 133, 138, 157, 160, 167, 169, 171, 174, 180, 184
Nykerk Hall of Music, 26, 30-32, 42, 45, 48, 62, 64, 89, 94, 98, 110, 117-18, 119-20, 121n, 151

O

Okada, Jun, 198
Olmsted, Nannette, 91
Oonk, James, 199
organizations: Arcadian, 149-50; Cosmopolitans, 103; Delphi, 149; Fraternal Society, 2, 76, 149; Knickerbocker, 109, 127; Musical Arts Club, 21, 26, 43, 78, 164; Sigma Sigma (Sorosis), 112, 119n105, 148
Osborne, Kenneth, 23, 126, 135, 156, 158, 161, 188

P

Paalman, Hazel M., 72, 79-80, 135, 164, 189

Palestrina, Giovanni Pierluigi da (Italian Renaissance composer), 91
Palma, Eleanor J., 196
Park, Soyeon, 193
Peale, Norman Vincent, 51, 177
Pease, Clarence Edward, 11, 184
Peeke, Harman Van Slyke, 34, 73-75, 184
Pellegrom, Ruth, 186
performances: concerts, 4, 6-7, 14, 16, 27, 44, 48-49, 53-54, 61, 63, 68, 81, 83, 85, 89-90, 94, 105, 126, 128, 130-31, 135, 138-47, 150, 152-53, 156-57, 160-62, 165-71, 173, 176-78, 180; recitals, 27, 78, 105, 133, 135, 138, 143, 152, 164, 167-68, 177, 180, faculty, 16, 37, 40-41, 47, 51-52, 54, 56-57, 60, 63-64, 94, 105, 117, 133, 135, 140, student, 11, 27-28, 41, 52, 65, 68-69, 89-90, 94, 111, 117, 126, 134-36
Pergolesi, Giovanni Battista (Italian Baroque composer), 151
Peterson, Arlene, 78
Peterson, Erich, 199
Petty, Neil, 117
Phelps, Frances, *73*
Phelps, Philip, Jr. (Hope president), 3, 99
Phelps, Lizzie, *73*
Phillips, Greg, 90
Phillips, Harvey, 199
Piippo, Richard G., 193
Pilon, Sherri, 198
Plantenga, Nancy Lummen, 107, 141

Pool, Nick, 52
Post, Henry C., 9, 11, 13-14, 184
Prins, Peter N., 76
Prins, Teunis W., 76
Prokofiev, Sergei (Russian Soviet composer), 140
Puccini, Dorival, 199

Q

Quackenbush, Palmer, 194
Query, Ann Van Dorp, 95
Quimby-Hopkins, Beth, 58

R

Rachmaninoff, Sergei (Russian composer), 52, 145, 158
Raiguel, Dorothy, 184
Ralph, George, 142
Rameau, Jean-Philippe, 69
Randel, Julia Phillips, 193
Ravel, Maurice, 52, 69
Renner, David, 140
Rensch, Colin, 90
Richmond, Brad W., 192
Rider, Morrette L., 23-24, 26, 28, 48-49, 49, 50, 59, 60, 83, 85, 116, 142, 145, 166, 174, 189
Rider, Wanda N., 94, 196
Rietberg, Roger J., 52-53, 53, 54, 55, 98, 141-43, 165, 167, 174, 181, 189
Ringwald, Roy, 149
Ritsema, Robert A., x, 50, 52-53, 55, 59, 59, 60-61, 64, 85, 87, 94, 107, 117-19, 141, 147-49, 166-67, 175, 178, 190
Ritter, Deckard, 126
Ritter, Walter, 187
Robbert, Iris, 195
Robbins, Martha C., 186
Roberts, Daniel, 158

Rogers, Richard (American composer), 144
Rossini, Gioachino (Italian composer), 140
Ross, Jimmy, 198
Roth, Raymond, 195
Ryker, Harrison, 52, 175, 190

S

sacred music, 38, 53, 66, 70, 72, 74, 86, 95-96, 125-28, 133, 143, 145-46, 156, 160, 180
Saint-Saëns, Camille (French composer), 133
Sanborn, Timothy, 192
Savaglio, Paula C., 193
Sayers, Dorothy, 181
Schaafsma, Kari, 54
Schaberg, Albert Roy, 189
Schaberg, Gail, 195
Schauffler, Robert, 41
Schekman, Joel, 200
Scholten, John, 198
School of Music. *See* Department of Music
Schouest, Scott J., 194
Schubert, Franz (Austrian composer), 63, 74, 130, 140, 143, 148
Schuelke, Ann S., 185
Schumann, Robert, 57, 63
Schuman, William (American composer), 133, 135, 140
Schuppert, Mildred, 72, 95, *98*, 104, 106, 131, 161, 163-64, 180
Scott, Charles, 34
Secor, Greg, 198
Sharp, Stuart W., 65, 142, 191
Shattenkirk, Ray, 151

Shepard, G. C., 6-7, 35, 99, 124, 160, 184
Sherman, Margaret, 197
Shields, W. A., 137
Sibelius, Jean, 143, 158
Simonetti, Achille (Italian composer), 78
Singleton, Mildred, 24
Skillern, Zella, 126
Smith, Marjorie H., 195
Smitter-Baker, Pamela, 199
Snow, Esther MacFarlane, 26, 39, 42-43, *43*, 44-45, 53, 79, 86-87, 107-8, 110, 134, 156, 158, 161, 167, 173-74, 188
Snow, Robert, 110
Snow, W. Curtis, 23-24, 38-39, *39*, 40-43, 55, 63, 68, 72, 82, 84, 94, 98, 107, 117, 125-26, 129, 133-34, 135, 157-58, 165, 166-67, 171, 173-74, 180, 187
Snyder, Donel, 198
Soeter, John, 86
Sooy, Julie, 199
Sousa, John Philip (American composer), 144
Southard, Robert G. (Gabe), 194
Southard, Sarah, 199
Spaulding, Albert, 51
Speaker, Robert, 197
Spencer, Daniel, 199
Spring, Peter, 197
Stainer, John, 131
Stalf, Denise H., 192
Stoppels, A. Dale, 71
Stoppels, Chuck, 89
Straus, Melissa, 200
Strauss, Richard (German composer), 140
Strouf, Linda Kay, 191

studios, 21, 99-100, 102-8, 110, 113-15, 118
Swart, Peter, 72, 84
Swets, Ethel Leestma, 41, 94, 107
Swierenga, Robert P., x, 159
Swieringa, Mary, 197

T

Talaga, Stephen C. (Steve), 198
Tallis, James H., 190
Tallis, Joan, 196
Tallis, Thomas (English composer), 145
Tammi, John, 61
Tchaikovsky, Pyotr Ilyich (Russian composer), 74
Tellman, Edwin, 129
Ten Brink, Dorothy, 167
Ter Molen, Edna, 52, 196
Thayer, Whitney Eugene, 4
Thompson, Robert, 190
Thompson, Robert F., 191
Timmer, Barbara Folensbee, 139
tours 4, 43, 54, 59, 61, 82-83, 85-89, 92, 128, 145, 152
Tower, Harold, 186
Tuller, Sherman, 186
Turbessi, Christopher, 90

U

Underwood, Roy, 29

V

Van Antwerp, Lucille, 194
Van Dam, Evie, 50
Vande Mark, Ray, 196
Vanderheuvel, Kenneth, 195
Vander Hill, Alma, 174
Vander Ven, Charles, 113
VanderWerf, Calvin A. (Hope president), 32, 50, 151

Vander Werp, Jeannette, 186
VanDeWalker, Rebecca, 199
Van Eck, Arthur, 71, 88
Van Hasselt, Herman, 184
Van Hees, John George, Jr., 5, 183
Van Katwijk, Paul, 176
Van Lente, Michael, 199
Van Oostenbrugge, Cornelis, 74, 156
Van Raalte, Albertus C., 137-38
Van Raalte Memorial Hall, 11, 17, 99-102, 114, 138
Van Vleck Hall, 113, 156
Van Wylen, Gordon (Hope president), 32, 151
Vennema, Ame (Hope president), 14
Viswat, Alma, 196
Vogan, Charles, 135, 188
Voogd, Helen, 138
Voorhees Hall, 14, 17, 21, 95, 101-5, 107, 111, 114
Votta, Michael, Jr., 191

W

Wagner, Richard, 144
Walchenbach, Lynne, 88
Waldvogel-Warren, Martha, 200
Walsh, Heber, 111
Walsh Music Hall, 31, 59, 89, 110-16, 121n
Ward, Kristin, 198
Ward, Steven D., 193
Warnaar, Donald, 197
Warnaar, Gail L., 196
Warnshuis, Henrietta, 186
Warren, George, 158
Washington, George (US president), 138

Waters, Ethel, 147
Wayer, James, 72
Webb, Christine Augusta, 187
Wecker, Karl, 186
Weid, Perry P., 186
Welmers, Thomas, 160
Welmers, William, 135
West, Elizabeth O., 193
Wezeman, Frederick, 96
Wichers, Wynand, 20, 23, 40, 42, 68, 151, 156
Wickstrom, Elizabeth, 171
Widor, Charles-Marie, 68-69
Wilkins, W. W., 185
William of Orange (prince), 157, 158
Williams, Vaughn, 54
Winants Chapel, 38, 76, 81, 89, 99, 101, 105, 118, 125, 131, 169, 176
Wing, Hazel, 185
Wolfe, Jennifer, 193
Wolf, Hugo, 140
Wopat, Dave, 148
Working, Julie, 197
Working, Thomas, 197
Woshakiwsky, George, 197

Y

Yates, Amy, 184
Yonkman, Fritz, 86
Young, Victor (American composer), 144
Yung, Chung Sun, 78

Z

Zwemer, Daniel, 194

Visiting Research Fellows Lecture Series[1]

Dutch American Identity Politics: The Use of History by Dutch Immigrants (2003)
Hans Krabbendam, Roosevelt Study Center, the Netherlands

The Rain of God: Reformed Church in America Growth and Decline in Historical Perspective (2004)
Lynn M. Japinga, Hope College

Reassessing 1857: Overlooked Considerations Concerning the Birth of the Christian Reformed Church (2006)
James A. De Jong, Calvin Theological Seminary

Disease and Death among the Early Settlers in Holland, Michigan (2006)
Netherland-America Foundation Visiting Research Fellow
J. P. Verhave, Radboud University Medical Center, Nijmegen, the Netherlands

---

[1] Several lectures are available for purchase at www.hope.edu/vri; for others, please email vanraalte@hope.edu.

Growing Up Dutch American: Cultural Identity and the Formative Years of Older Dutch Americans (2007)
Netherland-America Foundation Visiting Research Fellow
Peter Ester, Tilburg University, the Netherlands

The Dutch Equation in the RCA Freemasonry Controversy, 1865-1885 (2008)
Harry Boonstra, Calvin College and Seminary

"We live presently under a waning moon": Nicholas Martin Steffens as Leader of the Reformed Church in America in the West in Years of Transition (1878-1895) (2008/published 2013)
Netherland-America Foundation Visiting Research Fellow
George Harinck, VU University Amsterdam

Preachers, Pews, and Pupils: Commemorating the Past in Twentieth-Century Dutch America (2008)
David Zwart, Dordt College

"Pope of the Classis"? The Leadership of Albertus C. Van Raalte in Dutch and American Classes (2009)
Leon van den Broeke, VU University Amsterdam

Dutch Americans and the Rise of Heritage Studies (2010)
Michael Douma, Florida State University

Hope: The Legacy of Van Raalte (2011)
Rein Nauta, Tilburg University, the Netherlands

Documentary Films of the Netherlands Shown in the United States, 1942-1973: Viewership, Representativeness, and Visual Rhetoric (2013/publication forthcoming)
Henk Aay, Calvin College

Hendrik P. Scholte: His Legacy in the Netherlands and in America (2015)
Eugene Heideman, RCA staff member, retired

Seeds of Hope, Seeds of Hate: A Love Story (Begins) (2016)
Don Luidens, Hope College

"We made the Wilderness to Blossom": Nineteenth-Century Dutch Immigrants and the Natural World (2015/publication forthcoming)
Henk Aay, Calvin College, and Jan Boersema, Leiden University, the Netherlands

Ten Thousand Panes of Glass: The Crystal Cathedral and Religious Innovation in the United States (2018)
Published as: *The Glass Church: Robert H. Schuller, the Crystal Cathedral, and the Strain of Megachurch Ministry*, Rutgers University Press, 2020
Mark Mulder, Calvin College

Eleanor Calverley: First Doctor to Kuwait (2018/publication forthcoming)
Paul Heusinkveld, US Department of State 1984-2012

Making Music: Hope College's Music Department, A History (2018)
Marc Baer, Hope College, and Allison Utting, Class of 2019

Made in the USA
Monee, IL
21 August 2020